EXPATS

ALSO BY CHRISTOPHER DICKEY

With the Contras: A Reporter in the Wilds of Nicaragua

EXPATS:
Travels in Arabia, from Tripoli to Teheran

···

CHRISTOPHER DICKEY

THE ATLANTIC MONTHLY PRESS
NEW YORK

Portions of "Shadows on the Desert" and "The Prize" first appeared in slightly different form in *Vanity Fair*. Part of "The Stones" appeared in Condé Nast's *Traveler*.

Excerpts from Wilfred Thesiger's *The Life of My Choice* reprinted by permission of W. W. Norton & Co.

Excerpts from Wilfred Thesiger's *Arabian Sands* reprinted by permission of Viking Penguin, Inc.

Excerpts from Naguib Mahfouz's *Palace Walk* reprinted by permission of Doubleday. English translation © 1990 by the American University in Cairo Press.

Published simultaneously in Canada
Printed in the United States of America

Library of Congress Cataloging-in-Publication Data

Dickey, Christopher.
    Expats: travels in Arabia, from Tripoli to Teheran/Christopher Dickey.
    ISBN 0-87113-337-7
    1. Middle East—Description and travel. 2. Middle East—Politics and government—1979– I. Title.
DS49.D49 1990   956.05—dc20   90-151

Design by Laura Hough

The Atlantic Monthly Press
19 Union Square West
New York, NY 10003

FIRST PRINTING

ACKNOWLEDGMENTS

Any traveler accumulates debts of hospitality and friendship. Writers garner still more. And there are many people to thank for their help on *Expats*. It would never have existed if Gary Fisketjon had not asked me, in the middle of a war, to write a travel book. Nor would it be in print if his assistant at Atlantic Monthly Press, Garth Battista, had not shepherded it so diligently through the process of revision and production. To them both, and to my agent, Theron Raines, who found me in Kuwait to talk about the project, many thanks.

My editors at *The Washington Post* and *Newsweek* sent me out on many of the journeys recounted here and often helped me interpret what I found. Special thanks are due Bob Rivard, formerly *Newsweek*'s chief of correspondents, and Peter McGrath, its foreign editor, who took part in some of these expeditions. I'd also like to thank Katharine Graham, chairman of The Washington Post Co., not only for her support over the years, but for first taking me to Aleppo.

Elise O'Shaughnessy at *Vanity Fair* encouraged me on this project, deftly edited two of the chapters, which appeared in the magazine in slightly different form, and gave me valuable advice on the manuscript as a whole. She is a wonderful editor, and I owe her my gratitude and respect.

Pat Tyler, now defense correspondent for *The Washington Post*, and photographer David Mills were frequent companions in the Gulf. Their humor and friendship often made insane situations endurable.

For Carol, my wife, there can never be enough ways to give thanks. For a decade she has put up with separation and worry when I am away, my difficult temperament when I'm at home, lending our lives whatever stability they have. In the end, nothing would be possible without her.

For Carol, who shared everything

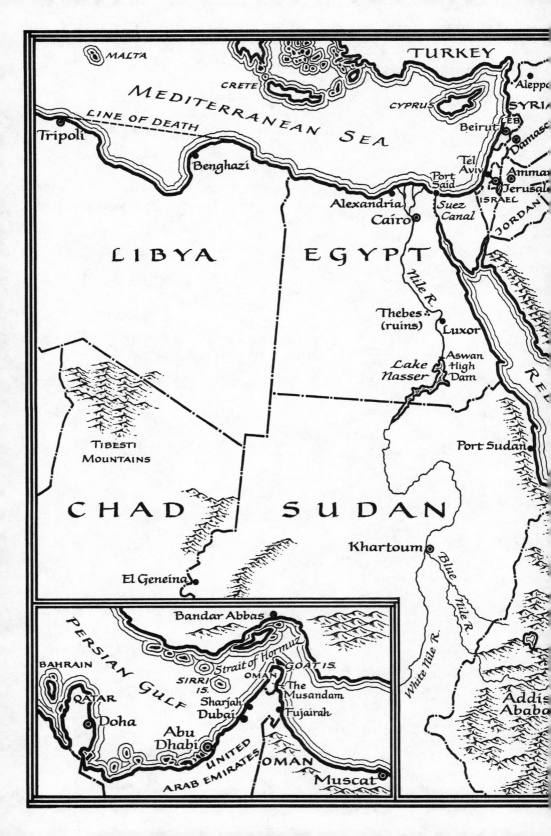

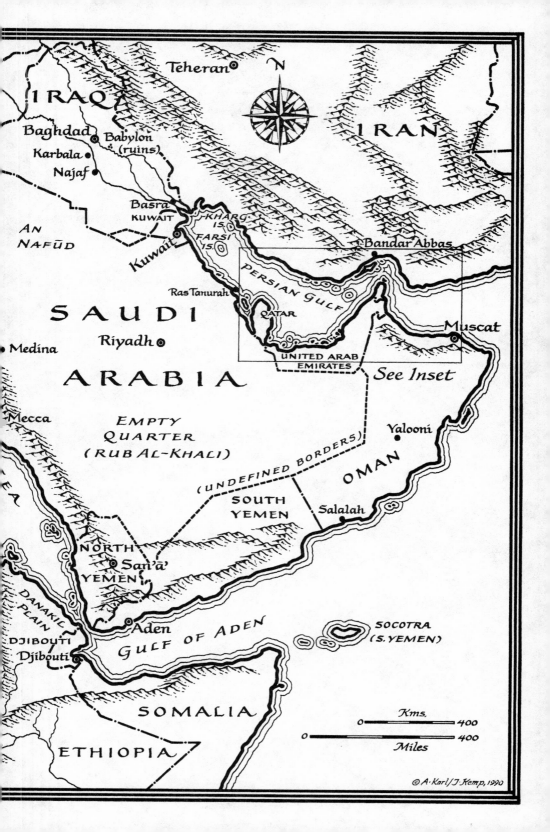

CONTENTS

EXPLORATIONS

GREEN MINDS

IT WAS HARD TO SLEEP IN TRIPOLI. THERE WAS TOO MUCH SUGAR IN THE fake Coca-Cola, in the fake Fanta Orange, in the cappuccino made with powdered milk. There was nothing else to drink and nothing safe to eat but the mushy pasta at the hotel buffet. The most common condiments had become treacherous. The butter served with the stale rolls, in its individual Kerry Gold wrappers from Ireland, was mottled green with mold, like Roquefort cheese, having sat for an indeterminate period on a dock somewhere, unrefrigerated, undistributed. This was the Grand Hotel on the waterfront, the best hotel in town. But by 1986 Libya, rich as it was, just wasn't working very well. Fresh food was hard to find, and much coveted. In the fall of 1985 riots began at the port when a boatload of bananas arrived from Nicaragua: a frenzy over fresh fruit.

I left the curtains open for the sun to wake me in the morning. But the golden glow of street lamps all over the city poured into the room. It was 1:30 in the morning, and I could feel the sugar surge, and adrenaline, too. A war was brewing somewhere there over the sea where the lights of the city gave out and dead black began.

Now this is not a story of war, exactly. It's about people caught out of place, out of their time, sometimes by chance and sometimes by choice and sometimes, as in Libya in that spring of 1986, caught in the middle of fighting. They are mainly American and British, but also Italian and Indian, Filipino and Pakistani, Russian and Polish. They are expatriates who may not be able to make their own countries work but who hire themselves out with the promise of making others' perform: the international brigades of efficiency. Some are explorers; others are drifters. A handful are artists and scientists. Many are businessmen. None of them fit into the surrounding culture, although they all have helped to create it. They are part of a new Arabia, a land of both Arabs and expats that blends the convenient and the exotic like a raj rooted in suburbia and Silicon Valley. It stretches from the Persian Gulf to the Straits of Gibraltar, wherever oil and opportunities are found.

During four years spent covering the Middle East for *The Washington Post* and *Newsweek* I ran into expatriates almost everywhere. But I first became sharply aware of their special world and its peculiar isolation in Libya in the months when a surreal rite of confrontation was being played out between mad Muammar Qaddafi and Ronald Reagan.

Qaddafi had come out of the desert and out of the ranks of the army in 1969 to bring a new vision of the world to his people, and of his people to the world. A bedouin steeped in the rhetoric of the Koran and the radio shows of President Gamal Abdel Nasser next door in Egypt, he raised the green banner of his faith, Islam, and he raised the price of oil, again and again, and at great profit. Within his government—a system he called Jamahariya—he created a kind of organized chaos where all responsibilities were shared universally, and all power devolved on him alone. In his relations with the world of foreigners, a world largely foreign to him, he defined himself by making long-term enemies and using short-term friends. The last vestiges of the Italian colonists had to go, but trade with Italy increased. Overt manifestations of American imperialism were eradicated. Businesses and air bases were taken over. Real cappuccino, real Coke gave way to their powdered-down, sweetened-up clones. But Americans and their oil companies were allowed to stay, under certain conditions, and work for the greater good of themselves and Qaddafi's state.

Throughout the 1970s Qaddafi's tactics worked. He could hire and buy the best, or at least the brashest, to pursue whatever goals he chose. He could try to buy Ed Wilson (fairly cheap) from the world of American intelligence services to give him the tools of the terrorist trade; he could pay off Billy Carter, the American president's brother, in a ridiculous effort to curry the administration's favor.

But by that spring of 1986—that April night when I was lying in the Grand Hotel in the dark trying to get to sleep—Libya's oil money was running thin. Ed and Billy were long gone. Foreign workers who weren't absolutely necessary, and many who were, had been pared away and replaced by Libyans, who, for the most part, didn't really know how to do the foreigners' jobs or didn't want to try. Eventually even the Tunisian bakers were gone, bread got scarce, and what could be found was stale.

The Grand Hotel was full of foreigners, but they were mostly revolutionaries and would-be beneficiaries of Qaddafi's political handouts: Chadians, Kurds, Filipino Moslems, dissident Palestinians, even the occasional American Black Muslim. Only a skeleton crew of highly paid, highly isolated foreigners remained to keep the country functioning, living in prefabricated settlements along the coast road west of Tripoli: Friendship Village, for the Eastern bloc workers and, for Westerners, the Tourist Village, or the National Oil Company compound.

In January 1986 President Reagan ordered all those Americans left in Libya to get out immediately. He had been sending warnings since 1981, when American jets first gunned down Libyan fighters over the Gulf of Sidra and the White House declared Qaddafi the most dangerous man in the world. The administration was determined covertly and overtly to rid the world of Qaddafi's regime. Bloody attacks at the Israeli airline ticket counters in the Rome and Vienna airports on December 27, 1985, fomented American pressure and rhetoric. The Abu Nidal Group of Palestinians had mowed down men, women and children, and Qaddafi was thought to be behind Abu Nidal. The Reagan administration was desperately afraid that Americans in Libya would be taken hostage, just as Americans had been taken hostage in Iran. But after four years, more than a thousand Americans remained. They were an enormous liability, a troublesome factor in the escalating confrontation. And many of them, it was said, lived in the NOC compound.

It's a long ride to the compound from the Grand Hotel. The driver of the run-down taxi spoke Arabic and Italian; I didn't. The sign language was shaky. Radio Malta wailed across the waves with a country-and-western song, something by Moe Bandy, as we cruised the corniche past stucco homes and the occasional missile site. At the compound high fences surround a cluster of houses poised together above the sea like so many shoe boxes on a shelf, tidy and neat with little lawns in front and, in the midafternoon, most of the shutters closed against the sun. Cars were parked by the curb. Occasionally, children on bicycles zoomed around a corner. In the early 1980s, when the dollar was strong, many of the Americans were replaced by Pakistani or Indian or Egyptian professionals, who cost the National Oil Company far less; but even they, in this suburban environment, took on American airs. The houses themselves were actually built by a Finnish company. But there was still the flavor of the States—patios and barbecues and carports—and there were still, in January 1986, several American holdouts. Mostly they lived in a large depression at the center of the compound near the tennis courts.

"We call it the Pit," said Charlie Lanier, from Houston, talking about the compound and, perhaps, the country. He was friendly and lonely, having been in Libya for a month with only pictures of his wife and kids and their split-level home on the little desk behind his shuttered windows. The oil boom in Texas had gone bust in the early 1980s. Company after company had folded. Lanier did computer programming for drilling firms, but the drilling firms had mostly quit drilling in America. "This is my survival," he said. "I'm fifty-four years old. I'm overqualified and overpaid, so I can't get a job." After several months he heard the Libyans were interviewing prospective technicians "outside the country." When he went to the meeting (he never would tell me where), three of his buddies gave him their résumés to take along. When he started talking to the Libyans, he liked what he heard. A man with his skills could earn twice as much as he was earning before the crash, and pay next to no taxes. Although the Libyans were frank about the problems that might lie ahead for Lanier, his choice—between no work and Libyan work— was all too clear.

The basic American government obstacles were easy enough to sidestep. At Tripoli airport you were given a slip of paper in your passport that you removed when you left. No evidence remained that you'd ever been to Libya. But living there was, by American suburban standards, a little rough. Lanier brought eight suitcases that he hoped held everything he'd need, from breakfast cereal to toilet paper.

"We don't get around much here. You have a language problem. You also have a food problem," said Lanier. "You have to go hunting, I call it, for food." On the edge of town were black-market food stands offering eggs, chickens, sometimes other meats. The vast supermarkets in the city were bare of almost everything except Korean-made Jamahariya gym shoes (size 12) and cooking oils. But, hell, at least the hunt was something to do. Most of the time Lanier worked straight through, six days a week, from 7:30 in the morning to 2:30 in the afternoon, then spent his time reading the occasional copy of the *International Herald Tribune* or *Newsweek*. Roughnecks at the drilling sites in the desert had it even harder for longer, working thirty days straight, then getting ten days off. Expats learned to listen to the shortwave—BBC, Voice of America—and they listened a lot. Maybe they brewed up some flash, bathtub gin that comes out pure fire and mixes with anything from Kool Aid to the local water. And they stayed just a little bit on edge.

"If I had to leave in twenty-four hours, I could take two suits and a flight bag and be out. That's the way you live in these foreign countries." That's why he didn't have a car. He didn't want to tie up his money in that kind of investment. His life was stripped down. No television, no video. "Where the hell you gonna get tapes for it? Sometimes you can't even get batteries." Always ready to roll. "You don't want to get involved."

Lanier seemed to enjoy the flavor of adventure. "I call this hazardous duty, and that's how you're paid." He could leave when he saw fit, he said. "Some people have no other chance, so they're going to stay here and stick it out. And some people more gutsy than I am come here with three kids."

It used to be that a lot of people came with their children, and down the street from the NOC compound there was a school. It looked like a junior high in southern California, with its open breezeways and its playing fields and its plaque with the school poem by the door of the little administration building:

> *In the midst of the sandy desert*
> *Beside the shining sea*
> *Stands a school that fills our hearts*
> *With pleasant memories.*

By suburban Tripoli standards it was an old plaque. The school had been founded twenty-eight years earlier. By 1986 its students came from fifty-two different countries, many of them Eastern bloc, but the English-language curriculum offered a daily diet of American-style education. Before 1982 there were about eighty American teachers at the school. By 1986 there were only two or three left, and one of those was Skender Brame, the recreation director. He and his wife, Carol, had lived in Libya for fourteen years. Their son, Greg, thirteen, was born there. They were never political, as they saw it. "We still play baseball. We still do all the typical American activities: aerobics, Little League, tennis," said Skender. But now they were thinking about leaving their comfortable, neutral life of American values on Libyan shores. "It'll be difficult. I'll put some résumés out," said Skender as we sat around the kitchen table. Of course, the American oil companies were still finding ways to work with Libya through subsidiaries that kept pumping Qaddafi's oil. "The whole thing is just so hypocritical," Carol burst out as the coffee water boiled.

The Brames weren't afraid of the Libyans. They were afraid of the Americans. "There are so many ways you can be got at other than being arrested." They worried about tax audits and about air raids on Tripoli. "That's the only way our safety is jeopardized. If they don't do anything militarily, we're safe." But Skender seemed to run out of breath and will as he finished his sentence. "We're going to comply with the policy. I'd hate to think we're doing anything to support terrorism. We might be a hindrance to the future development of the policy." They had come for the money, convinced themselves they were staying for something like the culture, but found that inertia had trapped them between a superpower and a madman. "We don't see any way out right now. No one wants to face criminal charges. But it's a helluva way for the U.S. government to treat U.S. citizens."

Seen from Libya—from the Pit or the School—the confrontation building between Reagan and Qaddafi required a willing suspension of disbelief. It was so often theatrical; it seemed so absurd. To try to keep some perspective, I kept a copy of the French photo-journal *Paris Match* in my room. It carried graphic color of the carnage at the Rome airport: the horror of a beautiful young woman, a child, a grandmother—wounded, dead and dying. But the flat reality of the horrors faded into the surreality of the Tripoli scene: this curious, hollow city peopled by zealots or, more often, people pretending to be zealots.

"Shit! Shit on Reagan!" they would shout. "Down! Down with USA!" they screamed, in English, at the biggest rally staged for the press, on Nasser's birthday. Thousands of young Libyans filled the auditorium that normally holds the People's Congress in Tripoli. All had green strips of cloth to wave or tie around their head like Islamic martyrs-to-be. Many wore fatigues. But as they waited for Qaddafi to come on stage—standing in the hallways, boys in small groups, girls in small groups, staring past each other or catching glances out of the corners of their eyes—the atmosphere was filled with the pure and universal ritual of high-school courtship. While Qaddafi waited in the wings, the kids could have been waiting for their basketball team to bound out or for an Alice Cooper concert.

I was at a corner of the stage looking across the crowd. Boys in the middle, young men to the right. In the balcony were the hell-raisers, all Ramboed up, with their green headbands and their fists waving and the spit sparkling at the corners of their lips as they vowed to die, sometime, someplace down the road. "We are the generation of anger!" they shouted. Among them were little boys, ten or eleven years old, their voices cracking with the slogans. Girls and women were on the left, many in tightly fitting uniforms. "Down! Down USA!" Toward the back a couple of girls in Western skirts and blouses were really getting into it, standing on their chairs, swinging their green banners. "Shit! Shit on Reagan and your Sixth Fleet! Down! Down USA!" shouted the one in the tweed skirt. She waved. She screamed. She took a breath and looked at her watch.

Qaddafi came out, the crowd got crazier, the noise higher, and he was ready for them. He walked down a carpet reserved for him. He led the chants, then stood and savored the scene, adjusting the microphone, irritated that it was placed too low. He looked up and around, to the balcony, to the boys, to the girls. One, two, five, seven minutes passed before he began to try to speak, staring at these young faces, his young faces, almost all of them born since he took power. And then he looked down, and he was looking at his own face.

Arrayed before him, like enormous footlights, were four television monitors showing him his image as captured by every camera in the hall. And as he spoke, throughout his speech, through the corner of his eye Qaddafi could see the faces of Qaddafi.

Gradually, a sense of the man's logic started to emerge. He believed in his *Green Book,* and the society he was building required people who had "green minds." America was afraid of the green mind, he told his people. His Third Universal Theory was intended to combine the best of capitalism and communism but created chaos that only he could control. His notion of freedom was summed up by his declaration that "democracy means popular rule, not popular expression." The symbolism of his state was simple and ludicrously literal. The green square at the center of the city was just that, nothing less or more: a vast tract of asphalt painted green. Qaddafi obsessively idolized Nasser and seemed to believe that he could model his confrontation with Washington over the Gulf of Sidra along the lines of Nasser's confrontation with Britain and France over the Suez Canal. He could eulogize an Egyptian border guard who went berserk in 1985 and shot down a group of sunbathers near an Israeli beach. And he could say with perfect aplomb that Abu Nidal was a fighter for a cause who had to be supported. Why talk of the people he killed? Why not talk about the Israeli killers? And so on and so on.

Each day, in search of analysis and facts, the assembled journalists made their rounds of the embassies. But dutiful interviews with diplomats soon turned to socializing. In the world of expatriates, diplomats and journalists hold special niches because, at least in theory, they stay in touch with the culture around them. But in fact, in countries where barriers of language and culture already exist and political and secret-police barriers are imposed, journalists and diplomats wind up talking mainly to each other. Then, too, embassies could offer a refuge from the abstemious rigors of the Grand Hotel. The British consulate seemed to have an endless supply of scotch and gin, especially for British journalists. It was a magnificent run-down mansion on the seafront, well appointed with elegant antique furnishings, even a grand piano in one room, and a swimming pool in the back. The House of Shame it came to be called by journalists ruefully remembering their performances there the night before. Eventually socializing even led to romance in the long, drawn-out weeks of headline stories that kept the press corps hanging on and hanging out in Tripoli. Several news organizations sent some of their most attractive women correspondents and field producers to Tripoli, trolling for exclusives with Qaddafi, it seemed. And if that was the strategy, it paid off. One American reporter virtually took up residence at the House of Shame.

It was a young Brazilian diplomat who provided the most interesting, if not always the most verifiable insights to what was happening in Libya. He was an avant-garde novelist by vocation, a diplomat only by appointment. "Libya is difficult, but it's not terrible," he used to say. "The problem is the desert is not just physical. It's this dryness in the minds of people."

He was fascinated by stories about one of Qaddafi's advisers, an East German who supposedly came to Tripoli in the mid-1970s as part of a force training Qaddafi's security apparatus, then converted to Islam and married into Qaddafi's clan. The German's name was Karl Haensch, as the Brazilian heard it, and later was arabicized to al-Hanish, which means "the serpent." In time he became the media adviser of the maximum leader. "Can you imagine?" the Brazilian marveled. "An East German image maker? But look at Qaddafi, and you will see it. The mannerisms, the way he poses and moves his head—it's pure 1930s German expressionism." The maximum leader as Nosferatu, filmed from four angles.

The Brazilian occasionally would invite groups of journalists to his apartment on Friday afternoons, when Tripoli was entirely shut down. His little liquor supply soon ran out. But he would serve feijoada and ham, defying Islamic dietary laws. "I always try to have something illegal." After lunch he would close the shutters and play a videotape or music that no one had seen or heard for a while. Bruce Springsteen would blast out "Born in the U.S.A." there in the suburbs of Qaddafi's city. Gene Kelly would dance through *Singin' in the Rain* there on the edge of the desert.

The Brazilian had several young Libyan friends and tried, as best he could, to make a life in Tripoli not entirely different from the life he would have led in Rio. But the beaches, vast and beautiful, offered little Ipaneman solace. In almost any Islamic society today one encounters mind-numbing moralism about sex. Qaddafi had confused the issue by revising Islam to suit his predilections. In his Jamahariya everyone was liberated. "It is an undisputed fact that both man and woman are human beings," *The Green Book* explained, although "woman is female and man is male." Young women were brought out from behind the veil and into the army. But the net effect was to make women more available only to the maximum leader, and simply increased the frustration of the boys in the street. "These people, they masturbate on the beaches in summertime," the Brazilian marveled. A Polish nurse or Bulgarian technician goes bathing in an Eastern European bikini, and the beach goes crazy. "Not just one of them. You can see the whole beach masturbating." But none of us was going to stay for the summer.

On March 24, Libyan missile batteries near Benghazi fired on American navy jets, and the Americans, unscathed, responded by blowing apart Libyan missile installations and sinking Libyan patrol boats. The Americans were baiting Qaddafi, and he was rising toward the hook. At a rally a few nights later Qaddafi emerged from behind a green door to stand on the guardhouse balcony at the entrance of the Bab al-Aziziya barracks, where he lived. His posture was stiffened by the bullet-proof Kevlar in his vest. As he started to speak, the rays of the setting sun caught him just right, like a light from heaven. The Americans had crossed the parallel at 32°30', which marked the top of the Gulf of Sidra. He called it the Line of Death. And they would pay.

There were no courtship rituals that night, no television monitors. In the fading twilight the hard glare of television lights deepened the creases on Qaddafi's face, and the crowd of men—soldiers out of uniform—exulted in his rhetoric, readying themselves for the climactic show. As the leader finished, suddenly a cow was led into the midst of the throng beneath the balcony. On its side was painted the word REAKAN. Across its throat went a blade, and the beast shuddered, gushing torrents of blood as its legs collapsed beneath it. Young men danced in the pools of red. Cameramen and sound men from the American networks sought steady footing in the slick gore. I looked up at the balcony. Qaddafi had disappeared.

Out at the NOC compound, around the Pit, the population was thinning. Lanier had left, and the Brames as well, as far as I could tell by knocking on their doors. In an afternoon I found only one American. I caught him shirtless and sunburned, mowing his lawn. He said his name was Lee and he was from Arkansas but had been in Libya fifteen years and he figured he'd stay on a while longer. He had been through the crisis in 1981 and held out. "I went round the road and come back again." But the drop in the standard of living was getting to him. "Gonna have to be a vegetarian. I haven't bought any meat in three and a half months."

Lee didn't really want to talk. "I wish I could offer you a beer," he said and shrugged. There wasn't any beer. It was a way of ending the conversation. But I didn't want to leave just then. After weeks of the green mind the smell of cut grass and the fumes of a lawn mower—the old smells of the Atlanta neighborhood where I grew up—were familiar and comforting. It was easy to understand why we take our suburban customs with us wherever we go, the way the British had taken high tea or the Japanese take cameras. The lawn ritual was such an assertive, American way to establish the comfortable frontiers of home. I wondered whether this building of barriers, real and imagined, was the only way for a Westerner to stay sane in this desert of the mind.

All over the Arab world, where the cultures of the West and the Orient are thrust together, one has a sense that they are powerfully attracted to each other but never quite capable of mixing. Proximity seems, on the contrary, to heighten frustrations and create reserves of terrible mistrust. Sixty years ago, when T. E. Lawrence had ended his wanderings in Arabia, he warned bitterly that to view the world through the veils of both cultures was to come near madness. He cautioned against "love of the glamour of strangeness." In Libya you could see mutual incomprehension building with seismic force, leaving a vast chasm between the trim lawns of the compound and the gore-slicked street in front of Qaddafi's barracks. I did not suppose that Lee could show me how to bridge it, or that he would be one to try. If I wanted to try reconciling my experiences of the two worlds instead of closing myself in my own, I would have to look elsewhere. Lee was taking one day at a time.

"Is your wife with you?" I asked.

Lee said she was in the States but was coming back. "I called her today and said dump all those dresses and just put food in." He bent down and adjusted the choke on the mower, getting ready to crank it back to life. "It's terrible," he said. The world beyond the edge of his lawn was closing in. But what could he do? "Business is so down the drain in the States. Hell, at my age I wish I'd never heard about the oil industry."

On the night of April 14 I was back in the Grand Hotel, back in one of those universal, unobjectionable rooms with desk and mirror and flame-resistant curtains and the phone on the Formica table by the bed, and sleep not coming and the long night stretching out in front of me. I had dozed only three or four hours in two days. The climax was coming in the showdown with Qaddafi. Everyone could feel it. A bomb had gone off on a TWA jet flying from Rome to Athens. Then someone had blown up a disco full of American servicemen in Berlin. And word was filtering out of Washington that this was Qaddafi's doing and a lesson would be taught this time. Anything could happen, but nothing had.

And then the phone rang. My office in Washington wanted

to know what was going on. And I said it was 1:00, no, 1:30 in the morning and what did they think was going on? Well, word had leaked from the National Security Council that "it's going to be tonight." What's "it"? An attack. "Either it was thirty minutes ago or in about thirty minutes from now." It looked quiet to me. I called the House of Shame, where a little party was going on, as usual. One of the reporters there was Marie Colvin, an American working for UPI who had become Qaddafi's favorite journalist. When he would talk to nobody else, he was talking to her. I figured she'd know where I might call him at this hour. Or maybe she had already heard where the American attack had hit.

She hadn't. Nobody at the House of Shame had heard anything. But then, all of us, at the hotel, at the House of Shame, in our beds or on our balconies, heard the distant rumble of the first bombs.

The sound rolls across the landscape, and then the sudden explosive roar of jet engines cuts across it. Among the streetlights, still on all over the city, comes the flash of the explosions. The air rips above our heads. The planes are so close the building shakes, but they are invisible in the dark. They exist by noise and vibration and impact, and the concussions are spreading. I retreat from the windows to the lighted hallway. A Kurdish rebel from Iraq, come to Tripoli looking for Qaddafi's subsidies, emerges sleepily from across the corridor. "Americans," I say, making my hand swoop like a dive-bomber. He shrugs, nods as if nothing else were to be expected of the evening and goes back into his room.

There is no place to go, really, nothing to do but wait. The antiaircraft fire is sporadic, as if the gunners were half-asleep. The city is still lighted. The flash of a single rocket goes up from the breakwater at the port below the hotel. Flares start to career across the sky. Bombs seem to be landing in all directions. But only in the last seconds of the strike do the lights go out. Cars pass in the street below, oddly unhurried. Suddenly the port erupts in a belated fury of ack-ack and surface-to-air missiles, and the smell of smoke and cordite seeps into the sudden dark of the Grand Hotel.

* * *

I never went back to the Pit. But from what I hear there are still some Americans mowing their lawn at the NOC compound, still working for Qaddafi, counting the days until their next vacation, counting their money and probably wishing to hell they'd never heard of the oil business.

SHADOWS ON THE
DESERT

....

WILFRED THESIGER IS THE LAST OF A BREED OF BRITONS, SPRUNG FROM THE traditions and ambitions of empire, who explored the most God-forsaken corners of the world, especially the Arab world, and came to love it and be obsessed by it and wrote beautifully about it: Sir Richard Burton slipping disguised into the forbidden city of Mecca in the 1850s, Charles Doughty in *Arabia Deserta*, Sir John Bagot Glubb—Glubb Pasha of the Arab Legion—who died only in 1985 and T. E. Lawrence, of course—mythical, mad, indelibly remembered from *Seven Pillars of Wisdom* and Peter O'Toole's Panavision portrayal. They suffered mightily to encounter Arabia's realities and succeeded in recording them, but their lives epitomized the romantic myths and aspirations of the nineteenth century. Generations of boys stayed up late in the night reading, rereading their accounts of desert crossings, imagining themselves facing the challenges these men faced, enduring what they did, triumphing as they did and, sometimes, having their triumphs snatched from them. This is the stuff of a boy's dreams—or at least the boys of generations as recent as my father's.

In fading green ink in my father's copy of *Seven Pillars*, which he gave me before I came to the Middle East, he had copied out a passage onto the title page. The penmanship is a schoolboy's. The romance is irresistible:

> We were wrought up with ideas inexpressible and vaporous, but to be fought for. We lived many lives in those whirling campaigns, never sparing ourselves any good or evil: yet when we achieved and the new world dawned, the old men came out again and took from us our victory, and remade it in the likeness of the former world they knew. Youth could win, but had not learned to keep, and was pitiably weak against age. We stammered that we had worked for a new heaven and a new earth, and they thanked us kindly and made their peace. When we are their age no doubt we shall serve our children so.

How adolescent. How compelling.

I came late to the excitement of all this, well versed in revisionism, somewhat suspicious of heroes, tending to remember about Burton that he was not in fact the first European to enter Mecca, tending to think of Lawrence as a desert queen. And I had not heard of Thesiger until early 1986, when I was in the Gulf. I first picked up a copy of his *Arabian Sands* in the well-refrigerated Kuwait Hilton, where the lobby shops sell compact-disk players and Louis Vuitton luggage. Thesiger's other classic, *The Marsh Arabs*, I bought in Bahrain's Intercontinental and read while sunbathing among some stewardesses from Cathay Pacific.

The first book is an account of Thesiger's travels, by foot and on camels, through the Empty Quarter of southern Arabia in the years just after World War II. This land is virtually uninhabited and completely inhospitable, even to the bedouin, but it had obsessed more men than just Thesiger. Harry Saint John Philby, too often remembered only as a footnote to the life of his treasonous son, was one of those to cross it, after years of preparation and anticipation. It is a moonscape of enormous dunes and utter aridity, and to traverse it as first Bertram Thomas then Philby and, finally, Thesiger did is an enormous test of endurance and will. If you remember the grim crossing of the wind-blown Nefud desert in *Lawrence of Arabia,* the "sun's anvil" as they called it, you can multiply that hardship a hundred times in the vast wastes of the Rub al-Khali, the Empty Quarter. And it is the trial itself that seems to have attracted Thesiger and those who went before him. He writes at one point that he spent one of his birthdays riding 115 miles on a camel, and someone later asked him why on earth he did that. "Well, it was just sort of to test myself and see if I could do it," Thesiger said. "Also to test the camel."

The son of a diplomat and nephew of Lord Chelmsford, who was viceroy of India, Thesiger possesses the self-assurance and under-statement of the upper crust. His writing style is spare and reticent but marked with frankness and an ingenuous authenticity. What is most appealing about Thesiger's books is that they were, very con-sciously, explorations of ways of life that were disappearing even as he encountered them: "I went to Southern Arabia only just in time," he writes at the beginning of *Arabian Sands.* "Others will go there to study geology and archaeology, the birds and plants and animals, even to study the Arabs themselves, but they will move about in cars and will keep in touch with the outside world by wireless. They will bring back results far more interesting than mine, but they will never know the spirit of the land nor the greatness of the Arabs."

When I found that Thesiger was still alive, spending most of each year living among the tribes of northern Kenya, I wanted to meet him. Just as much as the bedouins, Thesiger was part of a culture, a way of life and of looking at the world, that is just about gone.

I finally tracked down the old explorer of the Empty Quarter in the heart of London's Sloane-ranger-land, in Chelsea. The night before I was to meet him, I reconnoitered a bit. On the phone his old-school accent had left me inwardly chastened and I hadn't wanted to get lost on my way there, lest punctuality be one of his passions when he is in his British, as opposed to his bedouin, mode. The red-brick neighborhood is precious and, now, militantly upwardly mobile. A hotbed of real estate speculation, it affects an ambience of old salons, invokes long-dead literati. (A plaque on one just-sold townhouse announced that Oscar Wilde had lived there, a Henry and James real estate agency advertised widely, and there were Shelley Court apartments.) In Sloane Square, nearby, singles were on the prowl, rock and roll cut into the street, Budweiser was selling well: two bottles for two pounds sterling, a third one free. It was the Fourth of July, an excuse for a special offer on American beer. Couples drifted off into the night, still strangers, but drunk. Here by the National Army Museum things were more quiet. A couple of men in madras shirts passed by, talking of Jaguars. I found the old explorer's address. From his top-floor apartment only thin blades of light showed past the drawn shade.

I never could tell from the pictures in his books just what Thesiger looked like. So many of them are faded old prints taken with bad lenses there in the heartland of Abyssinia or out on the blistering sands of some African desert. He's tall. I knew that from the books. But when I stepped from the cage of the elevator the next morning, I was struck by the length of his face, so odd and distinctive, aquiline, but a sad caricature of an eagle. Every feature—the nose (broken while boxing for Eton), the ears, the chin—seems to have been stretched downward. The eyes are close together and deep set beneath ample, arched eyebrows. They're dark eyes, coated with that film of water that comes with age. He was seventy-seven. A week before Wilfred Thesiger had been released from the hospital, where he'd been operated on for cancer. But he did not tell me that until later, and I saw only small hints of stiff fragility as we walked down the hall to his rooms.

The flat was musty. His mother had taken it "during the war," and some of the decoration seemed unchanged since then. On the wall were prints and sketches from his travels and an oil portrait of

Thesiger as a youth, on top of a bookcase was a sword in a leather scabbard, and a dagger lay here and there. Small oriental carpets were strewn about, but the whole was as muted as the tweed of his jacket, and there was a patina of age on the place like the film on his eyes.

The window in the living room looked out on the Thames. As we began to talk a plane flew over. Thesiger, impatient with the intrusion, got up and closed the window. He called for coffee from the little gray woman who had kept his house for the last forty years. She came to the door with the tray, at the limit of her strength. He got up to bring it the rest of the way into the room. As Thesiger talked, his fingers moved constantly, twisting on one finger a gold ring that was so old the band was worn paper thin, rolling and unrolling his knit tie, picking up some amber worry beads and toying with them.

Wilfred Thesiger first saw the light of day in Africa, in Addis Ababa in Abyssinia, where his father headed the British legation before and during the First World War. It was a time when Ras Tafari—later known as Haile Selassie—fought tribal battles on a scale surpassing Agincourt to make himself, eventually, emperor of his medieval mountain nation. "I was born there, you see, and up to the age of nine led a very extraordinary life." He beheld the pageantry of soldiers wearing lions' manes, the grim imagery of gallows on the street corners, the excitement of hunting. Then he went back to England, to public school, and his father died.

"I was sort of odd man out at the school. Because here was a boy who claimed to have been on a tiger shoot, which I had in India, to have seen the armies coming past and had done camel journeys and everything else and yet had never heard of cricket or played a game of football. And certainly in this country you get ganged up on if you don't conform."

In that inimitable public school world of social Darwinism there were beatings, he writes in *The Life of My Choice*, at the hands of the headmaster of Saint Aubyn's, one R. C. V. Lang. "The school motto was 'Quit you like men: be strong,' an exhortation not without relevance to some of us boys. He beat me up on a number of occasions, often for some trivial offence. Sent up early to the dormitory, I had to kneel naked by the side of my bed. I remember crying out the first time, 'It hurts!' and Lang saying grimly, 'It's meant to.' " Yet, he writes, "Strangely enough I bore him no resentment for these beatings, accepting them as the penalty for what I had done. It never occurred to me how disproportionate was the punishment to the offense."

All in all, he seems to have found Eton and Oxford pleasant enough. But he was increasingly anxious to get back to Africa. He returned, finally, to Ethiopia at the invitation of the emperor and soon traveled into the country of the Danakil, fearsome cannibals who castrate their enemies. He joined the colonial service in Sudan and made his way to the Tibesti mountains in what is now Chad, then into the British Special Air Service during the war and rat-patrol combat among the dunes. Afterward, with an assignment from the Food and Agriculture Organization to search for the breeding grounds of the locust plagues that sweep across Africa, he found his way to southern Arabia and first conceived his passion for the Empty Quarter.

"There was the beauty of the sculptured sand dunes, there was a feeling of space, there was a cleanliness, there was a silence which we've driven from our world—which you realize now when you hear that bloody plane going over. But what mattered to me above everything was the comradeship of the desert people. What took me back? What made me want to go there? It was the companionship of these Bedu, and without it these journeys would have been just a meaningless penance.

"When I went to the desert, I was fairly tough by then, but I realized that I couldn't really compete with them on physical grounds because they were born to this sort of thing, the hunger and the thirst and everything else. But with my background of family life, Eton, Oxford, the Sudan government and everything, I did feel that I would be able to compete with them in civilized behavior—and that's really where I fell down.

"There was a nobility there which I've encountered nowhere

else. I mean, here in England, and I've no doubt in America and elsewhere, one finds—the qualities of nobility. But it's comparatively rare. And certainly you wouldn't think of the English people as a noble race. I mean you've only to read the papers to realize what's going on with the bulk of the country."

Are there people still alive who can talk about the concept of a noble race? I'm not sure even Leni Riefenstahl has used the phrase in her picture books since the war. But Thesiger did. And his conversation was, in its way, unabashed nineteenth-century romance. The virtues, the emotions, the passions he acknowledged were as noble and simple and alien to the modern world as Mallory's Arthur or Tennyson's Ulysses or anyone that Kipling ever wrote about. And it is from Kipling, of course, that he took the epigraph for his autobiography:

> *I have eaten your bread and salt,*
> *I have drunk your water and wine,*
> *The deaths ye died I have watched beside,*
> *And the lives ye led were mine.*
>
> *Was there aught that I did not share*
> *In vigil or toil or ease—*
> *One joy or woe that I did not know,*
> *Dear hearts across the seas?*

Indeed, one finds dear hearts in his books, particularly in *Arabian Sands*, where he writes often of the two boys who accompanied him through the Empty Quarter and Oman during the five years he spent there, staying with him until they were men. Bin Kabina one was called. The other was Bin Ghabaisha. They were his guides, his protectors, his friends. The pictures he took of them show barefoot young men with daggers and rifles, their hair streaming to the middle of their backs, looking like nothing so much as Comanche or Sioux, except for the long, simple robes that were then worn in that part of the desert. They were noble savages.

"Bin Kabina, or Bin Ghabaisha, any of them, could easily have got a job in the Hadhramaut if they didn't want to starve and if they didn't want to be continuously thirsty and at risk from raiding parties. I mean, you lived there with your rifle in your hand and your eyes scanning the horizon. It was a parlous life in a way, and you were continuously thirsty, almost always thirsty, and almost always hungry." But—"they would always scorn this easier life of lesser men. To them it was this challenge of the desert. It was the freedom of the desert which they needed, which was so important to them."

Thesiger never glossed over the general cruddiness of desert life. These are not Sean Connerys astride elegantly caparisoned stallions with flaring nostrils and flowing manes. He writes without untoward admiration about the primitiveness of their quotidian routines. But the gritty reality blends into a mystique of endurance, the notion that pain and hardship cleanse and improve. The boy who accepted the justice of sadistic beatings at school grew up to believe that the bedouin codes of conduct he admired "were formed by the harshness of the environment and the harshness of their lives." Without what he calls their "standards" they "would have all been at each others' throats." He thinks about this statement a moment. After all, much of the time they were indeed at each others' throats. "I don't say there wasn't a lot of raiding. But it was done according to standards of behavior."

The retainers who followed Thesiger in his long marches, including Bin Kabina and Bin Ghabaisha, were paid for their troubles. And what they did with their money was further proof to him of their worth. He talks of seeing Bin Kabina in a town at the end of their long last march together "shivering on the sands in just his loincloth." Thesiger asked him why he hadn't used the money he'd been paid to buy a blanket. Bin Kabina scoffed at him: "I'm Bedu. I don't want that. What I need is camels. I'm going to use the money you've given me to buy more camels." Thesiger smiles, delighted as he tells this story, repeating it. "Blanket? I'm a Bedu; what do I want with a blanket?" And the old man says, "It was one of the last times I saw him, in fact."

But he has blankets now, doesn't he?

"Oh, yes, they've got—well, there you are. But I mean the whole of their life has been turned topsy-turvy."

How often do you go back? You went back in 1977 and—

"I went back just that one time. I wouldn't go back again."

You wouldn't go back?

"No. I wouldn't set foot in Arabia again. It's meaningless to me. It's . . . this . . . this enormous wealth that they've got and everything, it means the place isn't . . . is . . . it means nothing to me. Bin Kabina and Bin Ghabaisha now have their Land Rovers or their Jeeps and things. They go off into the des—" He was not quite stuttering. His phrases and thoughts were shifting like sand. "They still, I'm glad to say, they still live . . . those two live in their black tents down on the edge of the sands. And they've got their camels. But, I mean, nobody ever rides a camel any longer. If you go anywhere you go in a Land Rover. And if they are far away out in the desert and they're short of water, imagine Bin Kabina saying to his brother, 'Look here, take the Land Rover and go back to Muqshin. It's only two hundred miles. Go and fill up all the jerry cans and bring them to us.' The hardship and the challenge and the everything which made them what they are—what they were—has gone out of their lives. There aren't any . . . I mean, as I knew them . . . there are no Bedu left in Arabia."

Thesiger cannot overcome his bitterness about this, and doesn't want to, really, though he knew even when he wrote *Arabian Sands* that the way of life he chronicled was disappearing. Nor does he blame his noble savages in the least for what happened to them. "There were the oil companies looking. It was the curse of this bloody oil, you see. They were looking like a sort of shadow on the edge of the desert, and within a year or two of my leaving they were in there."

At one point Thesiger reads from his book about hardship and challenge and how happy those things made him, and all this as we sit in deep old wing chairs looking out on the Thames. I ask him if he feels he led two lives. "No, it's one life." He looks around him as if he has just awakened to his surroundings. "Do you mean this?"

This is a long way from the desert.

"Yes, it is. And you can say that there are these two sides. One is the immense satisfaction I got in the desert when everything you owned would go into a saddlebag: a spare shirt, my field glasses, camera, a book or two. But it all would fit into a saddlebag. And that's your freedom. The more you own things, the more you lose your freedom, don't you?"

Here in the apartment, he says, the only thing he really cares about is his collection of sixty-five volumes of photographs. "My life, in a sense.

"I reject almost all the material manifestations of our civilization," proclaims the old explorer. "Even when I went to my prep school, I had no interest in cars and things at all. I loathed aeroplanes. I felt they were going to put paid to my world—which indeed they've done. Even back at the age of fourteen I realized this. When some wretched woman called what-was-her-name—Amy Johnson or some such—flew across the Atlantic, I hoped she'd fall into it. I could see this was going to reduce the whole world to nothing—as it has today, so that you can be in China eighteen hours from leaving London airport—and it would rob the world of all diversity. Well, it's done that."

You can't help but be struck by the misogynous allusions to women, who seem more or less an irrelevance, as insignificant, if not as hateful, as the aeroplane. Thesiger never married and has no children. "No. I couldn't have led the life of my choice if I had been married." After a long pause he changes the subject to the days of his lion hunting in Sudan. "But," I have to ask, "how about the companionship of women? There's a great lack of women in your books."

"Yes. You see, when I was in Arabia we hardly ever saw a woman. I mean, I was there for five years. We were always traveling about in the desert. It's been a life, on the whole, of male society. I agree."

Were you in love with Bin Kabina and Bin Ghabaisha?

"As long as you don't mean physical love. . . . They were

people who mattered to me more than probably anybody else has ever done. That is the sort of love which you give to your brothers and your family.

"I mean, when you are talking about men and then you use the word *love* in the context of today, it probably would imply a sort of homosexual relationship. And, I mean, the Bedu . . . it was one of the things that was sort of unknown there, really. There was a bit of it in Jidda and the town, places like that. Among the Bedu, no."

But what about T. E. Lawrence and his experiences?

"I think Lawrence was undoubtedly a homosexual. I mean, it emerges. But I think that in a sense one of his troubles was that he was a frustrated homosexual. Even with Daud or whoever it was I suspect that the relationship was never consummated and that Lawrence had a craving for a homosexual relationship, and the sort of thwarting of that may have contributed to his . . . uh . . . to his oddity."

And what of Thesiger?

"Sex," he says matter-of-factly, "has never been of any real importance to me."

Now there, I think, remembering the pubs on Sloane Square the night before, is a view of the world that's lost.

In the end perhaps Thesiger was looking in the desert for nothing so much as his childhood: the excitement that he felt as a boy watching the warriors of Ras Tafari parade in their barbaric glory through the center of Addis, that life in the British legation with his father or in imperial India with his uncle. The deserts of Arabia, the marshes of Iraq and mountains of Kurdistan, among the other places he explored, were paths back into that world of his childhood. This explanation is a commonplace among his older acquaintances, so obvious and so simple. His books and conversation hold ample evidence. But it is an explanation he never quite made for himself. For Thesiger adventure was what it was, is what it is.

And if anyone were left who had Thesiger's need for adventure and freedom, his thirst for hardship and danger, where would he find them? What could he do? The oceans remain. And outer space. But the explorers of those regions are limited by the enormous expense of technology, their adventures less a triumph of the will than of the microchip. The explorers themselves are conceived and chosen as elements of a machine.

"In July 1969," Thesiger writes at the end of his autobiography, "I happened to be in Kenya, on the shore of Lake Rudolf, when I heard with incredulity from a naked Turkana fisherman that the 'Wazungu'—as he called Europeans, including Americans—had landed on the moon. He had heard the news at a distant mission station. To him this achievement, being incomprehensible, was without significance; it filled me, however, with a sense of desecration, and of despair at the deadly technical ingenuity of modern man." Or, as Thesiger put it that morning in Chelsea, "I knew they were flying about in space, but I never had the slightest interest in what they were doing, and I barely even looked at the pictures. I mean, it's like looking up a woman's skirts to look at a photograph of the far side of the moon."

A few months after I talked to Thesiger, I was back in Kuwait, and found Dame Violet Dickson, who had spent her long, long lifetime there. I asked her about Thesiger, who had stayed at times in her house by the sea. "What was he like?"

"Very nice," she said. "I've rather forgotten what it is he was interested in, but he was interested in the desert. And . . . now I think . . . it was the wildflowers of the desert, too."

Dame Violet begins her story—even now, with the beginning so far back in time that only blurred corners of it are visible—at the British bank in Marseilles, where she worked after the "Fourteen-Eighteen War." As she once wrote the tale, in very proper prose, she was twenty-three years old. Her father was dead, and she was trying to make her way in the world more or less alone when

Captain H. R. P. Dickson of the 29th Lancers, Deccan Horse, Indian Army, came in to enquire if there was any

mail for him. He had arrived by train from London, he told
me, and was joining a ship which was to take him back to
the Persian Gulf via India. As there were no letters for him,
he spent a short time talking to me over the counter, and
asked me my name. I was naturally flattered by the interest
shown by the handsome young officer, but when he walked
out of the Bank I assumed that there was the last I should
ever see of him. Imagine my surprise, therefore, when
about a week later I received a cable from him from Port
Said asking me to marry him and go out to join him in the
Persian Gulf. The prosaic and unromantic interior of a
bank would hardly be thought of as the setting for a meeting which would lead a young English girl to travel to the
East and to make her home there for the next forty-five
years. But it was in such workday surroundings that I met
my future husband, whose love for Arabia and the Arabs
I was to share throughout our married life.

It was a tremendous decision for me to have to
make, and my hesitation was natural, but in the end it was
short-lived. After some heartsearching and some consulta-
tion with kind friends in Marseilles, I decided to throw in
my lot with my handsome suitor; I would cable "Yes." Our
marriage was to last for thirty-nine years, and I never had
cause to regret the decision.

Dame Violet Dickson was seventy-five when she wrote that
passage in her autobiography. When I visited her, in October 1987,
she was ninety-one. She and her husband had moved to Kuwait in
1929, and she'd lived there ever since in a house made of mud, its
walls two and three feet thick and whitewashed against the heat; the
doors and gates and open wooden stairs, linking its disjointed parts,
all were painted blue against the evil eye.

Harold Richard Patrick Dickson was the "political agent" to
Kuwait when the British still ruled India and this upper corner of the
Gulf was nothing but sand and sea, fishermen and a few traders. His
father had been in the Levant Consular Service, and he had grown

up speaking Arabic in cosmopolitan Beirut and Jerusalem. He had served the British Political Department in Mesopotamia and worked for a while as private secretary to the maharaja of Bikaner. But in Kuwait he found the fascination of the desert and its people, and he stayed even after he retired from the foreign service, in 1936.

If Thesiger wrote an evocation of bedouin life, H. R. P. Dickson wrote the technical manual. But it has been, in its way, as monumental and almost enduring. It is massive and rambling, and meticulously informed about the minutiae of daily life, the text mingling campfire tales with instructions on how to capture falcons or construct a tent or prepare a pearling boat to sail. There is no introspection. It is up to his daughter to tell us, in the preface to the third, abridged edition of *The Arab of the Desert*, that Dickson "never found much in common with the native-born Englishmen of his day," and at Oxford "he frequently felt himself an outsider, but usually won his way to acceptance when it was discovered that he had a great talent for cricket, tennis, and most other masculine pursuits." We might have guessed. But she also tells us that in the 1920s and 1930s, when life in Kuwait offered little attraction to most Europeans, "he enjoyed the challenge of disturbed local politics, warring tribes."

H. R. P. Dickson looks, in pictures, like the perfect pompous bore. Standing alongside the favorite falconer of the sheikh, he wears his pith helmet; one of his hands is in his coat pocket, one on his shotgun. But the personality that had set him at odds with his British peers was no doubt accepted by the Kuwaiti bedouin as typically British. He was, in the early years, one of the few standards by which they could judge. When Dickson died, in 1959, he had long since faded into anachronism. That his widow still lived in Kuwait in the mid 1980s everyone knew. But there were few visitors, and young British diplomats were quick to say, with a cursory shake of the head, that she was "quite dotty."

Fernando, Dame Violet's Sri Lankan houseboy, showed me in through the blue gate, and I found her in her study. She was, indeed, very old, but heavyset, with broad, strong hands. She wore a cheap, cool plaid dress and rubber-soled shoes with Velcro flaps across the top. On her right wrist—across skin blotted pink and brown from most of a century under the sun—she wore three slender gold brace- lets, like those of unwed Arab girls, and on one finger a heavy turquoise ring the same color as the sea beyond her windows.

The house looks out on a small fishing port full of graceful sambuqs, the ancient teak-hulled dhows once used for pearling and still used to trade up and down the Gulf. But between the house and the sea is a four-lane highway, and through the open windows comes the constant din of Kuwaitis in their cars. It doesn't bother her, she says. "I have nothing to do, you see." Sometimes she goes to sit on the veranda. There is a fresh breeze blowing in off the water onto the porch. There is a single chair facing out to sea. Its rattan is gray with age.

Dame Violet's memory lapses from one moment to the next. She tells me to come back the next day. She wants to check some things in her book. Fifty-eight years in Kuwait take some recalling. The appointment is set for 10:00, but when Fernando guides me down to the gate, he says to come earlier. "After 9:00 she begin to forget. . . ."

The next morning she begins to remember. "The Kuwaitis are still very friendly with the Europeans. But very few come here. They've all been 'educated.' " She mocks the word a little as she says it. "They've been educated, and they've been given jobs, you see. So they don't really come around like they used to when they were very poor and they would come to us and we would give them a chit for coffee and tea and things from a shop in the town." A room down- stairs in the house was especially for the visitors, who would drop in and sit and talk. There was a "coffee man" to pour the bitter carda- mom-flavored coffee for them, and the talk would go on for hours and hours, about all the details of their life, and the lives of everyone they knew. But now, says Dame Violet, "the bedouin who used to be out in tents—all were children then—and they're no more the same. You don't see them in the souk, or anything. Everybody's been ed-u-cated, and so they are all rather similar.

"Back in the old days everybody knew me as 'the mother of

Saud.' My son was called Saud. Hanmer York Warrington Saud Dickson. . . . Someone said if you have a son, be sure and call him after me—I forget who." Her mind is wandering, and she knows it's wandering. "I was thinking just a few days ago that this really would have to be my last winter here. I don't think next spring I shall be ready to come back. I'm getting very old. I'm—what am I now? 1896. Four years older than the year. It's '87 now? I'm ninety-one."

But as she talks, Dame Violet grows sharper, as if she is just warming up after a long, long silence. Somewhere nearby a rooster is crowing, though it is almost noon.

"This is one of the old houses. All the walls and everything are mud. The roof is mud, and when it got hot we slept out on the roof, you see. We put our beds out there. And it was very hot."

Again, the rooster.

"That's my cock that's crowing. He's seen a stranger. When he sees a stranger come into the house, he crows."

We walk out onto the balcony at the rear of the house, above a little courtyard. "That's the stable, where we kept horses. I had a nice horse. And we used to go out riding most afternoons, and we had a couple of greyhound dogs, salukis, and they'd come with us on our rides. . . . Now there are too many cars, really. I don't ride anymore, although I still have a horse. Too many cars now. But everybody's happy with their cars. They wouldn't know what to do if they didn't have a car now."

And then she said, as she would say several times that morning, "I think this will be my last winter in Kuwait."

It would be sad to leave this house to go live year-round in England.

"Yes."

In the living room there are leopard skins on the wall from hunts in India. There are massive wooden chests, braced with iron and covered with brass studs. "They were all made in Kuwait. I don't think they make them any more now. They were ideal when we went on leave. You put a padlock on and, you know, you can't just carry them away."

Windows are cut through the thick walls. "We've always had the same house with a nice view over the sea. And of course, we kept rather a big launch. For ships and things. . . . I always managed to buy one or two pearls. It was ideal, really."

Dame Violet stays in the world that Thesiger abandoned, but the new Arabia holds no more for her than it does for him. She shows me stairs leading from the barren veranda up to the roof and lets me climb them by myself. From the top of the mud house much of Kuwait City is visible. Behind the modern apartment blocks nearby sprawl vacant lots, cars cutting across them, ignoring the roads. In the middle distance are high-rise glass and steel offices and the Seeb Palace of the emir. I count nine minarets, all recently built and randomly scattered over the skyline. Closer at hand, a landing craft used for deliveries along the coast sits at anchor on the turquoise water. Beyond it are three enormous oil tankers. Industrial smokestacks loom from a point of land near the horizon, just visible through the haze.

Dame Violet is sitting in her gray rattan chair when I come back down the stairs. The nearest thing she sees, beyond the edge of her cool veranda, is a Dempster dumpster; beyond that, the highway—four full lanes; and only then the quiet little port with five elegant sambuqs at anchor. One looks beyond the dumpster, of course, to the distance, and the long past that absorbs everything.

THE GULF

THE BIG ORANGE

It was July 31, 1987, at 6:45 in the morning when I set out onto the hot blue water of the Persian Gulf aboard a boat called *Big Orange VII*. From a distance she looked like a tugboat, but bigger. One hundred and sixty-four feet long, with the superstructure squeezed onto the front third of the ship and a rear deck as big and flat as a river ferry—the *Big Orange* was ready to receive supplies to support any needs that men working on the offshore derricks or manning the supertankers might have: groceries, or tanks full of water, or replacement crews, or huge engines or air-conditioned trailers. The boat was owned by the Houston-based Intermarine Inc. (IMI) but was registered in Panama. She had a British captain and a Filipino first mate. One member of the crew was Sinhalese, another was Tamil. The cook, Manuel, came from Manila, and one of the seamen was an English schoolboy on vacation.

The amenities offered were better than might be found in

many a London bed-and-breakfast. The bunks were comfortable, the shower clean, the cabins smelled of sea and soap and the cold metal scent of polished brass. The officers' mess was graced with color television, a pirated poster of Madonna as the desperately-sought Susan and a lithe, linseed-oiled Chinese pin-up on a Taiwanese shipping company calendar. From the bridge international calls could be placed over the VHF radio to anywhere in the world.

We were headed into the southern Gulf from Sharjah, one of the United Arab Emirates. Moving slowly away from the docks, we passed the enormous market built in neo-Mogul style and the highways sweeping gracefully, chaotically around the city that had sprouted in the last few years from the bare sand. In the distance, from the lagoon, spurted a jet of water like the one in Lake Geneva. There is something remarkably quixotic about Sharjah. It is filled with ideas whose time will never come: an international airport only the occasional Eastern European carrier uses, this labyrinthine market newly built in an ancient subcontinental style without benefit of air-conditioning, spectacular hotels where no one stays. Its ruler, Sheikh Sultan al-Qasimi, is a man of culture and hindsight who has devoted much of his life to disproving the European assertion that his forbears were pirates.

But the long hook of land that runs from Abu Dhabi through Dubai and up to a point at the Musandam Peninsula, thrusting to the center of the strait at Hormuz, has been, as long as sailors have told stories, a coast of pirates and smugglers. From the emirates of Sharjah, Umm al-Qaiwain and Ras al-Khaimah they raided not only Western traders but each other, settling—and creating—vendettas on the water as well as on land. It was to curtail this chaos and the occasional challenge to its own authority that Britain in the nineteenth century imposed a series of restrictive treaties on the sheikhdoms of the coast. Eventually the British assumed all responsibility for these Trucial States' foreign affairs and, where expatriate Europeans were concerned, insisted on the Crown's jurisdiction in the courts. One law was created for the natives, another for everyone else. Gradually piracy and the slave trade were suppressed.

In 1948, when Thesiger visited the Trucial Coast, Abu Dhabi was a tiny settlement among the salt flats: "The castle gates were shut and barred and no one was about. We unloaded our camels and lay down to sleep in the shadow of the wall. Near us some small cannon were half buried in the sand. The ground around was dirty, covered with the refuse of sedentary humanity. The Arabs who had watched us watering [the camels] had disappeared. Kites wheeled against a yellow sky above a clump of tattered palms, and two dogs copulated near the wall." Up the coast, at Sharjah, the advent of Western influence was just being felt. "We skirted the aerodrome, passing piles of empty tins, broken bottles, coils of rusting wire, and fluttering bits of paper," he wrote in *Arabian Sands*. "A generator thumped in the distance, and a jeep roared down a track, leaving a stink of petrol fumes behind it. We approached a small Arab town on an open beach; it was as drab and tumble-down as Abu Dhabi, but infinitely more squalid, for it was littered with discarded rubbish which had been mass produced elsewhere." But at Dubai, Thesiger was impressed:

> Many native craft were anchored in the creek or were careened on the mud along the waterfront. There were booms from Kuwait, sambuqs from Sur, jaulbauts, and even a large stately baghila with a high carved stern on which I could make out the Christian monogram IHS on one of the embossed panels. This work must have been copied originally from some Portuguese galleon. I wondered how many times it had been copied since, exactly to the last scroll and flourish. . . . To the English all these vessels were dhows, a name no longer remembered by the Arabs. Once, however, dhows were the warships of this coast, carrying as many as four hundred men and forty to fifty guns. . . . Behind the diversity of houses which lined the waterfront were suqs, covered passageways, where merchants sat in the gloom, cross-legged in narrow alcoves among their piled merchandise. The suqs were crowded with many races—pallid Arab townsmen; armed Bedu,

quick-eyed and imperious; Negro slaves; Baluchis, Persians, and Indians. Among them I noticed a group of Kashgai tribesmen in their distinctive felt caps, and some Somalis off a sambuk from Aden. Here life moved in time with the past. These people still valued leisure and courtesy and conversation, they did not live their lives at second hand, dependent on cinemas and wireless.

Oil was discovered in the sea north of Abu Dhabi in 1958. By 1965 it was the third largest producer on the Arabian Peninsula, after Saudi Arabia and Kuwait. In 1966 Dubai hit oil, and eventually Sharjah also brought in a few wells. Development exploded across the sands. The elegant wind towers with their elaborate scrolled windows gave way to glass and steel and stucco that peeled after five years in the sun.

But life on the water has been slower to change. Enormous piers and harbors have been constructed; dry docks at Dubai were built to handle the most enormous of the supertankers. Yet the dhows remain, and life on the creeks at Dubai and Sharjah continues at a pace even Thesiger might have approved. Portuguese scrollwork is still copied on wooden ships that still sail the Gulf and the Indian Ocean on serious business. The gold souk is still dense with tribesmen from every corner of the Near East and southern Asia; it still caters to the taste of Indian brides.

Gold is heavily taxed in India and Pakistan, and heavily exported from Dubai. How it gets into India from there no one in Dubai cares to know. So extensive is the contraband that in 1987 the government in Islamabad proposed a salvage operation to recover millions of dollars worth of the metal regularly dumped overboard by smugglers when they fear capture. For decades some of the sambuqs and booms have been outfitted with high-power engines, like a bootlegger's car, ready to kick into high gear for a flat-out run across the water if a patrol boat approaches. Some are mounted with guns as well. In the early 1970s there was one gold runner reputed to have killed eighty-two Indian coast guard and naval officers during his career.

In the late 1980s in Dubai there was little sense of conflict, only of burgeoning commerce. At the airport the duty-free shop sold liquor at record low prices, and a pound of Iranian beluga caviar cost less than a hundred dollars. You could find it, fresh, just beneath the Kraft cheese in the delicatessen section. Along the creek the dhows were loaded to their dark-teak gunwales with refrigerators and air conditioners, rice and flour; Toyotas were lashed to their rough decks; dark-skinned sailors from Baluchistan or from Kerala in southwest India sat eating their curries among boxes and crates. Modern bridges handled a constant flow of Honda Accords and Mercedes 500 SELs across the creek between Dubai and adjacent Deira, but between the bridges wooden-hulled water taxis ferried crowds of women in veils and men in *thobes,* or sarongs, from one side to the other.

The war was more a business interest than a threat, a vast offshore account for contraband and a source of trade for the dry dock. But anyone who left the Creek to go out on the open water ran a chance of seeing it. And the big workboats that serviced the rigs and tankers on both sides of the Gulf saw more than most. Hundreds of ships like the *Big Orange* worked in the Gulf: some bigger, some smaller, some modified for special functions. Some were outfitted as salvage boats, spending weeks at sea, hovering near the coordinates of frequent Iraqi or Iranian attacks on shipping, offering to save a crippled ship, for a price. It was on board the salvage tugs and the workboats like the *Big Orange* that the most invisible of this century's vast and bloody conflicts sometimes suddenly loomed into view.

What became known as the Gulf War began in September 1980, when Iraqi troops rolled into southern Iran on a mission of conquest, revenge and overweening ambition. Iraq had invaded Iran but accused Iran of starting the war with border skirmishes and subversive attempts to overthrow the dictatorship of Saddam Hussein. Hussein's troops blasted their way across the Shatt-al-Arab waterway and deep into Iranian territory, then seemed to lose their way. As an article of faith the Iraqi commanders believed the twenty-month-old regime of Ayatollah Ruhollah Khomeini would collapse in the face of their onslaught. Instead Khomeini's people rallied, the Iranian troops regrouped, and with stunning disregard for their own or even their childrens' life, threw themselves, old and young, into the fields of fire. By 1982 Hussein was rolled back to the Shatt, where trench war took over on a scale rivaled only by World War I. Hundreds of thousands had died on both sides, killed by gas and killed in suicide charges and blown to bits in all the usual ways of modern warfare.

In 1984, with an apparently insurmountable stalemate in the land war, a new phase in the fighting began. Iraq and Iran were two of the world's greatest oil producers before the war, and if they were going to continue fighting they needed to keep pumping and selling their petroleum abroad. It was natural for them to go after each other's oil flows. Iran took the early lead, knocking out Iraq's only access to the Gulf, through Basra, and using a strategic alliance with Damascus to shut down Baghdad's biggest pipeline to the Mediterranean, which ran through Syria. Iraq built other pipelines through Turkey and Saudi Arabia, and it struck with a vengeance at Iran's oil production by declaring a killing field that consumed half the Gulf. Iran's main oil terminal was at Kharg Island in the northern tip of the Gulf. To get its oil out, it had to load tankers there, then run them the length of the waterway and out through the Strait of Hormuz.

By 1984 Iraq had acquired French Mirage fighters and a vital little piece of armament: the Exocet air-to-sea missile. From a range of forty miles, far out of visual contact with its target, a Mirage could cut loose an Exocet, then turn and run while the missile homed in on the ship's profile, heading straight for the biggest mass that registered in its monomaniacal circuitry. Iran was virtually defenseless against these attacks. Its air force was vestigial: its elite American-trained pilots had been decimated by the Thermidorean slaughter of suspected royalists in the early days of the revolution; its jet fighters were crumbling for lack of spare parts embargoed by the United States. Unable to fight back directly, Teheran began to retaliate against any available targets. There weren't any Iraqi ships left in the Gulf, but Iraq's allies, Kuwait and Saudi Arabia, had tankers sitting out on the water like enormous defenseless whales.

Iran also managed to develop a shuttle system to bring oil down from Kharg. A few well-rewarded if oft-attacked tankers shuttled it to makeshift terminals near the mouth of the Gulf then loaded it onto more cautious carriers for its journey to the rest of the world. The perilous route followed by the shuttle came to be known as Exocet Alley.

Each new phase in the war had been accompanied by apocalyptic predictions that the conflict would provoke astronomical rises in oil prices, superpower involvement, a region in flames. But after the first few years, and the first few scares, most of the world discovered it could live quite comfortably with the Iran-Iraq slaughter. Oil prices stabilized, then actually declined. The carnage was remote from the world's television screens and its conscience. No end was in sight.

Even in the Gulf it was possible to be very close to the fighting yet remain completely detached from it. Artillery battles along the Shatt-al-Arab occasionally rattled the windows in Kuwait City when the wind blew down from the northeast. But most Kuwaitis paid little attention, worrying more about scandals in their stock market, or shepherding their investments abroad. In the southern Gulf the Emirates quickly found ways to turn a profit from the conflict. They opened land routes for traders to truck goods up the northeast coast of Arabia without having to brave the Gulf passage and also shipped Iran just about anything it wanted through the free ports of Dubai.

At sea proximity to the war was largely a function of chance, and a hair's breadth could make all the difference. By the middle of 1986 Iraq's air force started to increase its range. Exocet Alley was being extended steadily south toward the strait, and Iranian retaliation grew increasingly desperate, increasingly vicious.

* * *

Captain Gerry Blackburn and his young chief engineer Phil Moir had just seen a lot of action aboard the little workboat *Anita* when I met them on my first trip to Dubai, in 1986. I was looking, even then, for a ride out onto the water. The *Anita* was tied up outside the Gulf Agencies Company offices, a huge Emirates flag painted across its rear deck as a talisman of neutrality to avert bombs and rockets. Moir was in the wheelhouse tidying up. "I'm not going back out there," he said in a thick Scottish accent. He pulled out the earplugs he had worn up from the engine room. He wiped his hands on his white coveralls. "It's just too dangerous." He looked tired; his chin was covered with thin stubble. Forty-one vessels had been hit by Iran or Iraq in 1984, forty-four in 1985. By August of 1986 the toll was already sixty-eight. Even as we spoke, the radio in the wheelhouse broadcast news of a fresh attack somewhere near Kharg. Moir had worked on the shuttle in Exocet Alley. I asked him about hazard pay. "Expats on the shuttles get eight thousand to ten thousand pounds a month—for officers. Quite an attractive salary if you want to get your head blown off." At Kharg itself Iraqi bombers roared overhead like the Germans in the blitz. Many of the shuttle tankers, rust buckets owned mostly by Greek and Cypriot companies, had been hit, repaired and put back into service, then hit again. And again. Burned out, Moir changed jobs, figuring it was safer in the southern Gulf.

On Moir's first day out on the *Anita,* August 12, 1986, they sailed for Sirri Island, where Iran had set up an improvised oil terminal. The *Anita* was delivering water to one of the many tankers scattered around the ninety-six square miles of anchorage. In the middle distance the *Klelia,* a mother ship used for storage, was sandwiched between the Iranian shuttle tanker *Azarpad,* which had brought oil down to Sirri from Kharg's beleaguered terminals, and the *Mississippi,* which was loading up the crude for export. It was 11:00 in the morning. "I'd just come up from the engine room," Moir remembers. "I was taking off my boots when I heard a whining noise and two explosions." Launched without warning from warplanes that were never seen, missiles had slammed into the *Klelia* and the *Azar-*

pad. "There was smoke pouring out of them." A rush of images came back to him as he talked. "There was two bodies floating past." Moir was only twenty-five. "I think it's time to get out of engineering," he said. "If they'd hit the tanker we were next to, I could have been one of those bodies. I don't particularly like being a messenger for other people's wars."

As Moir talked, Captain Blackburn came up into the *Anita*'s wheelhouse. He listened for a minute, and the expression in his sharp blue eyes was hard to read, but it was dead level and seemed to caution Moir against talking too much. If Blackburn had identified with the bodies in the water, he didn't say. He told the story his own way, in sparse phrases and hard facts. "We were on the wing of the bridge, and we just heard a crack, a couple of cracks, like they were testing the antiaircraft guns on Sirri. Then over the VHF we heard 'We're under attack.' We saw the smoke. We started steaming toward the three ships. From the way it was burning, I knew right away it was a mother ship. In fifteen or twenty minutes we were there. The fire-fighting tugs were coming up. The first tug on the scene was shouting over the VHF that people were in the water." Suddenly sailors were screaming in the sea around his boat. Two were hanging on desperately to a single life jacket. "I pulled eight of them out of the water," said Blackburn. "Three were from the *Mississippi* and four from the *Azarpad.*" One was a Greek, one a Maldivian, the rest Filipinos. "The *Mississippi* had never been touched. But it just became sheer panic. It was pandemonium. It broke free and ran, breaking off all the pipes and spreading oil all over the *Klelia*'s decks, around the accommodations. The *Azarpad* had a flaming hole just above the waterline."

"We collected the people we could get. We circled, looking for more. We passed a body." The Iranians on Sirri ordered the work-boats to pick up corpses. "But I said, 'I'm too busy picking up live people to go after a body. You don't go after dead ones when you got live ones.'"

I liked Blackburn, with his hard gaze and his ruddy face. He looked as though he'd been through some wars, and would just as soon talk about them. He was thirty-six years old; his wife and child were living in London. I figured he would know a good bar in Dubai, if there was such a thing, and I asked him to dinner. To which he replied, "Do you like Mexican food?"

The Keralan midget at the door was dressed like the Cisco Kid and called me señor. The country band inside was playing "Desperado." The air was thick with smoke and the smell of beer, and the light was low. This was Pancho Villa's up on the second floor of the fleabag Astoria Hotel, where sailors came to stay and much of Dubai came to drink. There was a story, often told and often embellished, that shaken mariners once came into Pancho's after their ship was shot up by Iranian gunboats, only to find themselves seated next to their attackers. The faces that hovered over the nachos in the dim glow seemed to be from everywhere. Texas faces. Teheran faces. Indians and Maldivians, Italians and Brits, Chinese and Arabs. The long-legged singer in stretch jeans and gleaming boots was trying to coax people onto the dance floor. Her voice was husky, and people must have told her a million times she sounded like Kim Carnes. There we were with "Bette Davis Eyes" in this bar at the heart of Dubai. Still there was no dancing. Then, appropriately enough, a little something from Dire Straits. Money for nothing and chicks for free. That got them moving: a middle-aged Brit and his teenage daughter twisting away, the mother watching from the table, sipping her pint of Foster's. Behind the band was a big blowup of the old Mexican revolutionary bandido himself, looking to raise some hell with some of his boys. Draped beside it were the Confederacy's Stars and Bars, the Union's Stars and Stripes, the Texas Lone Star—and the Union Jack. Filipino waitresses worked their way through the crowd to pick up pitchers of frozen margaritas at the bar. Sizzle and steam cut the air from hot iron plates full of steak *fajitas*.

Gerry and I got a table in the corner near the kitchen door, and we could barely hear each other, shouting over the music, the dishes and the chatter. He was talking about the *Akarita*. She'd been waiting three days to load off of one of the Emirates' offshore terminals when low-flying planes came in after her. "When I got there, she was well alight," said Blackburn. But she was lucky, in a way. One missile had gone into the sea. It was luck or marksmanship as well that had spared the oil complex only three miles away, with its living quarters full of workers. Gerry had called them on the VHF and offered to help. "Get the fuck out of here!" they told him. They were scared shitless, completely helpless. "If you're on a ship, you can kid yourself," said Gerry. "You can kid yourself that you can move. But if you're on one of those damn structures . . ."

For Gerry the war was getting close. He wasn't quitting, like Phil. But, still, you had to say it was close. A few days ago the Iraqis had hit a supply vessel about the size of the *Anita*. The *Abu Adil* it was called. "A total wipeout. Everybody was killed on that one." And the Iranians were using helicopters. "The damn things hover there." They were so bloody insidious. The Iranians had been challenging ships in the strait for years. But now they had this new twist, where they challenged the vessels, let the captain identify himself, his destination, his cargo, then just said "Have a nice day" and sent him on his way. A few minutes later a chopper would come at him. "The worst case we had was the Saudi ship the *El Safaniyah*, off Qatar. . . . The helicopter hovered right in front of her and fired right into the accommodation. Twice. They killed the British captain." We listened to the music. Ordered another beer.

That was the night I first heard about the Filipino Monkey. A disembodied voice with a Tagalog accent comes onto the hailing frequency of the VHF at odd hours to regale his listeners with obscenities. "You get a lot of fucking around on the VHF," said Gerry. "Filipino Monkey and like that. Well, as soon as they hit Sirri, it stopped."

Time for a piss. Out through the swinging doors, searching for the men's room. There. But who are these people? In the banquet hall, beyond the toilet doors, are all these women in chadors. Is this a wedding, a shower? Chadors, there, only a toilet's distance from Bette Davis eyes and Foster's lager.

* * *

Eleven months later I was aboard the *Big Orange* and headed out to sea with a handful of other journalists. She was in good condition, better than I remembered the *Anita*. The amenities made life easier than I had hoped. Manuel, the Filipino cook, served up a hefty breakfast of bacon and eggs. The mess, the sleeping quarters, the bridge were all air conditioned to an electrical chill. Step outside, and the sun hit you at one hundred plus degrees; your glasses fogged, and condensation formed on your cool arms before the sweat started.

Those first few hours at sea I spent a lot of time with my eyes locked into the rubber cone that shaded the radar screen. Beneath the sweep of the luminescent radius most ships looked alike. Enormous differences in size made little difference in the blips scattered across the glowing circles. It was the way they moved, and where, that drew attention: small fishing boats, sometimes traveling in groups, looked like a school of guppies in an electric fishbowl; enormous supertankers driving through the water with the brute force of a hundred locomotives blasted through the concentric circles of distance—five, ten, fifteen kilometers in a few minutes. The old dhows cut across the normal shipping lanes with the casual abandon of ships in home waters, as comfortable as boys in the souks running errands through the back alleys where they were born. As they came into view, no one knew whether the long, light fiberglass fishing boats or the wooden dhows had guns on board, whether there was a rocket-propelled grenade hidden beneath the tentlike shade over the rear deck, whether their crews were dropping mines in the water during the night.

Iran's helicopter raids on shipping had subsided by the summer of 1987, to be replaced by an even more reckless high seas guerrilla war. As Iraqi air raids now ranged the whole length of the Gulf, the Iranians were desperate to reply. Revolutionary Guards discovered they could pull a skiff the size of a Boston Whaler up to a tanker in the middle of the night, jacklight the bridge and fire away with complete impunity, using rocket-propelled grenades and fifty-caliber machine guns (anything lighter tended to bounce like BBs off the heavy hulls), terrorizing all the crewmen, wounding and killing as many as they could. Eventually the attacks started coming in broad daylight. There was nothing to stop them. The Iranians' other innovation had been the use of mines, usually laid from World War II landing craft, which also served countless peaceful purposes, delivering goods to the shallow harbors all along the Gulf shores.

Our captain was Alan Hatfield. He still looked like a kid, shirtless and in running shorts as he commanded the ship. He was laconic, cool and competent, and seemed the perfect skipper for this odd expedition; taking a bunch of journalists deep-sea fishing for war stories. He had come down to the Gulf with his father from Yorkshire and had spent most of his career in the waters north of Sharjah.

Gerry Blackburn had come from Yorkshire as well. There seemed to be Yorkshiremen all over the place. But when I asked Alan to tell me how they all came to be in the Persian Gulf, so far from home, he had little to say. "You should talk to my father." He was the one who had sailed with the Arctic Fleet. He could explain.

Ray Hatfield worked on shore in Sharjah as a manager at the company that chartered the *Big Orange* boats. His face showed years of weather and pain. Like Blackburn and many others, he had come to the Gulf from the stormy seas near the Arctic Circle once sailed by Britain's deep-water fishing boats. In the Gulf fourteen-foot waves are considered big. For a sailor with Hatfield's past, "fourteen-foot— that's like a summer's day." The veterans of the Arctic Fleet are now in their late forties or fifties, having gone to sea, for the most part, when they were about fifteen. Sailing out of Hull, England, in the 1950s and 1960s, they worked almost 330 days a year: three weeks out, two days in—one for tending to business and one for getting drunk, spending whatever money they'd managed to pile up. "Millionaire for a day," as Ray Hatfield remembered. He made skipper when he was twenty-six, but there was little hope for a long career. Few men worked into their sixties. Many died in the mountainous waters they sailed, where ice would crust up on the rigging and eventually just bring the boat toppling over. One black day there were more than sixty killed on three boats. This was the old, hard life of the sea, full of mystery, fear and superstition. Shaving was thought to be unlucky. "I've seen men stood there with a couple of weeks' growth and icicles hanging from it." The nets were pulled to the side of the ship by winches. But—"once you've got the trawl up to the rail, you'd have to pull it up with your fingers. They looked like raw meat when you was finished." The pay wasn't great. And for every one who made money, there were three who wouldn't. "You was only ever as good as your last voyage." On board the ship, "it was just work—and sleep when you could." But, as Hatfield would have it, "the genuine fishermen of years ago, they was a fine bunch. The finest crowd there was. We used to work together, drink together, sing together. It was good."

Then came the Cod Wars, the long wrangle between Iceland and Britain over fishing rights that Britain finally lost after years of tense standoffs at sea, cut nets and lost catches. And the fishermen of the Arctic Fleet, by the hundreds, lost their work. They became a kind of diaspora, scattered to ports around the globe. Men like Hatfield and Blackburn looked at every point of the compass—Nigeria, Tasmania—before they found their way into the oil service business, and the Gulf. "Before this job came up, when you came out of fishing there was virtually nothing for you," said Hatfield. England was still home, and wives and children were left behind, but they grew distant, became memories, unless, like Alan Hatfield, sons came to follow in their father's trade. Gradually, for the men of Hull, the trawlers were replaced by geological survey vessels. The business of petroleum replaced the business of cod; a life of storms and ice gave way to the sun, the desert and the shallow blue sea off Arabia. "A piece of cake," said Hatfield one afternoon as he sat among the radio transmitters that keep him in touch with the workboat skippers scattered in the waters north of Sharjah, Alan among them. "The people who left fishing and came to work on these ships never had it so good." Ray Hatfield found in the Gulf, for himself and for Alan, what so many fathers want for their children: a better life in the old tradition. No war between Arabs and Persians was going to take that away from either of them.

That night of July 31 was Alan Hatfield's birthday. He was twenty-six years old. We were a hundred miles out into the Gulf, headed north. We celebrated with a bottle of champagne in the mess of the *Big Orange VII*.

PINK SMOKE

....

OUR FOREMOST CONCERN WAS MINES. IN THE EARLY SUMMER OF 1987 they had become Iran's guerrilla warfare weapon of choice, the *punji* sticks of the Gulf. Big ships were on top of them without warning, and suddenly found themselves crippled. Smaller ships could be annihilated. The first big show of U.S. force to parade into the Gulf that summer of 1987—frigates and cruisers with flags flying proudly to escort the Kuwaiti-owned, U.S.-registered tanker *Bridgeton* toward its berth in Kuwait—was humiliated by these simple, deadly devices. While surrounded by its escort, the *Bridgeton* had struck five hundred pounds of high explosive. But that was not the worst of it. The accompanying warships quickly came to a terrified halt: their thin skins, their captains knew, couldn't take a blast like that. Their sonar couldn't find the things. They were blind, stumbling through a field of bombs. The warships had let the crippled tanker—the ship they were supposed to protect—take the lead. "The *Bridgeton* will be acting as a deep-draft minesweeper. He realizes that he can take hits easier than we can," Captain William Mathis explained to his crew on the cruiser *Fox*. They followed humbly, hunkering down at battle stations in the merchantman's wake. For the U.S. Navy even one mine was, in the skipper's words, "enough to keep the pucker factor up."

Washington's show of force looked ridiculous, as if the Pentagon had been suckered into a situation it didn't understand and couldn't handle. And the scene, already ludicrous, would have been hilarious if the path into the *Bridgeton*'s wake hadn't meandered through so many tragedies. The American navy was in the Gulf to expiate the sins and omissions and plain mistakes of the Reagan administration in the Arab world. Just as the bombing of Libya had been a bold, flailing blow against terrorism, calculated as much for its macho imagery as for its military efficacy, the deployment of a large number of American warships to the Gulf was supposed to be a demonstration of strength and endurance to American allies convinced, in the course of the previous decade, that the United States had no staying power.

In those first months of the deployment, diplomats and politicians often drew analogies with Beirut in 1983, where the Reagan administration had let events dictate its policy and stumbled into a confrontation with Iranian-backed terrorists that cost the lives of 241 Marines in a single horrible morning. After the suicide bombers took their toll, the American administration continued proclaiming its resolve to stay in Lebanon, but nobody believed it. There was never a clear reason why the United States got involved there, why it stayed for so long at the cost of so many lives, or why at last it left.

Now it all seemed to be happening again: the pattern of escalation so confused that even the identity of the enemy was obscured in official policy statements. Washington said it was in the Gulf to protect a principle: freedom of navigation. Or it was there to keep Soviet influence in the region from growing. Washington said it would protect only those ships flying American flags, then welcomed Kuwait's request to register its ships in Delaware. The U.S. Navy had had a small presence in the Gulf since 1949 and Washington said nothing more would be needed. Then an Iraqi jet hit the U.S. frigate *Stark* with two missiles that killed thirty-seven American sailors. The United States decided for its own protection to increase its naval presence in the Gulf by a factor of five. So it was—manipulated by the Kuwaitis, competing with the Soviets, attacked by Iraq—the U.S. Navy girded for war.

The enemy knew who he was. He was the same enemy as in Beirut, the same one who had humiliated the Reagan administration only a few months before by exposing its secret deals to trade arms for hostages. Whether Washington said so or not, every move it made was against the Ayatollah Khomeini. But Iran's leaders were careful plotters, well aware of limits on their actions, meticulously calculating the level of provocation, the dangers of retaliation. They knew the Great Satan well, and wanted to do nothing to provoke directly the massive American deployment in the Persian Gulf. The mine that hit the *Bridgeton,* said one of the Ayatollah's men, was simply the work of "invisible hands."

A week later we were out on the *Big Orange,* sailing toward the same hidden enemy.

We were headed west northwest from Sharjah. Dubai's Fateh oil field, far from the sight of the mainland, rose like an urban apparition from the surface of the sea; a city perched on stilts, with little derricks and pumping stations standing like silent sentries around its far-flung perimeter. Its high-tech practicality evoked imagined space stations; ungainly, bolted-together modules, seeming almost to float in the air. Supply boats moved among the towers, shuttling between the complexes and the platforms. A dhow was anchored near one of the derricks. A helicopter hovered in. Every few days choppers or supply boats brought new crews to the complex. A gas flare soared into the sky above the largest agglomeration of living quarters and machinery. Defense attachés in Abu Dhabi had told me there were antiaircraft missiles mounted on the Fateh superstructure, but if so, they were hidden. The whole complex appeared perfectly vulnerable, as exposed and fragile as an Erector Set anchored in sand.

In the distance, just at the northern horizon, rose another city above the sea. This one, the twin of Dubai's Fateh, was Iranian.

At dusk another complex appeared on our left, Abu Al-Ba-koosh. The flat sun was setting behind its two flares; a layer of smoke spread out in the sky above. Again, in the distance, an Iranian twin city rose above the sea. Through the binoculars we could see little supply ships anchored there. Far in the distance what must have been an Iranian tanker was fading into the night of the northeastern horizon. This was Sasson field, and we saw no activity as we sailed closer; only these three orange and white Iranian National Oil Company supply boats, tethered and dead still. No flare above the complex. No lights within. The colonels at the embassies in Abu Dhabi had said Sasson was often used by Revolutionary Guards as a lookout post, sometimes as an attack base. We passed, without incident, into the dark.

At 8:15 in the evening, nervous and bored, I started flipping through the channels on the television in the officers' mess: "Sesame Street" in Arabic, flip, a soap opera, probably Egyptian, from the look of the women, flip, a poster of Khomeini and a mullah standing before it, exhorting the faithful, flip, flip, Big Bird, Khomeini. It was going to be a long night.

On the bridge, in the dim glow of the running lights and the halo of the radar screen, nothing to see but the occasional gas flare welding the edge of the sky. Alan is at the wheel. He says that when men fly in space they can make out only two man-made features on the face of the earth: the Great Wall of China and the gas flares in the Persian Gulf. Alan, and the other men on that little sea, believe this.

Channel 16 coughs workaday communications, coordinates and cargoes, then suddenly begins to vomit obscenities. The *fuck you*s are Anglo-Saxon enough, but the accent is Tagalog. And then, there, in a drawn-out croon, the call-sign curse of the Gulf, blocking radio traffic, screwing around in the long dark hours of the night on the surface of the sea: "Filipino Monkey. Filipino Monkeeeeee."

At midnight, in my bunk, I kept thinking of the photographs in the record book kept by the insurance adjusters at the Dubai Tower. A workboat called the *Sedra* had been sailing these waters a few weeks before. Chartered by the Kuwaitis, it was about the size of the *Big Orange,* maybe a little smaller. While minding its own business, it was attacked with rocket-propelled grenades designed to blow apart armored personnel carriers and battle tanks. It was the middle of the night. The crew, mostly asleep, had no time to move or react. The photographs showed them, in the white flat glare of a Onestep flash camera, carbonized like the exhumed bodies of Pompeii, the flesh charred but still pink in places, the lips burned into rigid grins.

"Klingons!" someone shouted just after dawn. A warship, the first we'd seen. The photographers and camera crews scrambled for their lenses and battery packs. We were moving up on the channel that led to Bahrain, and, in the low-angled light the gray profile of a frigate took clear shape through the binoculars. Its flag was too small to see, but there was a distinctive bright white dome looking like R2D2 perched large on the heights of the superstructure. It was unmistakable: the Phalanx system, ready to lock on to any incoming missiles and shield the ship with a hail of uranium bullets. An American frigate. We moved in on it, making a pass about a half mile off its stern. Closer up the horizontal sunlight showed the surface of the thin, alloy skin dimpling against the steel ribs of the hull. Some of the crew members were back on the fantail, flak jackets over their T-shirts, fishing. On the bow, others were at battle stations, carbines in hand, helmets on, ready to clear the way of mines—by shooting at them.

Garbage bags look a lot like mines, and the Gulf has a lot of them, big and black and shiny and round, bobbing on the gentle chop, sometimes with a dusky brown sea gull aboard. You can't be sure, even with binoculars, until you approach within about a hundred yards. By then, if the bag were a mine, and part of a field, you would be in it. Quite a few garbage bags were sunk by the navy's marksmen that summer. Nothing on the surface of that sea was safe from the navy, nor was the navy safe from it.

I learned what little I know of mines from an ordnance-disposal man who had retired from the British military but was still working his trade in an office in a back corner of a Dubai shipping agency. Above his head was a chart, meticulously hand drawn in colored pencil, laying out the basic principles and structures that made these infernal machines so effective. They were as simple as a mousetrap, and attempts to make them better only elaborated basic themes. The weapon lies in wait at the bottom of the sea, then springs to life sometime shortly before its target appears. Some of the most sophisticated mines are programmed to identify the acoustic signature of individual ships. As early as World War II mines could actually count the vessels in a convoy passing above them before rising toward the surface and their selected target. Others were magnetically activated. But the basic mechanisms of a contact mine could be extremely simple: a plug made of salt and glass tubes surrounded by soft lead. A mine, said the old pro, is a "waterway denial weapon," that is, something "designed to deny passage to and from ports, a silent sentry, a sleeping policeman." It need only be sophisticated enough to perform that job.

The Iranian mines looked like Popeye cartoon parodies, old-fashioned and clumsy. But they were perfectly effective. The essential design originated in Britain just after the turn of the century and was adopted and mass-produced by the navy of the Russian czar. As this grizzled expert explained it, and the chart above his head made clear, the mine comes in three basic parts: the container that holds the explosives and fuses (the studded ball that looms through the mist in old movies), the "shoe" on which it rests (usually with wheels) and the tether that links the ball to the shoe. When this assembly is rolled, pushed, slid or dropped over the side of a boat—any boat will do if it can be fitted with a block and tackle—it sinks to the bottom and stays there, far below the waves and invisible to the sonar of the ships passing above it. The ball full of explosives is buoyant, but held to the weighted shoe with a plug or with glue that dissolves. "It could be made of salt or sugar"—substances just as simple, just as available as the contents of a kitchen cabinet. Depending on the thickness and composition of the plug, it could hold the mine on the bottom for minutes, hours, weeks. When it dissolves, the mine rises toward the surface, to the length of its tether—say, about forty feet beneath the surface. Often, the tension of the tether pulling taught triggers the mechanism that arms the mine. Detonation of roughly five hundred pounds of RDX or another high-powered explosive inside is almost equally simple. The "horns" of the mine contain glass vials of mercury. The metal that surrounds them is extremely soft. If it is hit or bent, the vial breaks, an electrical circuit is completed. Boom.

The name of the ordnance-disposal man was Happy Day. He had been at this job for more than thirty years. His manner was affable. He talked with the dark, bitter bravado common in the British armed forces, where humor is sick and predictable, where anybody named White is called Chalky, any Scot becomes Jock, any Day becomes Happy. On one of the walls of his office was a poster in the style of *Ghostbusters*. It said, "BODY BUSTERS." "A lot of black humor," I said, by way of conversation. After Britain's last war, said Happy, there was a T-shirt made up for one amputee: "I GAVE A HAND IN THE FALKLANDS."

Happy had found his way to the Gulf via Libya, where he spent his time clearing World War II mines off the beaches. Before that there were the mines washed up on Britain's shores or pulled up in fishing nets, left over from D day. When he retired from the service, he joined up with other former noncommissioned officers: "a group of specialists who offer unique services."

Above the Body Busters posters were other colored-pencil diagrams: air-to-sea rockets and their warheads, a rocket-propelled grenade and its explosive charge. "We've seen these missiles in all sorts of situations: stuck in bulkheads, in oil, on a boatswain's bunk. The most common misconception is that if it hasn't gone bang, it's not going to," said Happy instructively. "We have to be insured not only against killing ourselves but against damaging a ship with, say, $52 million worth of cargo aboard." After three decades working around volatile explosives, you have to have confidence in your abilities. The slightest mistake is the last mistake, said Happy, "unless you can run at 22,000 feet per second"—the speed of the blast. "If you're bad in this business, you're not bad for very long. You're awarded what's called the Order of the Pink Smoke."

We were just a few doors down from the office where I'd met Gerry Blackburn about a year before, and I remembered that before our drinking bout at Pancho Villa's we'd been looking through snapshots of ships that had been hit and the damage done to them. There was a photograph of a couple of men leaning over a rocket lodged under the steel beam on the inside of a ship's hull.

"That was probably the twitchiest one we've done up here," Happy allowed. It was a French AS-12 rocket, wire-guided from a helicopter, a weapon originally designed for attacks on tanks. It hadn't gone off but had gotten jammed up under a beam on the side of the ship, with its tip protruding through the hull, out of reach of Happy's tools, impossible to defuse, capable of going off at any second. There in the fume-filled hold of the tanker it was 126 degrees. Happy and his colleague were standing in two feet of oil. Except for their little spotlights trained on the missile, they were in a morass of darkness, straining for a movement of millimeters to pry the missile free of the steel beam without blowing themselves and the hull to bits—millimeter by millimeter, thinking of 22,000 feet per second. The steel would not give. They had no welding tools, and if they did those would have brought other, perhaps even greater risks. Millimeters, millimeters, hands sweating, sweat pouring. "If you want the closest thing to Dante's Inferno, you had it that day." One hour. Three. Five hours.

The noise rang in their ears like the end of the world. And then, in relief, they laughed. The beam had broken. And Happy was sitting there with the rocket in his lap.

When Happy Day left the service of Her Majesty, he was described in his discharge papers as an "adrenaline operator" who got high on the risk and tension connected with his work. But he kept it up, he said, because "the actual truth of the matter is it's the only thing I know how to do." In any given situation he and his colleagues had the "absolute right" not to take on a job. But to begin refusing assignments because your nerves are going means "it's a very short step after that before you get the Order of the Pink Smoke, before you say, 'Play Misty for Me.' "

I looked up and studied the charts of mines and missiles, and there was a little uncomfortable silence unbroken by the laughter that was supposed to be there. "You become incredibly tired. Not morose. But very tired," said Happy Day. "It's not a good living, and you're always in a war zone." And as good as you might be, there was always the possibility of something unexpected turning up, such as a trap worked into the wiring of the mine just to throw off an ordnance-disposal man, just to kill him. In the Gulf the very simplicity of the devices encountered was frightening. High-tech mines, the mass-produced ordnance of the modern powers, had manuals and specifications that could be learned. But the essential device was so rudimentary that, in Happy's words, "a workshop could produce mines. They could be forty-gallon drums. It's just a container for explosives." A terrorist device of any kind, whether a mine in the Gulf or a car bomb in Belfast, had a kind of personal touch that was disconcerting, and at first terribly unpredictable. "It's the product of one man's mind." Happy had met his counterpart on the other side of the Gulf, the man who disposed of ordnance for Iran, if not the man who made it. He respected him. Hell, he identified with him. "He is a very well trained, very courageous man who looks about one hundred years old." The Iranians were no fools.

The danger of the work still brought a thrill. Sure. "You tackle one of these weapons, and you're on a real high. But as soon as it's over, it subsides very quickly." Afterwards, Day would head off to one of the pubs in one of the smaller Dubai hotels for a couple of beers, "and I mean a couple." There's no percentage in hangovers and shaky hands when faced with the choice of which wire to cut. And as he sat there over a pint of beer the last of the adrenaline would drain away. A moment would come when this dangerous life in an alien land seemed terribly ordinary. "We become middle-aged men," said Happy Day, "who wish to God we were doing something else."

SHEEP LATITUDES

EVEN THROUGH THE BINOCULARS THEY LOOKED A LOT LIKE MINES, AND A thrill of excitement and fear went through the bridge of the *Big Orange*. They seemed to be scattered at random—the random pattern of a minefield—there in the afternoon light. Certainly they were not garbage bags. Were those the detonating prongs that projected from their sides? And yet . . . and yet there was something unminelike about these things. As we drew closer and their shape and color in the water grew more distinct, they appeared to have heads, and—feet. And they were not black, after all, but the color of raw wool. They were sheep, quite dead sheep, bloated from the sun and brine, scattered by the dozens across the surface of the sea, like the horse carcasses that littered the subtropical latitudes of the Atlantic in the days of becalmed sailing ships. Born in Australia, these sheep had been bound to Saudi Arabia for sacrifice, died en route and been thrown into the sea. They would never make it to the Plain of Arafat.

On the Eid el-Adha, the great feast that marks the end of the Muslim pilgrimage to Mecca, thousands of sheep, bullocks and camels are slaughtered outside the holy city, and in echo of that ritual an orgy of killing takes place throughout the Islamic world. In Cairo blood runs through the streets in little scarlet rivers, coagulating here and there in the dust as men who claim to specialize in the trade of religiously sanctioned killing walk up and down at dawn among the houses with knives in their belts and spattered aprons. They slit the throat of a sheep or goat, then slit the skin on its legs and blow up the animal like an inflatable raft, forcing the hide away from the flesh. Then they strip the skin away and butcher the animal into parts.

Horrified European hoteliers, especially in the early days of Arab wealth, told stories of guests, unaccustomed to modern establishments and devoted to the rigorous duties of their faith, who would slaughter animals on the balcony of their high-rise room. Yet at the heart of this spectacle is a philosophy of charity and generosity. By tradition and law, which are much the same in Islam, those who have bought the animals for slaughter keep only a third of the meat, another third goes to family and friends and the remainder is distributed to the poor. To be wealthy enough to participate in this ritual is a matter of pride among those whose fortunes are increasing, a matter of grave obligation among those whose wealth is assured. In Jidda alone more than 250,000 sheep are killed during each year's celebration. At Mecca special abatoirs built for the pilgrimage are capable of slaughtering a thousand head an hour.

It was not the slaughter of sheep, however, but the slaughter of people at Mecca that caught the world's attention in 1987. We first heard about the incident over the BBC shortwave at 9:00 in the morning on our second day at sea: "Thousands of Iranian pilgrims have been involved in violent incidents in Mecca, and there are reports of many casualties."

Holy war. Islamic Jihad. In the 1980s those words were heard so often, associated with so many atrocities, that to many Western minds the Muslim faith itself came to seem a source of terror. Whole sects were condemned in the popular imagination. "I just stepped in some shiite," read the redneck bumper stickers in the United States. But for the Westerners in the Gulf, the real threat at hand was more complex. Few understood Islam except in terms of dress codes and drinking rules. They lived and worked among worshipers, and proximity tended to mitigate bigotry. But in the back of their minds, many expats dreaded a moment of terror in which they would become symbols for all that the zealots feared and loathed. The world of the fundamentalists was being changed by the products, the skills, the values brought to it by these foreigners. Yet there were very few attacks against expatriates in the Gulf. Islam surrounded them, but they lived at peace. At the center of the war, through most of the conflict, the Muslim faithful were too busy fighting each other to bother the infidels in their midst.

The essence of Islam, and the literal meaning of the word, is submission. With the promise of everlasting life in paradise held out before him, a man of faith surrenders himself to the will of God, his future to the fate that God has written for him in a book that ordains the destiny of every human being. His law is the law of God delivered by the Prophet Muhammad in the Koran. There is no recourse or appeal: there is no god but God, and Muhammad is his messenger. But as a believer gropes his way through life to discover his fate, he must observe certain rules, perform certain duties. Five, known as the pillars of Islam, are essential: he must abandon all other gods, pray five times a day, demonstrate charity, fast during the holy month of Ramadan and make the hajj—the pilgrimage to Mecca—at least once in his life. From this narrow foundation there rises, like an inverted pyramid propped up by these few strong columns, a vast array of lesser duties, rules, regulations and certain carefully prescribed punishments to be meted out for infractions.

More perfectly than any religion or ideology known before or created since, the design of Islam served as a political framework for conquest. Though its Prophet delivered the last word on monotheism, it is explicitly tolerant of the other "people of the Book," Christians and Jews. Thus followers of the two greatest organized religions in Muhammad's day could save face, surrender and survive when they faced the conquering armies of Islam. At the same time the Muslim faithful were promised that if they died in the jihad, the holy war waged to spread Islam and punish the infidels, they would instantly enter the gates of paradise.

But with the spreading of the faith and the passing of time inevitably there was an accretion of contradictory interpretations around this code of conduct designed for the needs of desert nomads and villagers. A constant tension developed from Islam's earliest days between the need to adapt to a changing world and the fundamentalist desire to strip away the layers of theology and interpretation to return to the powerful, basic quid pro quo: surrender to God in the present, be assured of paradise in the future.

When powerful and disparate cultures blended with this powerful faith, the faith divided. Within twenty-five years of the Prophet's death his followers were split by a violent struggle for leadership. The group that later came to be known as the Sunni maintained the basic aggressive simplicity of the faith; the other, the Shia, developed a much more pronounced clerical structure and a cult of persecution. The seventh-century struggle for the future of Islam was a war between the rich, worldly rulers of Damascus, who claimed the legacy of the Prophet by force of arms, and the followers of Muhammad's grandson Husayn, finally slaughtered by the Damascene armies at Karbala, in what is now Iraq, abandoned and betrayed. Each year the most devoted of the Shia faithful scourge and beat themselves on the anniversary of Husayn's death. Eventually the Sunni faith became identified with the Arab cause, while the Shia sect took on a distinctly Persian caste.

Within each group, voices always remained—sometimes in the background, sometimes erupting into prominence—that called for a return to the simplicity and power of the basic faith and, often, for the jihad that would cleanse their ranks and spread their beliefs. For much of the last eighty years that tension has expressed itself as hostility toward Western ideologies, particularly communism and Arab socialist variants and, more generally, toward the onslaught of "modernity" impelled by the growth of European, American and

Japanese technological empires around the world. In the United States, in the popular imagination, *Shiite, fundamentalist* and *terrorist* became virtual synonyms for Iranian. But all sides in the Gulf War believed God was with them, and Washington's most important ally made the holiest claims of all.

The first Islamic fundamentalist to command the attention of the twentieth century was Abdul Aziz ibn Saud, who forged a nation—Saudi Arabia—with his faith, his saber and his rifle. The Saudi flag bears a sword and the Arabic phrase from the Koran "There is no god but God and Muhammad is his messenger" emblazoned in white on a field of green. Ibn Saud's followers were fundamentalist Wahhabis, a Sunni sect, and they fought their way from Riyadh in the center of the peninsula, to Hejaz, on the western coast. They defeated other bedouin tribes, then Turkish armies, then British designs, to capture the holy cities of Mecca and Medina. But who is righteous enough to rule over Mecca and Medina? Upon assuming the role, someone always claims to be holier than the current ruler— and may mobilize fundamentalist forces to act on that claim. This is the danger of having the masses talking directly to God: they may hear God reply and demand changes on earth.

Or they may demand that nothing be changed at all. When the Wahhabis entered Mecca in 1924, they smashed the mirrors in the houses because they had never seen such things before. Less than five years later, some of Ibn Saud's best generals rebelled against him, objecting to the telegraph network he was establishing in the country and to the visit of his young son, Faisal, to the infidel nation of Britain. As late as 1962 there was fierce opposition to the abolition of slavery. When Faisal as king introduced television, one of his royal nephews attacked the station and was killed trying to destroy the transmitter. Ten years later the brother of the dead zealot murdered the king for revenge. But it was always the holy cities that aroused the greatest passions. In November 1979 a fundamentalist Wahhabi zealot and the would-be messiah he had anointed turned the Great Mosque of Mecca into a battleground for two weeks, seeking to abolish the now-worldly ways of the House of Saud, to seize the shrines and to transform Islam itself. The rebellion ended, that time, with sixty-three executions.

July 31, 1987. This time it was the Iranians.

Reports in the first few hours of the massacre came over the shortwave radio and on the Gulf television stations picked up on our little set in the officers' mess. Along with bits and pieces we could glean from conversations over the ship-to-shore telephone, these told us as much as anyone knew just then. For several years Iranian pilgrims had staged political demonstrations during the hajj, but this year the Saudis had banned such activities. The Iranians marched anyway. Maybe they were prepared for more extensive violence; later reports spoke of explosives and weapons smuggled in. The shooting war at sea and the propaganda war on the airwaves, the ongoing competition over oil prices—a vital element in financing the fight—all had raised tensions between Saudi Arabia and Iran to unprecedented levels. The Iranian leadership was waging a holy war in which holy cities—the Shia shrines of Karbala and Najaf in Iraq as well as Mecca and Medina in Saudi Arabia—became political, moral and potential military objectives. Yet with all this, the Saudi King Fahd, Custodian of the Holy Shrines, could not forbid Iranians' taking part in the pilgrimage, one of the five fundamental duties of Islam.

At first the Saudis conceded that a couple of dozen people were killed, while the Iranians claimed hundreds. The Iranians proved to be right. Two days later Saudi television showed only scenes of Mecca, with peace restored. Here were men dressed in white towels, like makeshift togas: the humble attire affected by all male worshipers, rich or poor, who are equal in the eyes of God. Women, too, were all in white, but their heads were covered. There was a great mix of faces: Oriental, Arab, black African. The pictures showed perfect tranquillity.

Eventually the Saudis conceded that the price of this peace had been the death of more than four hundred people: shot, beaten and trampled. The vast majority were from Iran. In Teheran, Prime

Minister Mir Hussein Moussavi declared, "Those behind the incident will have to pay dearly for it."

Throughout the ten years of his rule, Ayatollah Ruhollah Khomeini's greatest gift was his ability to turn a people perpetually aggrieved into one of the most aggressive religious forces in modern history. Their righteousness was based not only on their faith in God but on their sense that the world had wronged them for centuries: thirteen hundred years ago the Imam Husayn was killed at Karbala; the day before yesterday they were mowed down at Mecca. Khomeini and his followers in Iran, along with such influential Shia clerics in Lebanon as Mohammad Hussein Fadlallah, threw off a millennium of restraint. Before, the Shia faithful had been called on to contemplate the caprices of power; now they were encouraged to seize it. Where once they were told to practice taqiya, the dissimulation that concealed their faith if they felt it was threatened, now they were told to stand up and fight for it. "Civilization does not mean that you face a rocket with a stick or a jet-fighter with a kite, or a warship with a sailboat," wrote Fadlallah. "One must face force with equal or superior force. If it is legitimate to defend self and land and destiny, then all means of self-defense are legitimate."

When the momentum of the Iranian revolution flagged, persecution by its enemies merely helped it to revive. This had been Saddam Hussein's miscalculation when he rolled across the border from Iraq in 1980.

If all means of self-defense are legitimate, then there are no moral or physical limits to the scope of a holy war. Soon Iranian revolutionaries and their Shia followers were linked to a stunning array of actions that shattered international norms—Western norms—of behavior. In December 1981 the Iraqi embassy in Beirut, a seven-story apartment building, was blown off its foundations by more than five hundred pounds of TNT. Seventy-two people, including the ambassador, were killed. After the Israeli invasion of Lebanon and the complete collapse of order there, new opportunities for expansion arose. The country's Shia majority was radicalized under the Israeli occupation. Iran sent Revolutionary Guards to Beirut and the Bekaa Valley to begin building a new Islamic republic on the shores of the Mediterranean. Again terrorism was the tool, and the enemies of Iran its victims. Twice the United States embassy was bombed. The marines were slaughtered.

By the mid 1980s, however, the causes of Iran, of the Islamic revolution, of emancipation for the Shia of Lebanon, Iraq, eastern Saudi Arabia and the Gulf principalities were muddled together with the personal vendettas of various Lebanese Shia families, clans like the Hamadis and the Mugniehs. Their actions had less and less to do with the Gulf War, and more with settling scores.

In December 1983 a group of Iraqi and Lebanese Shia terrorists serving Iran's interests launched a coordinated series of suicide attacks in Kuwait planned by Imad Mugnieh. Their targets were the American and French embassies and several economic installations. Their apparent goal was to create enough chaos to provoke a coup or the collapse of the Kuwaiti regime. In this they failed. Beginning with the print off a severed finger of the suicide bomber at the American embassy compound, investigators were able to unravel the network and arrest most of the conspirators. In the spring of 1984 seventeen were tried and imprisoned. Three of them were condemned to death. The judgment was issued in Kuwait, but the effect was felt almost immediately in Lebanon. Suddenly the practice of kidnapping foreigners intensified. The CIA station chief in Beirut, the AP bureau chief, and more than a dozen other Americans and Frenchmen were abducted. Airline hijackings by Shia terrorists escalated as well. The kidnappers and hijackers wanted to trade their hostages for the seventeen imprisoned in Kuwait. One of them, on Kuwait's death row, was Mugnieh's brother-in-law. But Kuwait would not budge. There was no deal. As the United States grew more desperate and sent out more feelers, Iran decided to enter the picture directly. It offered its "help" with the hostages in exchange for arms from the United States that might prove vital in its war with Iraq. Iran's failure to bring down the Kuwaiti regime, or to free the men imprisoned there, turned to success of a different kind as the Americans started shipping TOW missiles to Teheran. The loose ends were the lives of the hostages. Those who held them still wanted their relatives freed. They still had scores to settle. The CIA chief died, tortured to death. The AP bureau chief remained—and remains—a prisoner of his abductors year after year after year.

Our ship of journalists was headed toward the speedboat islands of Farsi and Harqus. All afternoon we had been in contact with American warships. The guided-missile frigate *Crommelin* overtook us at midday. Then the U.S. destroyer *Kidd* came past us about two hours later; much bigger and more impressive-looking than the frigate, it had two Phalanx domes gleaming on its superstructure. For hours we could hear the warships challenging any and all boats that might get in their way. Both vessels had been doing twenty to twenty-five knots. Our top speed was eleven. Yet in the late afternoon suddenly we found ourselves overtaking them. We checked our position and saw we had arrived at the edge of the suspected minefield where the *Bridgeton* had been hit. A navy helicopter was working the area, eyeballing the surface of the sea, approaching us with the door gun ready, warning us away. I sat on the prow of the *Big Orange*. A dead sheep floated by, then a garbage bag. A sea snake, striped black and yellow, wriggled toward the boat. There are times, I was told by one man, when these highly poisonous snakes are mating in schools as thick and twisted as Medusa's hair. But this was only one, and he soon disappeared beneath the prow. If there were mines in these waters, we couldn't see them.

And then, in the sunset light, the reflagged Kuwaiti natural gas carrier called the *Gas Prince* suddenly emerged on the northwestern horizon, heading toward us, coming unescorted through the minefield. The American warships were waiting to meet it once it had passed the threat of the mines. When the warships had left, and the *Gas Prince* with them, we headed into the field.

That night we anchored off Karan Island, a little sandspit at the southern edge of the Iranian attack zones around Farsi and Harqus. All our lights were on. Other correspondents and photographers on deadline for Britain's Independent Television Network and Agence France Presse had been hanging for hours on the radiotelephone, dispatching the story of the *Gas Prince* and trying to transmit photographs as well. The calls were open for anyone to monitor, as everyone did there in the Gulf. They pinpointed our position, made it clear that we were a bunch of Brits and Americans on a supply boat called the *Big Orange,* there in the dark in the middle of a possible minefield, well within the proven radius of a dozen Iranian speedboat attacks.

There was nothing to do but go fishing with one of the crew's handlines, to look up from the folding chaise longue out onto the big, flat rear deck, study the Dipper and the Milky Way. And wonder what that little light was in the distance, wonder whether a speedboat would move in on us, how much we would hear before we were hit. If we would survive. How one might endure, or not, if taken prisoner.

But nothing happened. This battlefield was quiet. No speedboats came. No fish bit. The water at the anchorage was slick with oil, and my T-shirt was streaked with the sticky crude that came up on the handline. In the late, late night, when the other reporters were off the radio, the Filipino Monkey came on. "Fuck you, Filipino Monkeeeeee."

By the end of the following day we were headed back east southeast, past Ras Tanurah, toward the other end of the Gulf, and the straits themselves. Iran had announced major naval maneuvers by Revolutionary Guards there, raising the possibility of some lunatic effort to seal the entrance of the Gulf. At eleven knots, it was a voyage of almost two days. I passed the time with what I could find on board—an assortment of bad novels, old magazines and a copy of *The Daily Express.* I looked for a column by Ross Benson, who used to bill himself, quite rightly, as the only foreign correspondent on this dreadful British paper. We had covered the hijacking of the Italian cruise ship *Achille Lauro* together, and I had been amazed at some of the stories I heard him dictating about the plight of a few British dancing girls trapped aboard. "Make it live," he joked, "make it sing, make it up."

The most widely passed-around book was a paperback called *Survival*, a sort of combination how-to, true adventure and Ripley's "Believe It or Not!" For those who believed, it offered inspiration and hope that some people could live through almost anything. For those who weren't convinced, it gave practical tips on how. Its separation of fiction from reality was, appropriately for those of us on board, rather hazy.

Meanwhile we did a fair amount of sunbathing. Sebastian Rich, the ITN cameraman, worked out fanatically and wore little on board but bikini briefs, a sweatband and a Walkman. He'd been in love with his body, said his soundman, John, for about four years. That would be since about the time he recuperated from a chunk of shrapnel he caught in the gut when an RPG blasted into the truck he was on in Lebanon.

At dawn on our fifth day at sea I looked out the little porthole beside my bunk and saw we were in a sparse forest of drilling rigs on the outskirts of an offshore field. I ran up to the bridge. There in the middle distance were orange and white workboats. This was Sasson field; these were Iranian waters; those were Iranian boats. Having gotten bored, someone had decided to get daring, and we were making a pass at this installation so often described to us as an "attack base" for Revolutionary Guards. Certainly the Iraqis seemed to believe that. Their warplanes had attacked the platform several times. The structure was a wreck: windows were broken; a gangway leading from one section to another had collapsed. A voice came over channel 16 on the VHF: "Get away from the field." A few miles away we could see the flares of the Emirates' Abu Al-Bakoosh field burning bright in the early morning light.

Suddenly an Iranian workboat revved its engine and came

after us. We altered course quickly, heading as fast as we could for United Arab Emirates waters. The Iranian boat pursued us for a few more minutes, then turned back, like a dog rushing out of his yard at a passing car.

We headed on toward Hormuz.

H.M.

······························

Arrival at the end of the earth is, of course, a subjective notion. But the few places I've been that qualified for that distinction were inhabited by a handful of people one might plausibly suspect of links to one or another of the Western intelligence agencies. The thing about the ends of the earth is that someone somewhere—usually in Langley, Virginia—will imagine they have strategic value.

In the case of Oman's Musandam Peninsula someone was right. Iran is less than twenty-six miles away. Between the territorial waters of Iran and the territorial waters of Oman there are no international waters at all; and through these staked-out seas travels much of the oil that keeps the developed world developed.

From the sea the peninsula reveals almost nothing of itself. Rounding through the Strait of Hormuz, past Salamah rock, all that can be seen are the towering contours of the cliffs, capable of hiding almost anything that floats among their shadowed folds. It is a place where civilization itself might lose sight of you.

This peninsula that juts into the duodenal curve of the Strait of Hormuz is mostly vertical land. Hard-edged cliffs shoot straight up thousands of feet, from the clear sea toward the clear sky. They provide the perfect aerie from which to observe the waterway. Stone forts built by the Portuguese and by local pirates attest to this. The ancient masons, though, could never have imagined the cliffs' utility for electronic monitoring of what goes on beyond the water, beyond the horizon. Jebel Harim, a mountain towering more than a mile above the troubled surface of the sea, is surmounted by a small mosque reserved for women and by two enormous flat antennae reserved for the West. And it is doubtless a considerable advantage, for the watchers and listeners, that very few people are around to observe what they do. Perhaps twelve thousand people are native to the Musandam; small, weathered, leathery men and women, they are used to lives as primitive and rough as rock and sand. The few roads through the valleys take precarious courses along fragile ledges. Schools of fish are visible in the blue abyss beyond the friable edge of the track. Fresh water is scant. The rare rainfall is collected in cisterns hollowed out of the rock. The winter is mountain-cold; the summer is desert-hot. On the coast the people traditionally work the sea in slender, gondola-like *houris* or the larger dhows. Inland they live in caves or one-room windowless houses among the cliffs, their lives built around a vertical migration from the valleys in winter to the cooler slopes in summer. The men carry walking sticks mounted with small, finely wrought axheads. The women wear black cloaks and cover their face with stiff cloth masks that have the sheen of metal, like the visors on an ancient helmet.

"You come here. You civilize them. And they lose a lot," said Janice Dymond one afternoon in 1986 as the sun was getting low on the edge of the Musandam's mountains. I had flown from Muscat up to the little bare landing strip at Khasab that morning. Janice's husband, John Dymond, had spent the day showing me around the peninsula and now he was in the kitchen loading a cooler with ice and beer. It was time for a Hash—an athletic social rite observed by the handful of Americans and Brits who lived at Khasab. They were to go up the wadi for a run, to chase like harriers after a dragged bag of scent up and down the hillsides until they had a thirst that only a freezing can of lager could cut. Paddy O'Shea, the commander of the local Omani air force unit, might be there; or Rick Hardy, who headed the Omani army's operations in the area. But the expat population had thinned a bit over the last year. The boys who built the big satellite dish in 1980 and 1981—"We just called them the Texans," said Janice—had long since gone. The Americans who remained were specialists in fisheries, engineering or agriculture. John and Janice, as affable a middle-aged British couple as you could ever care to meet on a country lane in Wales, had lived in the Musandam for almost six years. Before that John, a navy engineer, had served three years aboard the sultan's royal yacht. They were making payments on a little forty-acre farm back home. Janice had a picture of a thatched cottage on the wall of her office. "It's the sort of place you always think you'll end up," she said. But she and John had ended up here.

"We keep a fairly low profile, as it were," said John, "but obviously people know there are white people up here." The cooler went into the back of the Jeep. We piled in after it. Janice was talking: "It's a strange thing, I feel, foreigners running government agencies." But that is what the Dymonds did. Their business was development, the side of it that used to be called hearts and minds. Working for a private company owned by one of the founding fathers of the CIA, John was "coordinator" for the activities of eight different ministries in the Musandam, in a situation that even he conceded was "a little peculiar."

During the 1970s the people of the Musandam were abandoning the peninsula. Their slight contact with the outside world had led them to believe a better life was to be had almost anywhere else. Their loyalties, though fierce at the family and tribal level, were shaky when it came to national identity. Villagers identified with the people they dealt with most regularly, and the Omani government in Muscat had dealt with them very little. "Originally the tribal elders pledged allegiance to Oman," said Dymond, "but they were surrounded by the United Arab Emirates."

A forty-mile corridor separated them from the rest of the country. A little settlement like Bukha, inaccessible by road, was nearer by foot and by sea to the emirate of Ras al-Khaimah than to anything Omani. Meanwhile Iran's influence and its presence were strong. The biggest village, Khasab, had a population that was 40 percent of Iranian descent; and for commerce virtually everyone looked across the water, not over the mountains. "In 1980 a lot of trade was carried on and a lot of holidays were taken on Larak Island, which is in Iran. It still is. You might say it's semi-legal," said John.

As the delicate wooden *houris* gave way to the long, light fiberglass dories, Iran grew closer still. "You put twin engines on the back, and you can bang across in an hour and a half." Given all this emigration, isolation and these relations with nearby countries not always friendly to Oman, the challenge of the 1980s, a British colonel in Muscat told me, was to keep the Musandam from "floating away."

Oman has always had an air of mystery and inaccessibility. Even Thesiger was kept from penetrating deep into its interior. The Musandam, until this decade, seemed pure terra incognita. "Until we came here," said Janice as we careered past the little motel where I was lodged and up the wadi, "this was really purely a military area. That's where all this mystery probably started." But there is more to it than that.

Along the wedge of Indian Ocean that comes to a point at the Strait of Hormuz lies a forbidding array of military installations known only to true cognoscenti of geopolitics. Down the coast south of Muscat the island of Masirah has become a virtual American air base, although the technicians are nominally civilians employed on contract, and elaborate protocols have been worked out to keep the U.S. profile as low as possible. Farther south and west, off the coast of the People's Democratic Republic of Yemen, the Soviets have a massive base on the island of Socotra. Continue on the same trajectory and you hit Djibouti at the tip of the horn of Africa, declared independent in 1977, but almost indistinguishable from the French colony and Foreign Legion outpost that it was.

The British military has a relationship with the Omanis as symbiotic as any in the postcolonial world. No elaborate access agreements are needed, a British officer once told me. "At the moment, the sort of person who's going to make a decision about whether a Royal Air Force aircraft can come in is a Brit anyway, isn't he." Militarily, the Musandam is their baby, and Goat Island, just west of the tip, is the apple of their eye.

"It is the key," said a British colonel. "All that's required as far as the Musandam is concerned is the guarantee of Omani territorial waters, which is ipso facto the shipping route. At Goat Island they are well aware of any ship passing. They make sure the Iranians observe the letter of the law, and amazingly, it works."

The Iranian revolution, then the Gulf War, gave this point of control even greater importance. There was constant talk of Iran's "blocking the strait." They couldn't very well do that unless they could control the Musandam.

While the Omani military under Paddy and Rick were securing the peninsula militarily, an Arlington, Virginia, company headed by one of the Central Intelligence Agency's veteran Middle East operatives got the assignment of keeping the Musandam's people in place, and keeping them loyal to the sultan. James H. Critchfield had retired from the agency, where he was national intelligence officer for energy during the 1973 oil crisis. He was one of the "barons," an old hand who had joined just after World War II. He ran agents in Eastern Europe in the first years after the Iron Curtain dropped, then turned his attention to the Middle East. Like many other aging senior CIA agents, when Critchfield left government service he went into business exploiting decades' worth of contacts and expertise he had built up in Langley's secret world. First he formed a company called, simply, Tetra Tech, which specialized in underwater technologies, including weaponry. Its domestic operation subsequently was sold to Honeywell, but Critchfield held on to Tetra Tech International. At the request of the sultan, TTI set up the Musandam Development Committee in 1976, and through the committee was given supervisory control over the work of most government ministries there.

Dymond was Critchfield's main man on the ground from the beginning. He supervised everything from road building and port construction to the minor details of everyday life. His men inspected the few restaurants for hygiene. They tied up goats found wandering in the streets and fined their owners (five rials, or almost fifteen dollars). They implemented, as well, the sometimes rather capricious uniformity imposed on Omani society by a sultan with a decided penchant for interior decorating—including the interior of his nation. A decree was issued prohibiting brightly colored gates. "They were trying to get a uniform tone to the country, I suppose," said Janice. The local Omani governor went a step further and banned any foreign insignia, including Islamic symbols and Koranic sayings, from the gates. Then there was the rule against hanging wash out of the windows.

John and Janice had the good sense to wonder about the kind of civilization they were bringing to the Musandam. Earlier in the day, as John and I made the de rigueur visit to the little port, then up the wadi all the way to Jebel Harim, he had expressed satisfaction with Tetra Tech's accomplishments. Its first five-year plan had been met in three years; its second was accomplished in two. In this region, where there had been no roads at all, a wide gravel highway now linked the peninsula to the rest of the country. Where there had been no water, each village—and, in most places, each house—had big water tanks, filled regularly by delivery trucks from Khasab. The coastal towns still inaccessible by road were serviced by *Rosie,* a modified landing craft more or less like the ones that stormed the Normandy beaches. Elsewhere, scattered through the mountains, were helicopter pads for the quick access of rescue teams or, of course, the military. TTI had tried to make improvements in the basic patterns of life rather than transform them altogether. The *birqat,* or cisterns, had been modified and cleaned and improved. Farming had been encouraged, and in what were once hidden valleys, along the Khasab-

Dibba road, alfalfa and flocks of goats seemed to be thriving. But the Musandam's culture, bit by bit, was fading away. "The traditional meeting places tend to die out," said Dymond as we drove around the village of Sal as Ful. The people got electricity, they got televisions. They got water tanks near their houses, so there was no longer any need to go to the *birqat*. There was less need to talk, to meet, to work, to be a family.

At the site chosen by the Hash House Harrier club for their party that afternoon, the expats already were bringing out the barbeques. We were in the shade of the sheer mountains around us, but the sun was still high enough on the meridian to light a vast evanescent assemblage of clouds rolling off the ocean. Other places in this world may have landscapes as spectacular, but the confluence in this remotest corner of Arabia of such primordial spectacle and these hard-running, sweat-dripping, beer-swilling joggers chasing hard along a course over rocks and gravel, wadi and mountain, made the moment, finally, unforgettable. These little Western men were as insignificant and alien in this terrain as field mice scurrying among the columns of a cathedral.

As the beer started to work its magic, we lapsed easily into the old camaraderie of drinking by a fire, telling jokes and singing bawdy songs. For the expats of the more remote reaches of the Gulf, beyond the domain of golf courses and tennis courts, the Hash had a riveting appeal. The rituals were as set as a fraternity party, an *Animal House* on the run, built around a steady flow of beer—over bodies as well as into them—and humor as raw as home-brewed gin: racist, sexist, not-giving-a-fuck-about-the-wogs, for a few hours at least, stewing in sweat and hops there by the campfire.

In Bahrain, for instance, they'd been running the Hash since 1972, and it was a local obsession. Everyone went out with a vengeance, including many of the U.S. Navy commanders stationed there. A few locals joined in as well—Salah, Kamal, Eddie; they were known as the Hash Browns. In 1987 the Bahrain club published a special magazine for its fifteenth anniversary, its eight hundredth run. Admiral Hal Bernsen, commander of the American fleet deployed in the Gulf, turned out for the race. He was a regular and affectionately nominated for Wanker of the Year. The program included a letter from the *Stark*'s commanding officer thanking the Hash for contributing T-shirts to members of his crew who had lost all their belongings when the *Stark* took those two Iraqi Exocets in its gut. The shirts "helped lift our spirits during this devastating tragedy." Another veteran reminisced about the good old days in Iran, before the revolution, when they projected *Deep Throat* against the crumbling walls of a shepherd's hut in the desert. As the drinking went on, the rhyming began, with limericks and verses, some original, some remembered or half-remembered, like the tale of Bionic Fred, with his high-tech prosthetic penis. And so on, and on, until hangover time.

In the Musandam, the bawdy is a little less blatant, but only a little. The society is smaller, the sense of responsibility greater. "We don't do anything to upset the locals because they're nice," said Janice, nicely, as we drove back down the wadi through this night at the end of the earth.

"The people shall not have what they want but what I think is good for them," the old sultan, Said bin Taimur, used to say during his thirty-eight-year reign in Oman. Education? The people would have none of it. Automobiles? Only if he approved each one, and only rarely would he do that. Did they want to go outside the walls of Muscat after dark or wear dark glasses against the glare of the sun? These things were not allowed. At night, within the forbidding walls of the old city, each man had to carry a lantern to light his way through the narrow streets. No flashlights were permitted. And a hundred eyes were open, always waiting to report if the rules were broken, even after the sultan himself moved to Salalah, far in the south, for a sojourn of twelve years. Along the flat coastal streets in that land of monsoon rains, green fields and frankincense trees, he would travel in a car pushed by his retainers. He did not bother to have gasoline brought in. And so he ruled, running on empty, until 1970.

His was a country that history passed by and the world had forgotten. Its days of glory were in the eighteenth and nineteenth centuries, after Oman's navy and its raiding parties had driven the Portuguese from the east coast of Africa and taken it for themselves. The capital of their empire was moved to Zanzibar, and Omani sailors dominated the sea and the trade in spices and slaves from Madagascar to Bahrain. But the spread of the British Empire and the British abolition of slavery brought an end to the economic power of Oman. By 1861 its African and Arabian domains were split; and by the time Sultan Said bin Taimur took power in 1932, little was left but memories of glory, crumbling like the mud-brick castles in the sun. Its exports fell away to nothing—a few lemons, some firewood. The tribes of the interior broke with Muscat and pledged their allegiance to an imam ruling in the ancient town of Nizwa and hostile to all infidels. A handful of foreigners were allowed into the capital, but they were closely watched to keep the locals away from them, and they were not permitted to travel outside the confines of the tiny capital without the sultan's express permission.

It was in the worst of those bad years, before any whiff of oil surfaced in Oman, at the zenith of the sultan's eccentricity, that Donald Bosch and his wife, Eloise, and their three small children moved from Ho-Ho-Kus, New Jersey, to Muscat. Bosch had been born in China, the son of missionaries, and he inherited their vocation. In 1954 he and his wife volunteered for the World Ministries branch of their Reformed Church in America, to serve—wherever, whomever—exclusively on the basis of human need. "I was a trained surgeon and my wife a trained teacher. They said it looks like the Gulf is where there's the greatest need."

Before the Bosches, no hospitals existed in Oman. "There were some years when I was in fact the only surgeon in the country."

The land, and the sea as well, seemed virginal then, unexplored and undiscovered. The Bosches found seashells that no one had found before. One beautiful spotted species is now called *Actaeon Eloise* after Mrs. Bosch. Other species are named for each of the children, and for Donald as well.

Bosch talks about the old sultan with genuine sympathy. "His major problem was that the country was very poor. He did some very good things. He gave power to the mission to develop a tuberculosis hospital and a leprosarium." The old sultan did not rule out oil exploration, and eventually he encouraged it. He began the construction of a major hospital at Nahda. "But as time went on I think he developed an honest conviction that too much of the Western world could have a negative impact on the overall society in this country."

But why had he banned sunglasses?

"You know, I think he wanted to be able to see peoples' eyes."

His window into their soul was lost when their eyes were hidden behind green glass. Why did he ban flashlights at night?

Again, because they were too easily turned on and off, while a lantern identifies the person who carries it. Sure, it all seems silly. But—"when the tide is coming in and you've developed a policy where you're going to slow the incoming tide, it leads you to take actions that in retrospect seem foolish, like building barriers of sand."

The sultan's world was falling apart around him in ways he could sense, but could not know. "He was certainly an extremely charismatic person, a person who could sway other people to the validity of his policies. But he didn't have people around him who were ready to tell him the truth."

And he had only one son.

Qaboos bin Said was born in 1944, and by the time he was a young man the sultan was persuaded the child should know something of the world. Major Leslie Chauncy, personal adviser to the sultan, took the boy on "a slow, round-the-world trip that took a whole year." Later Qaboos went to Sandhurst to become, in effect, a British officer and served in Germany with a regiment of lowland Scots. In a picture book called *Old Oman* is a photograph of Qaboos in 1963, when he was nineteen years old and just out of Sandhurst. He has a neatly trimmed mustache, in the style that modern, educated Arabs affected in those days. He is wearing steel-rimmed dark glasses.

* * *

The fifties and sixties were decades of war and threatened war throughout the Middle East. Egypt's Gamal Abdel Nasser was spreading his doctrine of Arab revolution with relentless radio broadcasts and conspiracies that fired the people with dreams of socialist modernity and frightened the West with threats of crypto-communism. They were also the years of burgeoning oil exploration, when the world first began to realize how vast the wealth might be that lay beneath the desert and the sea. These were the days of the cold war in Europe, the Suez crisis in the Near East, the pitting of East against West, Europe against the Arabs. But along the ill-defined borders between the domains of the sultan, the princes of Abu Dhabi and the Kingdom of Saudi Arabia the superpowers at each others' throats were Britain and the United States.

In 1952, not long after Thesiger visited the Buraimi oasis to go hawking with Sheikh Zayed of Abu Dhabi, a Saudi official arrived at this outpost where conflicting territorial claims converge. The Saudi brought sacks full of silver—centuries-old Austrian Maria Theresa dollars that were still the coin of desert realms. He declared himself governor at Buraimi, and the sultan, hearing of this, prepared to declare war. The Saudis were backed by the Arabian American Oil Company—Aramco—the American oil consortium. The sultan of Oman and Sheikh Zayed of Abu Dhabi were supported by the British.

Colin Maxwell was a young army officer who had been assigned to the Somalia Gendarmerie in Mogadishu, then to the Eritrean police force after World War II. "When things packed up out there, a lot of us were out of jobs." When the Buraimi crisis brought him a new assignment, he didn't even know where Muscat was. He arrived in Oman in October 1952, as the tribes were gathering on the coast. "The sultan and the men of the interior were in tents near the beach." Hundreds of men that a British officer could only call "irregulars" appeared; long rifles in hand, bandoliers crossed over the chest, their curved daggers and swords at their belt. The sultan, having arrived in his big red Dodge Power Wagon, looked on confidently. They wandered among camels on the strand, shooting off so much ammunition that Maxwell wondered whether enough would be left for Buraimi.

Then the British consul, Major Chauncy, arrived. Orders had come from the Foreign Office, and probably from the State Department, to find a negotiated solution. Talks dragged on. The tribes returned to the hills. The battle for Buraimi was averted, but war was still in the air. Maxwell was becoming a key adviser to the sultan, a commander of forces that began to take on some of the polish and discipline of regular troops, in the tradition of the Arab Legion created for Jordan a generation before by Sir John Bagot Glubb.

The Saudis did not give up their designs on the borderlands—the Empty Quarter that promised to be so full of oil. They were spreading their money and buying influence all over the Omani interior and spreading the word, as well, that the Oman of the imams was meant to be free of the sultan of Muscat. The fighting they provoked was never intense, but it did drag on around the Green Mountain from 1957 to 1959. Then several units of the British Special Air Service, having finished off the Communist guerrillas in Malaysia, stopped in Oman on their way home. "They stormed the mountain," Maxwell recalls, "and that was the end of that."

In 1958 Sultan Said bin Taimur retired to Salalah, in the province of Dhofar, in the far south of the country. For the months of the monsoon, almost half the year, Dhofar is a place that looks a lot like heaven to men of the desert. Today Arabs from Kuwait and the Emirates come just to picnic on the grass that covers the hills and on the escarpment behind the town, wiggling their toes, letting their children run. Camels grow big and sturdy and give milk frothing with hot, thick cream. The sea comes off the Indian Ocean in big, curling waves over wide beaches that rise to groves of palms. Here and there on the routes into the mountains are twisted trees exuding the sap of frankincense. The sultan's grandfather established his dominion over Dhofar only in 1897, accompanied by a British consul and a British warship. Its people had often been subject to capricious local rulers. And Sultan Said bin Taimur was no exception. He made Dhofar his secret garden, reserving its beautiful landscapes for himself, treating its people as his servants. By 1965 he had the beginnings of a war on his hands. Backed by the Communist Yemenis next door, the Dhofaris launched a rebellion that eventually swept to the hills around Salalah, sending mortar rounds pounding onto the city streets and the grounds of the sultan's palace.

With this new war, and then the beginning of commercial oil production in 1967, the sultan "really had lost his grip on the country," remembered Maxwell. He was trying to move Oman forward by inches, always apprehensive about going too far, never going nearly far enough. Now that oil money made his nation worth something to the world at large, he lacked even a modicum of technical expertise to develop it. There was no way to keep the country closed.

"All these peculiarities," said Bosch, the surgeon and shell collector, "came to the point where they became public problems." Oman was so primitive, and of the few educated Omanis, most had left. "There weren't a lot of people around who could be reasonably useful." Once again, British troops arrived, including, once again, the elite units of the SAS. But this was no one-stop war.

By 1970 "things were looking very grim indeed in Dhofar," Maxwell recalled. The sultan was politically and militarily isolated, and he kept his only legitimate heir, the prince Qaboos, a virtual prisoner in the palace.

Why his father had confined Qaboos on his return from military service in Germany is not a matter much discussed outside the royal family, if indeed it is discussed at all. "Sultan Said said that Qaboos had gone off to England at a stage when he should have been learning more about religious matters." A marriage had been arranged that "didn't come off," as Bosch put it. Qaboos never did take a bride, or produce an heir. Pictures taken in the gardens of Salalah show the young man who had sported a trim mustache and Ray-Bans three years before now wrapped in white robes and turban, a dagger in his belt, his beard, long, bushy and unkempt, framing his delicate mouth. His quiet eyes stare straight into the camera. It is said that

Qaboos spent much time in those days listening to tape recordings of music, especially the Western classics. Few visitors were allowed.

One of those few was a young British officer named Timothy Landon. He had been more an acquaintance than a friend of Qaboos's at Sandhurst. But as the war worsened and the British presence increased, "he went down as an intelligence officer to Dhofar and renewed his friendship," remembered Maxwell. There are stories that Landon would send tapes to Qaboos—Beethoven, Mozart, whatever his favorites might be—and that buried deep on the reel between movements were messages meant only for the prince's ears. Maxwell said he didn't know about that. "But Tim saw a lot of him, and he of course was very much in the know of what was going to happen."

The coup came in July 1970, discreetly assisted by the British. One palace guard was killed, and the sultan, grown fat and clumsy, shot himself in the foot while trying to drag a pistol out of a drawer. He was forced to abdicate and flown into exile. Qaboos became the sultan, Landon became an Omani general and, it is said, very rich.

On the first glorious national day of Sultan Qaboos, four years after the coup, Omani soldiers played triumphant airs on bagpipes, their khakis and kilts sharp-creased beneath the leopard skins thrown over their shoulders. The war in Dhofar had been turned around. British aid had continued, and the shah of Iran had sent his air force. But the coup changed more than that.

"Attitudes and the spirit of man, so to speak, changed immediately the very first day that Sultan Said was deposed," Bosch recalled. "People said, 'Now we've got a chance for a whole new start.' I'm sure it's safe to say that never in the history of mankind has any country changed so much so fast." Sultan Said had been holding back a horse. "Once that barrier was broken," said the missionary from Ho-Ho-Kus, "Whamo!"

Schools were turning up everywhere, not just for men and boys, but for women and girls. "You had young girls going to school sometimes with their mothers in the same class," said Bosch. Muscat began to develop quickly; the port and then the airport were expanded. The growth was explosive—but carefully watched by the fastidious sultan. As air conditioners started arriving in large shipments, he decided he didn't like the way they looked, sticking out of the sides of buildings. Now, by decree, all air conditioners in Oman are covered with wooden latticework, more in keeping with traditional architecture.

For the first few years the place was a godsend to British expats. If the colonial world had been fading when Colin Maxwell left Eritrea in the early 1950s, it had collapsed completely by the early 1970s. Walrus-mustached former functionaries from the British colonies began washing up on Oman's shores by the hundreds, men in their mid-forties with no time left to go back to England to make a new life. They defended, none too loudly but nonetheless steadfastly, the virtues of the old empire. They were like a secret society, the last survivors of Kipling's world and Maugham's. They enjoyed referring to His Majesty Sultan Qaboos bin Said as H.M. for short. Not to his face, of course; just within the club of his close advisers. They had standards, and they intended for the Omanis to keep them. H.M., at first, seemed quite happy with them.

In 1985 Oman was home to 11,000 British citizens. But the old hands of the empire were tending to give way to young men and women on the make, fresh out of London with skills the sultanate might need but not quite the standards it wanted. They could be found carousing at the Nel Gwynne, next to the sushi bar at the Falaj Hotel, or eating their fish and chips at the Intercontinental's pub, where lager and bitter were served on tap and fourteen different brands of single-malt scotch whiskey were available at the bar.

Perhaps inevitably, as his country's wealth and his experience grew, Qaboos began to chafe at the high British profile. The American partnership became more important. "The sultan knows that if the chips are really down, England's not going to save him but the United States could," speculated Donald Bosch. But the American link was not without problems. When Egypt signed the Camp David accords with Israel, Oman was the only Arab country of the Gulf that supported the peace. It was not a comfortable position, nor a very profitable one. More and more the sultan listened to his Arab advisers and put Omanis into top jobs as soon as—and, in a few cases, before—they were trained. He was ready to take his place as the leader of an Arab nation, not a halfway house for ex-colonials.

In 1985 he made his formal debut, hosting the rest of the kings and princes of Arabia at a summit of the Gulf Cooperation Council in Muscat. To receive them, he built a hotel—a palace—the likes of which the world has rarely seen, on the beach at Bustan. The price has been debated, but without question it was more than three hundred million dollars. From the immaculate sands and swimming pools to the six suites with gold bathroom fixtures for the six heads of state, it was a spectacular enterprise. Muscat was draped in lights, and the Bustan Palace was the crowning star.

The village that previously was on the beach at Bustan was simply removed, and with it the homes of two old expatriates: Donald Bosch and Colin Maxwell. Qaboos did not forget their services. He built them mansions, side by side; pristine and well appointed, tastefully designed with individual touches suited to their occupants. In Bosch's, of course, there is an aquarium for his shells and fish. The new homes, grander than anything their occupants could have imagined thirty years before, are nestled above a little cove, looking out to sea. They are alone, invisible from the road, so discreetly situated that a young Omani driving by would never know they were there at all.

On the morning of August 5, 1987, no Iranian warships could be seen in the Strait of Hormuz, at least not from aboard the *Big Orange*. Our trip was coming to an end. We had found no mines. We had seen the navies deployed in the Gulf but missed them in action. We had sailed past Sirri Island, where months before Gerry Blackburn had pulled survivors from the water around the burning tankers *Klelia* and *Azarpad*. We had seen, too close up, the oil-pumping cities suspended above the sea that would be the targets of any heightened fighting. Now, we were ready to go home. We started thinking about getting videotape flown back to land, a case of beer flown out to us. At the end of the shipping channel coming out of the strait, Alan wheeled the *Big Orange* around in a hard-banking nautical U-turn.

The gunboat seemed to appear out of nowhere. It was a corvette, fast and light and mean. It wove like an enormous water-skier behind us, first coming up toward one side, then swinging back to come up on the other, now rushing our stern. At first we couldn't make out the flag. Then, as the steam cleared from my binoculars, I could see the Omani colors and crossed swords. I made out the rocket launchers on the deck, then the dark-skinned crewmen looking more Indian or Baluchi than Omani. On the bridge the faces were European, and the voice that ordered us to hold our course, letting us off with a short-tempered warning, was distinctly British. For serious business out to sea, it seemed, His Majesty's forces were still served by Her Majesty's men.

THE OLD COUNTRY

THE CLUB

WE LIVED, IN CAIRO, IN AN OLD APARTMENT BUILDING THAT STOOD BE-
tween the two greatest expanses of open air the heart of the city had
to offer. One side of the apartment looked out on the Nile, and
beyond the river to a skyline of government buildings, hotels and
minarets. In the evening the muezzin's call to prayer came across the
water. For some reason we didn't hear it at other times. Perhaps it
was lost in the background noise of traffic, or something about the
movement of the air changed at sundown. Breezes moved above the
stifling alleys in the middle of the city, we knew. No one on foot could
feel them there, but from the little balcony of our apartment we could
always see in the afternoon light two or three—if you looked very
closely, you might see five or six or seven—little kites being flown all
around the city by children somewhere out of sight below the level
of the rooftops. The breezes that kept them aloft went on, it seemed,
forever.

On the other side of the apartment was the club. We looked down directly onto the croquet courts. Neither my wife, Carol, nor I ever played the game. But sometimes after dark we would look out the rear windows, and the whole croquet lawn would be lighted, and a small crowd would be standing around the edges watching distinguished-looking gentlemen and ladies swing their mallets. Most of the people there were Egyptian, as they would not have been in the years before World War II. Only a few were as finely dressed—in white linen, say—as they might have been back then. But the image of the croquet courts, seen from above and from a distance, was as pure an evocation as I could want or imagine of what the club must have been like when Egypt was a different country in a different, colonial time.

"The original idea of forming a sporting club in Cairo was put forward by the officers of the army of occupation," says the rule book of the Gezira Sporting Club of 1933. "The High Commissioner shall be President of the Club." British military officers, members of the Sudan Civil Services and "British clergy in the Diocese of Egypt and Sudan" were entitled to be admitted without election, I read one afternoon as I sat waiting for the club's secretary, Nadia Farahat. Her desk was behind a column at the far end of the crowded club office. She processed membership applications as children of wealthy Egyptian families wandered in and out wearing Walkman headphones and color-coordinated jogging suits. Old men and women shuffled papers, bending low over them to read the laboriously lettered forms. Flies bustled around glasses half full of hot, sweet tea. One ill-kempt employee sat by the machine that laminated membership cards, looking a little puzzled by the wisps of sulfurous fumes that seeped from beneath the roller. There was a sense, as there always is in Cairo, of faded glories subsumed by age and disorganization. But Madame Farahat, who had worked at the club since 1952, sat trim and dignified behind her desk and gave me the old rule books to read: this one from 1933; another, still earlier, from 1906, when it was still called the Khedival Sporting Club. She kept them handy in a pigeonhole.

In the years before World War II, and before Nasser's revolution, the club had taken up most of the island of Zamalek, which lies just in the middle of the Nile, in what is now the middle of the city. The few homes along its streets were villas for foreigners and the very rich. The poor were not allowed across the old iron bridge onto the island unless, as servants or making deliveries, they had a pass. The 1933 by-laws decree that "no dragoman is allowed in the Club Grounds"—no personal interpreters or guides were permitted. By the same token, "the conduct of a servant of the Club shall in no instance be made a matter of personal reprimand by any member."

"It is essential," Lord Cromer, the de facto ruler of Egypt, used to say, "that each special issue should be decided mainly with reference to what, by the light of Western knowledge and experience tempered by local considerations, we conscientiously think is best for the subject race." But in 1952—as it happens, the year that Madame Farahat went to work at the club—all this elaborate system of elitist checks and balances was torn apart. The British had come to Egypt in 1882 as debt collectors and had stayed as occupiers, convinced that the country could not otherwise run itself and pay them back. They came to protect the rule of the khedive, they said, even though he had not invited them. And they stayed to rule in what was known as the Veiled Protectorate. But around the world, in the aftermath of World War II, the white man's burden proved too heavy for the long haul. The British were rolling back, and the Egyptians, whose sense of pride and nationalism had been building for seventy years, wanted them out. When the British said they were staying, at least along the Suez Canal, Egypt went mad. After British troops fired on rioters in Ismailia, mobs in Cairo swept through the city, burning, looting, killing, until seventeen Europeans and fifty Egyptians were dead and seven hundred buildings had been razed or pillaged.

The club, on its island, was spared. But when Gamal Abdel Nasser took power in a coup six months later, the club's days, as the institution that it had been, were suddenly quite clearly numbered. In 1955 Nasser's council of ministers ordered the golf course and the race course expropriated. Within hours workers heartily set about demolishing the fences. By then the club president was an Egyptian, but a man raised in the ways of the old school. His impassioned telex to Nasser, a copy of which Madame Farahat drew out of her pigeon-hole, declared what this establishment was and what it meant to Egypt, and pleaded for its existence:

> THE GEZIRA SPORTING CLUB OF EGYPT AS IT STANDS TODAY IS ONE OF THE THREE MOST FAMOUS INTERNATIONAL CLUBS IN THE WORLD (THE OTHER TWO BEING THE WESTCHESTER OF NEW-YORK AND THE HURLINGHAM OF LONDON)   STOP
> LIKE THE GREAT PYRAMIDS, ABDINE PALACE, OR SHEPHERD'S HOTEL, ALL OF WHICH ARE IN THEMSELVES USELESS STRUC-TURES, IT RENDERS THE WHOLE NATION A UNIQUE SERVICE IN INTERNATIONAL PRESTIGE WHICH HAS TAKEN SIXTY NINE YEARS TO BUILD UP, AND WHICH IS VASTLY MORE SIGNIFICANT THAN THE NUMBER (12000) OF ITS MEMBERS MIGHT INDICATE. YOUR EXCELLENCY MAY KNOW THAT AN AVERAGE OF 4500 FOREIGN BUSINESS MEN, TECHNICIANS, SCHOLARS, AND DIPLOMATS HAVE RECEIVED TEMPORARY MEMBERSHIP IN THE CLUB IN EACH OF THE TEN YEARS SINCE THE WAR   STOP   . . . ONE OF THE MAJOR ATTRACTIONS OF LIFE IN EGYPT FOR IMPORTANT FOR-EIGNERS INVITED OR SENT HERE WOULD BE ELIMINATED AT ONE STROKE. . . .

As usual in Egypt, a compromise was found. A large portion of the land was taken, but the racetrack was allowed to remain on it. Soccer fields were established where polo once was played. The age of exclusivity had come to an end.

"I wanted to show you what was the Gezira Sporting Club," said Madame Farahat, standing up from her desk and leading me past the clerks poking at flyblown files to a little wood-paneled conference room chilled by an air conditioner. "During the war we had two houseboats, the *Puritan* and the *Niagara*," she said, looking from one shelf to another in the bookcases. She seemed distracted, quietly upset, before, finally, she said, "Ah, it disappeared. What a pity." There had been a book of the minutes of special meetings, a little history of the crises the club went through before and after the revolution. She shook her head, still looking. She found another volume. Thick and yellowed, full of photographs and letters from the war, when British troops on leave would come to Cairo and the officers would come to the club, or its boats, to relax. This was a collection of thank-you letters from polite British captains and colonels. One picture showed a party being held to celebrate the coronation of Her Majesty the Queen. "We always had gymkhanas," Madame Farahat said, and she believed there was a picture somewhere and began to look for it, too, but knew in advance, it seemed, that it would not be found. "There are things that disappear—like that," she said with a wave of her hand. "You don't know where they go.

"They don't like it. They want to cancel it. They don't want it to exist," Madame Farahat said suddenly. What? Who? The club, the memories? The government, the fundamentalists? "You don't know. So much has been burned, sometimes by ignorance, sometimes by religion. As long as we have to live with them, we have to take them as they are."

She seemed so frail, so tired, so bitter, and I imagined, though she did not say it, that she had seen too many indolent Egyptian teenagers with designer sweats, too many unshaven bureaucrats stinking after squash without a shower, too many of the servants, still in the dark blue and gold *gelabiyas* of the official livery, blowing their noses on the hems—too much equality. I asked how many people are members now. Twenty thousand families. And are they really so different from those who came before? Madame Farahat finally found one of the pictures she was looking for, buried in the pages of the book of thank-you notes. "There were a few Egyptians—the aristocracy, the pashas. There were landowners, you know, some businessmen. But merchants, no. No. That was crossed out. It was a very selected club." She looked at me and at the picture. It was of a group of soldiers sitting in wicker chairs having drinks and tea, just outside the main clubhouse. The chairs and the location were familiar. I passed them every day when I went running at the club's track except on Fridays, when part of that area was turned into a makeshift mosque. The faces, though, were of bright, handsome British men in sharp uniforms, smiling, elegant and so young so long ago in a society that seemed, from this remove, as fresh as the sprig of mint in a glass of iced tea. "Now what it has become . . . ," said Madame Farahat, "If you come on Fridays, this square is like . . . Mecca."

THE PRIZE

It was almost a year since the old man had won the Nobel. Yet as he sat in the Ali Baba Cafeteria just above Tahrir Square, nothing, on the surface, seemed to have changed about the life of Naguib Mahfouz. He had not left Cairo, except for the occasional summer week in Alexandria. He sent his two grown daughters to the award ceremony in Stockholm and then split the $390,000 prize four ways: a quarter for his wife, a quarter for each of the girls. The quarter for himself he gave away to charity.

The Ali Baba is a dreary café advertised by an electric sign out front, at once garish and nondescript. Mahfouz comes here because it fits his routine. It is open twenty-four hours a day, and he likes to get his first coffee as early as 7:00 in the morning. No one bothers him here, although he is only a couple of yards above the crowd as he sips the thick, sweet coffee, *masbout*. They are oblivious, running for the buses that never quite come to a stop, or winding their way through the traffic that presses en masse through red lights. Mahfouz had not planned much work for the summer. "I will consider myself very fortunate if I can manage to write some short stories." He is alone with his newspapers, his memories and, it is fair to say, the presence of death.

The threats began just a few days after he won the prize. Over the months they grew worse and became more public. At the height of the furor raised by the Ayatollah Khomeini against the British author Salman Rushdie for his blasphemous best-seller *The Satanic Verses*, an "imam" in Egypt who had been tried and acquitted in the fatal plot against President Anwar Sadat told his followers it was time that Naguib Mahfouz, in the name of righteousness, should die.

This was serious business in Egypt. Presidents, cabinet members and newspaper editors had been lined up in the sights of revolutionaries over the last decade, and some had died. At the street level Egypt is a police state that is never quite in control. And the government offered Mahfouz round-the-clock guards, as if he were a politician or, perhaps, a national treasure, a relic in the Egyptian Museum. He refused.

"I never thought about asking for protection." His face creases, smiling. "It's like being under arrest. We would be sitting here now with somebody next to us. It would be worse than death." He shrugs at allegations of bravery. "Look, at my age a threat of death is not really that frightening. I might receive a threat on Sunday and die of natural causes on Monday."

The Islamic grudge against Mahfouz goes back decades, to the late 1950s, when he first started publishing his novels serially in the newspapers. Nasser's government was looking for some liberal credentials by allowing writers a certain freedom of expression. But one of the first serials Mahfouz published was *The Children of Gebelawi*, an allegory about the search for faith and eternal truths in a poor sector of Cairo. Certain characters seemed to be modeled after Moses, Jesus, Muhammad himself. To the sheikhs beneath the minarets of Al-Azhar, it was a blasphemous tale. In a sense it was *The*

Satanic Verses of its time, although Mahfouz says he intended no blasphemy, and in those days such issues were a matter of debate, not death sentences. The sheikhs denounced the book, and it has never since been published in Arabic in Egypt. In the early 1970s Mahfouz was one of the first Egyptian intellectuals publicly to call for an end to war with Israel—another strike against him in the eyes of Islam's self-appointed holy warriors.

But it was not Mahfouz's views on God or Zion that most offended the righteous. In the fundamentalist societies of young men with long beards and short robes, with the bright eyes of the faithful and the will to die for paradise, Naguib Mahfouz is known as Sex Teacher.

Especially for Americans, who are so curious and uncomfortable about the Old World, this oldest corner of the world is a disturbing place. Outside influences come and stay and are absorbed, leaving only vague, disturbing allusions. The result is a cultural tension between the expectations of modernity and the weight of the past that cannot quite be resolved. Life here is tinged with constant disillusionment and confusion. In his strongest works Mahfouz uses this atmosphere to play the traditions of family, love and faith against the politics and the social upheaval that are imposed, most often, from outside. The people in the streets don't change much. But the people in the palaces and the Parliament do, courting or defying the British occupation, experimenting with revolution, trying to transform the immutable, fostering expectations difficult or impossible to attain—creating currents of politics that sweep over and through the masses like wind roiling the surface of the Nile. His characters are always searching: for affection and respect and happiness, of course, but, above all, for some sense of order. And the search for order and reason, in the midst of chaos and blind faith, can be dangerous.

"I had loved the village but could not bear to live there. I had educated myself," recalls the aged journalist in *Miramar,* one of Mahfouz's best novels, "and I had been wrongly accused and many people had said . . . that I should be killed. . . . I had been entranced by love, education, cleanliness, hope."

The life of Egypt, of the modern Egyptians themselves, was never presented in great works of English literature. (You will say Lawrence Durrell's Alexandria Quartet, and Mahfouz replies, rightly, "It is very beautiful, but it is about foreigners.") The Orientalists who helped build the magnificent myth of the desert Arab loathed the sedentary effendi of Cairo. "Egypt, being so near Europe, is not a savage country," T. E. Lawrence wrote to Robert Graves. "The Egyptians are very bestial, very savage: but you need not dwell among them. Indeed it will be a miracle if an Englishman can get to know them." Those who extolled Egypt's glorious pharaonic past were disturbed by the seedy decay of its present. They professed, as Lord Balfour did in 1910, to admire "great races like the inhabitants of Egypt" even as they took up "the dirty work, the inferior work, of carrying on the necessary labor" to run a country the Egyptians couldn't run themselves. It was always a country for tourists and travel writers, not for artists. So this Egyptian novelist was dealing with sensibilities the West knew little or nothing about in a society where men wear suits at the office, *gelabiyas* in the home.

Until you come to Cairo, the books seem to be full of odd, fantastical characters. In Mahfouz's *Midaq Alley* a self-taught dentist steals dentures from the dead, assisted by a golemlike creature called "Zaita, the cripple-maker." But this grotesquerie is the stuff of the present. On a bridge that leads from Nile Street to the café in Tahrir Square where Mahfouz likes to take his morning coffee, one particular beggar can often be seen working his way among cars stuck in the city's perpetual traffic jam. One of his legs is missing, and he hops up to the windows of the Mercedes and Fiats on his remaining, bare foot. The charitable must put their alms in the breast pocket of his *gelabiya*. He has no arms at all. My driver in Cairo once called him the Venus de Milo.

*　*　*

Mahfouz writes with the authority of age as well as art. He has lived the experience of Egypt, its political frustrations, the personal privation. He was born into the warren of ancient alleys behind the Khan Khalili bazaar in December 1911. His father had worked for the government in a minor job, back when officials proudly donned the red tarboosh as a badge of distinction; later he took work as the business manager of a copper merchant in the souk. Naguib was the baby in a family of seven children, the youngest by ten years, and his mother, Fatima, raised him almost as an only 'child. His first memories are of her songs as he fell asleep at night, and of her tales about the djinns. There are vague recollections, too, of feast days, of dervishes who twirled like tops in the streets, their long skirts becoming circular wings that seemed to lift them into the air, of wedding processions and of what he thought were family celebrations in the ancient and enormous cemetery known as the City of the Dead. "It's open country from here to Bab al-Noor. All around here is the cemetery," he wrote. "That's why the air isn't polluted."

As a young man he knew the exaltation of a cause. His university years in Cairo in the 1930s he remembers as "the golden age of patriotism." For boys at school, an end to colonialism seemed the beginning of all possibilities. "The university was a beehive of patriotic and intellectual movements. We were interested in what was going on around us more than we were interested in ourselves." *The times themselves were listening to you.*

Mahfouz had always written. As a little boy he would copy European detective stories he had read, putting in his own, Egyptian characters. In his first novels, fresh from the ferment of the university, he took pharaonic settings and tried to work into them modern political issues. But gradually, studying Proust, invoking Hemingway but evoking Dickens, he developed a style suited to the streets of his city. The novel, as a form, was something new in Arabic. It dates back less than a century in this language of poetry and prophesy. Even the idea of naturalism was alien. But slowly, slowly, Egyptians began to find themselves in Mahfouz's books, grabbing them up with the fascination of villagers seeing their image emerge for the first time from a Polaroid photograph. Here was a man who understood them, in a new form they could understand.

In Cairo you are surrounded by the creations and recreations of Mahfouz. Go to the entrance of Midaq Alley in the Khan Khalili, and the air is dense with the smell of herbs, the dust of spices. The narrow street runs thick with merchants, pushcarts, peasants in from the delta. The corridor of sky directly overhead darkens as the sun goes down somewhere behind and beyond the minarets of Al-Azhar. The human traffic in the street thins quickly. "The noises of daytime life had quieted now and those of the evening began to be heard, a whisper here and a whisper there"—just as he wrote they would more than forty years before. A coffeehouse he called Kirsha's is still near the entrance to the alley, the elaborate Arabic calligraphy crumbling from the walls, "light streaming from its electric lamps, their wires covered with flies." The old proprietor speaks through strings of mucus, monosyllabic, suspicious, half-shouting above the hiss of the gas jet boiling a thick mud of coffee in a little pot of black-crusted brass. *Midaq Alley,* the novel, is one of Mahfouz's best known in the Arab world. The film, made and remade many times since the 1950s, is one of his most popular, in theaters, on television or video. The characters of the alley have been spread not only across the screen but across this city on crude watercolor movie posters, where all movie-star skin is the color of jaundice, all lips the color of blood, and raised knives, smoking *shisha,* the faces of sullen, violent husbands and supplicant wives are the constant caricature of the streets teeming beneath them.

Yet for most of his life Mahfouz made little money from the books. Royalties traditionally are meager in Egyptian publishing, and he was forced to find jobs with the government, sometimes in the Ministry of Religious Endowments, more often in the state's film production business. "I was an employee for thirty years, despite myself. I lived like a student all that time. The job during the day, writing at night." He was thirty-nine before he married. "I didn't have time for marriage; there was no room for family life." His life was not very different from that of the characters he created.

In 1952, when Mahfouz was forty-one, he finished *Trilogy*. In the same year the long-awaited revolution finally came. Nasser "embodied all the dreams of those who went before him," Mahfouz remembered. "The old society which I used to criticize disappeared from existence." Or so he thought. He left off writing novels and concentrated instead on film scripts. But the promises of the revolution faded quickly, as revolutionary promises almost always do, and popular movies were not the place to say what Mahfouz now needed to say. When his novels started to appear again at the end of the 1950s, they were more spare, the style more compressed and unleavened by hope. "Heaven is any place where you live in dignity and peace," says a character in *Miramar*. "Hell is simply the opposite."

These were no longer vast books about the masses and for the masses. Increasingly they were hard-edged novellas about the rising despair among Egypt's political and intellectual classes. Mahfouz's reading had embraced the existentialists and the French "new novel." His notions of democracy, freedom, dignity, even of despair were influenced by the world of ideas far beyond the confines of the Egyptian desert. Yet the world beyond Egypt was, in fact, entirely imagined for Mahfouz. He had been out of the country only twice in his life: once to Yemen for three days, and once to Yugoslavia for three days. The world at large was gleaned from reading and talking to others who had read and traveled, meeting them in coffeehouses, for weekly talks on boats or in tea gardens by the river. *Chitchats by the Nile* is one of his (badly translated) titles, one of his own favorite books, and was specifically cited by the Nobel committee as "an example of Mahfouz's impressive novellas. Here metaphysical conversations are carried on in the borderland between reality and illusion."

It is just this borderland between a dissonant present reality and a world outside, dimly remembered from secondary sources and mostly imagined, that Mahfouz creates in all his greatest books. And his familiarity with this territory may help explain, in part, the empathy he feels for the women in his writing. The first paragraph of *Palace Walk*, the first volume of his trilogy, is a metaphor for Egypt's uneasy awakening to modernity, but also for the literal reality of daily life, still, for many Egyptian women:

> She woke at midnight. She always woke up then without having to rely on an alarm clock. A wish that had taken root in her awoke her with great accuracy. For a few moments she was not sure she was awake. Images from her dreams and perceptions mixed together in her mind. She was troubled by anxiety before opening her eyes, afraid sleep had deceived her. Shaking her head gently, she gazed at the total darkness of the room. There was no clue by which to judge the time. The street noise outside her room would continue until dawn. She could hear the babble of voices from the coffeehouses and bars, whether it was early evening, midnight or just before daybreak. She had no evidence to rely on except her intuition, like a conscious clock hand, and the silence encompassing the house, which revealed that her husband had not yet rapped at the door and that the tip of his stick had not yet struck against the steps of the staircase.

It is the straightforward sensuality, and the deep, painful and at times violent sexual frustration of his Egypt—of Egypt—that Mahfouz captures and conveys and that cuts into the nerve of the fundamentalists. No society is so fraught with confusion about fucking. Virginity was, in the 1930s and 1940s, and remains today, the badge of gentility among girls of the petite bourgeoisie. It was also the commandment of their God. Little girls are regularly mutilated by self-taught barbers in the alleys of Cairo, their clitoris removed and placed on a piece of cotton like a baby tooth, proudly displayed to the parents. Men dictate the terms of desire, then are thwarted by the system they create: forced by their society to remain celibate until they marry, unable to marry until they can buy and furnish an apartment, unable to do that, in many many cases, until they are in their thirties. Frustration and anger breed a still greater desire for domination. The key event in *Palace Walk* is the wife's daring decision to leave her house to visit a mosque after a lifetime of virtual imprisonment.

Yet for all this, Mahfouz's women still feel and love and want and build their lives, for better or worse, on something like their own terms. His narratives are often chronicles of seduction and the sorry fate of fallen women—who are in turn his most sympathetic creations. In *Midaq Alley* and *The Beginning and the End* the heroines become whores. For the fundamentalists, who seethe with repression and codify it into a world where a woman cannot step onto the street without cloth over every inch of her flesh, from the gauze over the eyes to the knitted gloves on the hands, the sensuality Mahfouz writes about—the idea of sensuality itself—is the threat. They can watch "Flamingo Road" and "Dynasty" on television. They can see German backpackers, their asses hanging out of cotton shorts, hiking across the Tahrir Bridge. And sometimes they are revolted and sometimes they are attracted. But that is from another world, the world of the infidel. To write about Egyptian women who might want to get laid— mere blasphemy pales by comparison. Mahfouz has, in the eyes of the intolerant, this damnable ability to understand.

Now Mahfouz lives across town from the ancient alleys, over a little branch of the Nile from the island of Zamalek. I first went to see him the day after the prize was announced. The Nubian janitor sat passively at the entrance watching cars career by on Nile Street; he wore the traditional long Egyptian robe, a turban and Ray-Ban knockoffs. Along the hallways Arabic graffiti was etched into the stucco. A black cat sat near a pair of rubber sandals outside the apartment door. Mahfouz was just getting back home, a plastic bag full of newspapers in his hand, when he was surrounded by reporters. "No lights," he apologized in English as he arrived at the darkened door.

Inside the apartment the sitting room was shaded from the sun by lace curtains, and the furniture, Egypt's own notion of Louis

XIV, was swaddled against the dust by white slipcovers. "The room is very quiet and dim, drowsing in a light that does not reveal the time of day." The author, diabetic and frail, had come to appear like the octogenarian writer in *Miramar:* "I look at my hand and think of the mummies in the Egyptian museum. . . . There's nothing left for death to devour—a wrinkled face, sunken eyes and sharp bones." Mahfouz's wife was fifteen years younger than he; sturdy, protective, declining to talk to the strangers, she constantly proffered soft drinks, tea, coffee. Her hair was covered, in apparent deference to Islamic modesty. His daughters were both grown: Oum Kalthoum was thirty-one; Fatima was twenty-nine. They lived at home as good unmarried girls do in Egypt.

Before the Nobel, Mahfouz and his family had long since settled into a quiet, well-regulated life. Mahfouz would spend part of each day in an office at the semi-official *Al-Ahram* newspaper and much of the rest of it in his favorite coffeehouses in the center of the city, a world not without cares but with little urgency. News of the prize broke over the wires hours before anyone from Stockholm could reach Mahfouz. "I was having my daily siesta after lunch when my wife woke me up and said 'Somebody wants to congratulate you on the phone. He said you won the Nobel Prize.' I told her, 'Enough of dreams.'"

The Egypt of today is a nation of faded reveries, where ideologies, faiths—love, education, cleanliness, hope—have been found wanting. And little is left but a kind of endemic fatalism that resides, permanently entrenched, just this side of despair. In his most recent writing, and in his many interviews, Mahfouz ignores, rather matter-of-factly, the myths that the West has built up to try to understand his country. Europe and the United States most often pin Egypt's identity to a single name—the decadence of King Farouk, or the dashing, dangerous, demagogic Colonel Nasser. Sadat's was the strongest image of all. But for Mahfouz he was "a very strange character." Few Egyptians mourned his loss. "When you look at Sadat, you would think he was really very insignificant and nothing good would come from him. But you would have been wrong." Mahfouz publicly advocated peace with Israel as early as 1972, when Egypt was too weak and too humiliated to admit how desperately it wanted to end twenty-five years of fighting. Mahfouz's books were banned in much of the militant Arab world; like Coca-Cola and Hertz Rent-a-Cars, they were tainted by compromise with Zionism. But then Sadat embraced peace, won a Nobel Prize for it. And he decorated Mahfouz as the great writer he had long since been recognized to be.

Mahfouz has the medal in a little display case with other tokens of esteem, next to the front door of his apartment. But his feelings about Sadat are mixed. On the one hand: "We owe him two things: a successful war, and peace. And also a trend toward democracy." But Mahfouz loathed Sadat for creating an "open-door" economic policy that made Egypt's rich filthy rich and the poor increasingly desperate, their envy tempered only by the preoccupations of survival. And still the economy is left like a humiliated beggar waiting for American largesse—more than two billion dollars a year—to be stuffed in the pocket of a *gelabiya*.

If you mention President Hosni Mubarak, Mahfouz speaks of him pleasantly. The air force pilot who inherited Sadat's mantle was long derided in the coffeehouses as La Vache Qui Rit, for his blandness and his bovine public presence. But Egypt has gotten used to him. He has given intellectuals more freedom than they enjoyed, certainly, under Nasser's token nod to liberty. Mubarak may be learning from his mistakes. "But it's like somebody being thirty feet under water. He can bring you up ten feet, but there are still twenty feet to go." Maybe there is nothing to do. Mahfouz has been through so many phases of hope and despair—"this is not the first time we have had troubles. There have been famines and plagues before. Perhaps we will have to go through others."

So, with the kind of comprehension that infuriates the true believers and the easy humor that turns their eyes to incandescent hate, Mahfouz can be perfectly philosophical about the men who want him dead. Who is this fundamentalist preacher, this Omar

Abdel Rahman who languishes in jail for his affronts to the government and, perhaps indirectly, for his threats against Mahfouz? "Ah,"
says Mahfouz, nodding as he bends toward each word of the question,
"he represents the disillusioned youths; the unemployed who think
religion will have an answer for their problems." Mahfouz sits back
and thinks for a moment. "And within the groups themselves they
do help each other, finding jobs and getting married. It gives them
a sense of belonging and productivity—which only they enjoy in
Egypt now, compared with other young people. It's a rejection of the
corruption that surrounds them." *I had been wrongly accused, and many
people said that I should be killed,* comes the remembered voice.

But corruption has been around so long. There have been so
many crusades, so many causes. "Weren't you the ones who pro-
claimed the holy war?" a young soldier screams plaintively at a government official at the beginning of *Autumn Quail,* set during the bloody
riots of 1952. "Yes," the anguished official replies, "that's why I'm
standing here in the middle of nowhere."

The buses career by on the square below. People leap on,
stumble off. They never quite stop. The old man barely watches now
from the second floor, at the Ali Baba. He goes back to reading his
paper. *There's nothing left for death to devour.*

THE STONES

....

THE PROFESSOR STEPPED LIGHTLY OVER THE PALM TREE. IT HAD STOOD FOR years above the Nile, swaying with the other palms in the garden of Chicago House at Luxor, shading however slightly the scholars who lived and worked and studied beneath. And now it lay across the yard, no longer bending with the winds, soon to be taken away to disappear in smoke. "Well, these trees don't have very deep roots," sighed the professor. It was just a fact of life. The wind, the sand eventually take their toll. But Carol came away oddly distraught. At least there's a photograph of the garden, she said, wanting an image to remain of the place as it was before this little calamity. At Chicago House, that seemed important.

It was the business of Dr. Lanny Bell, professor of Egyptology at the University of Chicago and field director of the Epigraphic Survey of the Oriental Institute at Luxor, to record—not so much to preserve, because there is little hope of that—but to record what can be recorded, as faithfully as possible, of the writing and the art that lived for five thousand years in stone at Luxor but now is fading and crumbling almost as fast as a newspaper left in the sun.

For more than twenty winter seasons he has come to this old mansion along the eastern bank of the Nile, bringing with him teams of colleagues, volunteers, students, artists—all working frantically to trace the disappearing hieroglyphs, as if they could hear the ticking of a clock that measured time in brief centuries. When Carol and I first wandered in off the Nile corniche one November morning in 1986, still marveling at the spectacle of Luxor and Karnak temples nearby, the professor cut short the pleasantries. "In 200 years there will be very little to see here," he said. "The shells of the buildings may remain. But the inscriptions will be gone." He introduced us to one of his colleagues, Carlotta Maher, and got back to his work.

This was when we had first moved to Egypt, and Maher struck me as a curious figure. She was the kind of woman I had often seen attracted suddenly in middle age to poetry or abstract painting, drawn by the emotional intensity of the works and of the artists. But I did not imagine then the latent passions in archaeology.

She led us into the old library, where the air was heavy with the smell of paper and buckram, heat and dust, and she let us pause there for a moment. In the upper reaches of the vaulted ceiling a thin breeze from the river stirred black cobwebs. "There's a monastic feel to this place," she said, pleased.

Maher's job was to file negatives and prints dating back to 1924, when Chicago House began its work. Even this chore was imbued with the fatalism—the almost lurid fascination with decay—that pervaded the project. "We have wonderful photographs back there," she said, motioning toward the darkened hallway at the end of the library. "But they're decomposing, too. So we have death and destruction going on right in our midst." Then she singled out a pair of pictures from her archives. "This is the real horror story." One photograph of a door carved for Amenhotep II was taken in the 1920s. Another picture, of the same red granite monolith, was from the last decade. In the course of fifty years the beautifully detailed inscriptions worked on its surface thirty-four hundred years ago have been destroyed, sloughed off by the stone like unwanted skin.

Such deterioration generally is linked to the rising level of underground water in the Nile Valley. In 1970 the Aswan High Dam created an enormous body of water, Lake Nasser, in what had been arid desert. Humidity increased, and the annual flood of the Nile ended. Irrigation was expanded, and the water table crept closer to the surface. Moisture penetrates the stone foundations of the ancient monuments and is carried upward by capillary action, dissolving the salts inside the rock and erupting on the surface like a white crystalline cancer. But the dam alone is not to blame. Egypt's population has grown virtually unchecked: a million more people every eight months, who produce sewage, who need new housing. Industrial and automotive air pollution are scarcely regulated, and the acids they precipitate can devour stone. Mass tourism is another problem: the tramping feet and rumbling buses generating thousands of little seismic shocks; the hot, moist bodies exuding carbon dioxide and humidity in ancient tombs. Even the sonic blast of grand opera played on stages set up at the Pyramids and at Luxor has been blamed for damaging monuments. "Whatever it is, it's happening and it's happening very fast," said Maher. And it is happening almost anywhere you look.

Long before the High Dam, Egypt was an epic of decay. Cairo and neighboring Giza, under the weight of eleven million people and forty-five hundred years of civilization, are a compost heap of history, with Christian monuments built atop pharaonic foundations, then Shia, then Sunni monuments atop those, all scattered under and among the slums and skyscrapers of the last few years and all seasoned by dust, all—even the newest—distinguished by disrepair.

In Luxor, more pristine, less populated under the hot, dry Upper Egyptian sun, the past stands in bolder relief; and so does its deterioration. At the temple a nineteenth-century mosque built to honor a thirteenth-century holy man is perched high in the air atop a wall thousands of years old. When the mosque was built, the level of the sands had reached up nearly to the top of the temple. But the sands have been cleared away in the last century, leaving the mosque as an elevated curiosity. Beneath it the excavations exposed what archaeologists call bathtub rings, formed as debris piled up around the columns, absorbing the waste of man and animal. Some of the stone still has a greasy look, and the particles of sulfate salts, expanding and contracting with changes in moisture and temperature, eat wide grooves into the rock.

The process of destruction is not limited to ruins above ground. The tomb of Queen Nefertari, favorite wife of Ramses II, is one of the most beautiful in the Theban necropolis. It was discovered in 1902 but closed to tourists a few years later because of the extreme fragility of its vivid, delicately drafted and colored murals. Maher pulled books of photographs from the library shelves, some from the 1920s, some from the 1960s, to show the damage. The paintings in Nefertari's tomb had continued to deteriorate, in some places chipped off the walls by the buildup of salt crystals behind the plaster, in others badly retouched by incompetent restorers. Now a new project was under way once again to try to save the tomb. I had talked to one of the conservationists. He was deeply depressed by what he saw. "It is as if you have a child and it is dying of something you can't do anything about," I recalled him saying. Maher shared that sense of tragedy. "You do this for love," she said.

Egyptologists live in a whole world reconstructed from dust. Treasure hunting long ago gave way to the meticulous exploration of daily life in the time of the pharaohs. Scientists search not only the store rooms of royal tombs but the garbage dumps of the slaves, sifting for bones that tell them pigs were eaten often, though they rarely appear in paintings; discovering fleas in straw sleeping mats; extracting pollen that shows what crops were harvested, what flowers bloomed. As they peer through microscopes and catalog shards, the rituals of life as well as those of death are performed before them. But the record hidden in the dirt is now so full of potential for chemists, botanists, conservationists, archaeologists, environmentalists (looking to document the deterioration of the Earth itself in the last five millennia) that each new excavation is approached with excruciating care.

"Archaeology is a process of destruction," says Egyptologist Michael Jones, a Welshman with a good ear for his own epigrams. "Once you dig up the ancient remains you start to destroy them, and if you don't do it properly they're gone for good." He and his wife, Angela Milward, have been working for a decade in Saqqara, near the site of ancient Memphis, about an hour's drive south of Cairo. Funded by the American Research Center in Egypt, they spend the winter season in a little house near their dig, surrounded by their work and by the still-primitive life of the Egyptian countryside. Donkeys plod along the street nearby. Peasant families still regulate their lives by the seasons rather than the hours, their world a narrow strip of green along the banks of the Nile, bounded by the vast hell of endless desert. In his slide presentations at the research center, Michael shows photographs taken of peasant farmers in the last few years to illustrate, almost exactly, the parameters of agrarian life five millennia ago.

Their cats run freely in and out of the work room as the Joneses meticulously record in photographs, drawings and ledgers each new fragment of pottery they have found in the precinct of the Apis, a sacred bull, the living image of the lord of Memphis. Having come to visit the site, I watch politely but in numb boredom as they work. Angela, a Scot, asks me if I want to see a picture of the treasure they had found after about eight years of digging. She presents me with photographs of thirteen small silver coins. She is proud of the find, and proud, too, that the hunt has never really yielded more conventional, vulgar treasure. She goes back to recording shards for the detailed catalogs that eventually will be written. "Excavation is like the tip of an iceberg that you see," she says. "Publication is the nine tenths you don't see."

When finally we go out for a walk in the digs, excavated temples stand in marshy pools, ominous salt crusts plainly visible along their sides. "You suddenly realize something you were looking at a year ago just isn't there anymore," says Michael. If one could immerse the affected rock in constantly flowing distilled water for months on end, perhaps that would cleanse the stone. "But how do you immerse a temple in a water tank?" Angela looks on with hardened cynicism, like a surgeon knowing there is nothing she can do. "They are ruins," she says, "and they are going to go on being ruined."

In the Valley of the Kings across the Nile from Luxor, in the tomb of Seti I, the rock beneath the paintings on the ceiling is beginning to flake off. The netherworld's sky is falling. Tourists, overwhelmed by the cavernous majesty of the pharaoh's resting place, take little notice. Nor do they pay much attention to the pit in the floor and the narrow shaft that leads down from it into obscurity. Bits of Kleenex and cigarette butts mingle in the dust at the opening, so neglected one assumes it leads nowhere. But no man alive knows where that tunnel leads, whether to a dead end or, perhaps, to the "real" burial chamber of Seti I, still grander than the one that is open.

Kent Weeks, a big, bluff redheaded professor from the University of California at Berkeley who leads a project mapping the Theban necropolis, was one of the last to try to find the end of the tunnel in the early 1980s. Already, by then, he was something of a mythical figure in the Valley of the Kings. He was, after all, the man who brought the balloons to the burial ground of the gods. Searching for the entrances to five royal tombs identified in the nineteenth century and since lost in the chaos of badly managed excavation or covered over by the wind and dust, he spent several seasons in the basket of a hot-air balloon drifting slowly along the cliff faces above the valley. His colleagues took to calling him the Red Baron.

Later he brought in other high-tech gear: seismic devices, electronic resistivity machines and sonar to try to find the hidden tombs. He discovered some likely prospects in the shadowy readouts of his instruments. One of them is next to the septic tank for the Valley of the Kings rest stop. "God knows what kind of shit is in there," he commented. "It used to be said that the safest antiquities in the world were the ones that hadn't been dug. But they are in some instances as endangered as those that have been excavated." More secrets that will never see the light.

So when you are faced with a mystery like the tunnel, sitting there right before you, open but unexplored, it becomes almost irresistible.

"The tomb of Seti I was excavated in 1802 by Giovanni Belzoni," Weeks explained one afternoon as we sipped tea in the garden at the American University in Cairo. "But Belzoni was an enormous man, six feet eight inches tall, three hundred pounds. He could only squeeze down the passageway about 100 meters." Howard Carter, who discovered Tutankhamen's tomb nearby in 1922, tried to penetrate the Seti tunnel but descended only about sixty meters before he was stopped by falling debris. Then, in the 1960s, one of the Egyptian families that worked in the excavations (first as grave robbers, later as archaeologists) got permission to clear the passageway. "They got down about 175 meters before they had to give up," said Weeks. "There was too little air, choking dust, it became extremely dangerous as bedrock started falling in around them."

In 1981, confident of his expertise and skills, Weeks decided to make the descent himself. Crawling, sliding, inching downward, he and his team moved into a passage where the stone was extremely fragile and soft—"like pudding with raisins in it." They attained, just barely, the 175-meter depth reached by their predecessors. Then blocks of stone started falling, almost blocking the way out. Weeks, too, had to give up. "We didn't find the end of the passageway," he said, "but we did find it extremely well carved down there." Certainly it is no simple well, although it might have been an effort to link the tomb with groundwater, the primeval earth, as part of the complicated symbolism of Egyptian death. "We just don't know how much farther it goes," he said. "To find out, we'd have to use the techniques of mining engineering to shore up walls and clear debris." The dust and vibrations could play havoc with the existing chamber. There is no money for the project.

Bureaucracy is as old as civilization in Egypt, and intramural politics are always an element as archaeological bureaucrats vie for power. Funding is low, jealousies high. There are tensions between local experts and foreign scientists. Egyptian officials retaliate for perceived slights with barrages of red tape, holding up permits for digs because a middle initial instead of a full middle name has been written on an application form. Debates about priorities and protocol begin and seem to go on forever, while the business of archaeology grinds slowly to a halt. The greatest discovery in recent years—five large and perfectly preserved statues found at Luxor in 1988—was made accidentally, by cleaning men.

Something else was hiding in the rubble of the temple. Ray Johnson could see, on bits and pieces of sandstone, an outline taking shape among two thousand stone blocks scattered near the entrance to Luxor Temple. Here was the blade of an oar. There, hideous and cruel, were the severed hands of defeated enemies skewered on spears. "If you have a running story, you can restore the entire scene around it," he thought. And there was a story here. During his lunch breaks the young American artist working at Chicago House would study the stones, matching and rearranging them, sketching the results over the course of months, until forty pieces came together to suggest the whole: a frieze sixty feet long that had stood in the colonnade court of the temple, the one known depiction of King Tutankhamen leading his troops in battle.

As Johnson labored to fit the pieces together, to fill in the gaps, he began to talk about the people in the stone as people he knew. Tutankhamen, the child-king with the short history and the rich tomb, "was a very significant pharaoh," Johnson would insist, "not the tragic little boy who played with mummy dolls."

Affected by the proximity of loss, the mortality of the monuments, an intimacy often forms between the scientists and the stone they study. But at Chicago House there is a peculiar intensity to the drawn-out labor. The technique of the surveys is extraordinarily meticulous, even by modern standards of Egyptology. A photograph is taken of the inscription to be recorded. But photographic lenses cannot interpret, and sometimes they actually obscure what they are meant to record. So an artist, often working on a ladder several yards above the ground but with his face only inches from the inscriptions, inks onto the photo what he sees with his eyes. Then the photograph is bleached, leaving only the lines the artist has drawn. Blueprints are made from these, and then Egyptologists go up the ladders to check on their accuracy, making notes and amendments until the record is as perfectly preserved as it can be. In the course of these labors they spend days looking at the feathers of a sacred wing or into the eye of a god.

"It's always a race against time," says Johnson, who has spent a lot of weeks on the ladders at Luxor Temple. Even as he was piecing together the frieze of Tutankhamen in battle, Egyptian antiquities officials were carting away some of the stones, scattering them to different sites and distant museums. The drawings at least keep the whole intact. "In many cases these will be the only records that survive into the future—to show the sensuality of the drawings and of the carvings."

Sensuality?

Johnson smiles. "Figures are leaping off the wall. There's energy, movement—life, in other words." He was in his early thirties, talking about imagined lovers more than one hundred times his age. "The hair of each of these women, every strand, has been carved in the most sinuous wave." Johnson had no epigraph before him as we talked in the high-ceilinged library of Chicago House, but a vision was clearly there before his eyes. "You see the way the stone has been carved : . . in these gentle curves. . . ."

Yes, there it is. You walk back to Luxor Temple and you see the sensuality of the stone. And there is this desire, almost a compulsion against your better judgment—because touching these inscriptions only hastens their destruction—to reach out. You want to hold on physically somehow to these paintings and the carvings and the inscriptions, to freeze the present so that no stone decays, no monuments crumble, so that not even a palm tree falls nearby. To defy time. Before it's too late. Before it is all overwhelmed by rising water and bad air and urban blight, before all that is left is a blueprint of the past.

THE OLD BOYS

THE LEVANT HAS LONG BEEN A LAST RESORT OF PERSONAL LICENSE, A PLACE where repressed Westerners might aspire to decadence on a grand scale. Caesar found Cleopatra; crusaders discovered unimagined delights of silk and skin. You read in wonderment Flaubert's letters about his cruise down the Nile, screwing his way from Cairo to Aswan; counting off the times he comes in Esna with a great black whore-mother of the earth; watching his boatmen pee on the naked Christian monks who, dog-paddling alongside the felucca, beg alms from the Christian tourist—and you think how wonderfully far that must have been from Normandy and Emma Bovary. Or one imagines Rimbaud, the apostle of disoriented senses, retreating to the mountaintops of Cyprus, leaving poetry and leaving Verlaine to lose himself in the silent Levantine snows of Mount Troodos and the stifling heat of the Red Sea coast. One thinks of Saint John Philby, the great explorer, and his son Kim, the great spy, rambling drunk as hell through Beirut on a long night in 1960 and the old man falling down dying. The spy sat by the explorer's bed the next day and heard him utter only one phrase. "God," said the explorer, "I'm bored."

I think of a French diplomat I knew who collected old photographs taken by licentious European artists with forgotten names in the late nineteenth century, photographs of young girls, young boys, depilated, smooth as polished teak, their faces smiling dumbly, unsure of what to expect from the Western lense. There is a licentiousness to the Orientalist's mind better reflected on the paperback cover of Edward Said's scholarly treatise than in his text. A young boy stands naked before old men, a snake winding its way around his shoulders. This was the land of license, a masturbatory Xanadu. *"Kula haga mumkin,"* the Levantines would say to anything asked; "everything is possible."

That sense, for the foreigner, is mostly gone now or mostly imagined, as exotic pleasures have been repressed by the resurgence of Islam or in that most seductively decadent of capitals, Beirut, bombed out of existence. By the late 1980s most of what remained of the old style and sensuality—and it was very little—was to be found in the Christian enclave radiating north from East Beirut and the overgrown fishing village of Jounieh, where wine, women and song were still cherished as symbols of a defiant stand against Islam. On a mountaintop above Jounieh Serge Hochard, a Maronite engineer educated in Bordeaux, was creating a world-class wine from cabernet, *syrrah* and *cinsault* grapes grown in the Bekaa Valley. Madonna videos played on the television station, whiskey and cigarettes were still advertised, with sex appeal, by the Christian Lebanese broadcasters.

Earlier in the decade the American television evangelist Pat Robertson had worked with the Christian Lebanese Forces to set up their little empire of the airwaves. He seemed to have thought they would like his brand of wholesome programming. They had no use for it at all, so he was reduced to running a station out of the Israeli-occupied security zone, broadcasting his "700 Club," old movies and tag-team wrestling bouts to the Shia of southern Lebanon.

* * *

The television was on in the bar of Jounieh's Montemar Hotel. But the sun was going down over the Mediterranean, and the view, over the edge of a scotch on the rocks, was a straight shot to the sinking disk at the other end of the sea. The Old Boy had come to join me. He was a British journalist I had met on the boat from Cyprus to East Beirut. He was coasting on a long magazine assignment, working on a book. He had come to Lebanon to check in with the families he knew in the hash, heroin and coke business. On the boat the faces all around us were Lebanese, and he had been looking to strike up a conversation with anybody who wasn't.

It was my first time on this odd ferry. When the Moslems and Syrians closed the Beirut airport, the boat became the only major link between the Christian enclave and the rest of the world. The *Empress* and its sister ship, *Sunny Boat,* sailed each night for Jounieh staffed by young recruits for the Lebanese Forces. Near the bar there was a little casino with blackjack, roulette and slots to while away the long cruise. One of the woman pursers was said to offer late-night services for a reasonable fee.

In the hallways were posters from Tasmania. One, found in several of the ship's corridors, showed fashionable young men and women taking a stirrup cup, foxhounds snuffling among the hooves of their great Irish hunters. The *Empress,* it seemed, had once been a ferry from Australia to Tasmania. Nobody had changed the posters. Perhaps they liked the incongruousness of the image. Christian Lebanon was in touch with the world in this strange way.

High, rolling seas tossed the ship that night. I slept badly and woke early and went out on deck at first light to watch as the Lebanese coast approached. I had looked closely at maps before we set sail and had a good idea of where Jounieh was positioned: to the north of Beirut, just south of historical Byblos, far from the Green Line snipers. Once before I had seen Beirut from the sea. A Shia banker had taken me water-skiing and blasted his boat right up to the dividing

line between East and West. It was not an experience I wanted to
repeat. But as we neared the coast this time, I got the distinct impression that Jounieh was off to our left—far off to our left. And we were
sailing straight for the shell-battered port area of Beirut itself, near the
headquarters of the Lebanese Forces at Karantina. The Christians
had seized the area in 1976, slaughtering the PLO fighters holed up
in the nearby Sleep Comfort mattress factory, forcing the Muslims
out, bulldozing their homes. Jon Randal, one of the great veteran
correspondents of the region, would later remember the Christian
soldiers' joy "in popping champagne bottles or playing mandolins
over a corpse as smoke poured out of a gutted house."

From the docks the old high-rise hotel district was clearly
visible, deserted now except for sharpshooters. The hotel towers had
been vertical killing fields in the early days of the war. There had been
a battle of the Holiday Inn, leaving the building a charred ruin. Where
Philby father and son had wandered, by the Saint George Hotel along
the waterfront, nothing remained but piles of rubble, collapsing signs,
burned-out cars, sandbags and craters. This was not where I wanted
to be after a long night. But in the token customs shed the driver I
had called to meet me arrived on time. I was overjoyed to see him and
noticed only out of the corner of my eye that the Old Boy was being
met by uniformed men with guns. For a moment it appeared he was
being arrested. But he seemed happy to see them as well.

A few nights later the Old Boy gave me a call at the Montemar. He was staying in East Beirut with one of the leading hashish-
and opium-trading families of Lebanon, and they had assigned him
a twenty-two-year-old Lebanese Forces bodyguard, a Catholic
named Samir. He drove us to dinner in a big Range Rover with
stereo speakers mounted in its roof, Christian FM blasting at us
through the night: an old song by Don McLean, "American Pie,"
about "good old boys . . . drinking whiskey and rye, singing this'll
be the day that I die." We were cruising past the stone homes and
newly built resort apartments sprung up with balconies, pools and
tennis courts all along the Jounieh littoral. Beirut wealth had moved
out here, first to play and then to survive, in style. We were headed

toward the Dog River, a traditional barrier that has inhibited invaders since prehistory. But instead of heading through the tunnel beneath the cliffs we veered off and up into the ravine itself, to a little restaurant called the Dog River Café. It had an American Western motif: fake wagon wheels and branding irons, steak-and-potatoes-and-catsup cuisine. The Old Boy said he thought this would be an interesting place to eat. But it was almost empty. By the third slice of gristle the evening was beginning to drag, and the Old Boy started wondering what else might be arranged for entertainment. Samir would have something in mind, he said, when Samir got back. "Something like dancing."

We piled back into the Range Rover, shouting over its FM blast, rolling now to a heavier beat. Samir was delighted to have a chance to show us a good time. His brief was to keep the Old Boy happy. But he couldn't think of any discos open just then. He had another idea, but, he had to add, he did not really have much experience with this sort of thing himself. He never paid for sex, he said. "Maybe you could introduce us to some nice girls—you know, with no brothers," I said, feeling a little uneasy about the direction the evening was taking. Samir laughed, looking back over his shoulder at me as he drove. "You take care of the girls," he said, pulling his Browning nine millimeter out of its holster. "I'll take care of the brothers."

I was never comfortable when, out drinking with correspondents from an older generation, we wound up touring the clip joints and whorehouse bars of Athens or Cyprus. These men in their late forties and fifties, the generation that had covered Vietnam, drank hard and screwed recklessly. ("He'd put his dick where most people wouldn't put their umbrellas," an estranged wife said of one.) They wrote with surprising elegance, living somewhere between Ernest Hemingway's machismo and Evelyn Waugh's bitterness. I envied them their passions and, in small doses, I enjoyed their company tremendously.

A few days before, in Cyprus, one of them had slid a note under the door of a colleague newly arrived in the area:

My Dear T——,

You will wake up imagining that you loaned me $100 last night. It is possible that you did. I went to a whorehouse with several hundred dollar bills in hand, but in a moment of utter abandon, I tore them all in half and promised the ladies that they could collect the other halves upon appearance in my room.

Unfortunately, none of them showed up to collect!

Now—I will be happy to return to you what is left of your original whole $100 bill, but you must be able to recall its serial number. Otherwise, dear boy, you're plum out of luck, and thank your lucky stars you didn't lend me the $500 I asked for.

P.S. This is not an I.O.U.

There weren't many like that around anymore.

The Jounieh whorehouse where we ended up was the second on Samir's list. The first, rather more presentable, had been taken over by a private party. So Samir took us to this place in a run-down block on one of the town's few main streets. I remember thinking, in the last few inches of light at the top of the stairs as I glanced down at the shredded, faded, all-weather red carpet on the treads (dirt and grit worked permanently into it, through it), that I was glad I wouldn't be able to see any more as I descended into the dark. We were in a cellar. The deafening whine of a woman's voice, a cappella and atonal, droned on in Arabic. A stench of beer and body odors filled the place. The blackness was broken only by a few dim red lights. A handful of customers were scattered about in the obscurity. Two men wandered with a proprietary air. Suddenly one of them was welcoming us. Tall and young, his whiskers fair, he wore a fatigue jacket and he was solicitous in a way that seemed unnatural to him. His hands talked and the movements were exaggerated, obsequious, as he tried to make us feel—what?—comfortable? The other man was short, slight of build, gaunt through his shoulders and legs, but with a pot belly, a thick black mustache and black stubble. In the dim red glow, in the air full of shadows, they looked Boschian and sinister.

Few girls could be seen. The one who came to sit next to the Old Boy wore a large white sweater that clung tight on her ass and was pulled close around her waist with a belt. She sat with one bare knee pulled up, as if she would rest her chin on it, but she was never quite that relaxed, or quite that coy. She did not have to wait long before the Old Boy took her off to the back of the bar, to the black cubicles there, darker than the red-shadowed room where I sat nursing a drink with Samir. He checked on the price: four hundred Lebanese pounds for fifteen minutes. In those days that came to about twenty dollars.

Samir told me that he had met a girl from this whorehouse. She was seventeen years old, and "she is an angel," he said. And he had gotten her out of here—got her a job making dresses in a factory. Uh huh, I thought, trying to imagine this seventeen-year-old angel in a sweater and belt, here in this red hole, then trying to imagine her in a dress factory in a denim apron. I wondered whether the story was all made up, a tale to pass the time. Fifteen minutes had passed a while ago.

The tall young man with the talkative hands—What was that obsequious motion? It was as if he were rolling up a napkin and tucking it into his stomach—wants more money from Samir. Seems the Brit can't get it up. We hear that she's going down on him. The skinny guy with the pot belly goes back to check, comes back from the cubicles, reports that the Brit is sprawled out, almost passed out as the girl is working him up. The Lebanese pimp delivers the news with an air of superiority and vindictive glee.

Samir starts to tell me again about the angel he saved from this place. And now a heavy, coarse-featured Arab whore sits down at a table nearby. Samir says he fought alongside her brother in one of the endless battles here. The girl is crying, strung out. She grabs the fatigue jacket of the host, then collapses in the ritual exhaustion of Lebanese despair, putting her head on the table, crying. Samir watches passively. Whatever his allegiance was to her brother, he has no interest in this girl. A customer comes in, tall, good-looking guy. She smothers his face with wet kisses.

The Brit finally emerges. His face would be a little pink, I suppose, if there were any real light to see by. His hair is mussed, schoolboyish, bad-boyish. He grins as he walks stiff-legged back to the table.

Samir thought the Old Boy ought to have something to fortify him after the ordeal of the black cubicle. Somewhere on one of the highways heading into Beirut we found the pastry shop he was looking for. I don't remember what Samir called what he ordered, but it seemed like—and I guess it was—curds and whey, with candied fruits and syrup on top. Samir said this always restored him after sex. As we waited for the order, two women walked in with two middle-aged men. The women were attractive, or at least they were not unattractive. The Old Boy made as if he would go talk to them. Samir said, straightforwardly enough, "The men are armed." The Old Boy, after a couple of feints to suggest he didn't care, or that this was Samir's problem, was persuaded to be still. He sat quietly in his chair, eating his curds and whey.

I had about given up looking for the old Levant, about lost my taste for the faded romance of Arabia. I was still feeling the lure of "the glamour of strangeness," to use T. E. Lawrence's phrase, but it was not remotely the same glamour or the same strangeness that he had known. The experience of the different cultures swirling around and through each other, or crashing and exploding, had begun to define my time in the Middle East. To try to recapture Thesiger's world seemed increasingly futile, as indeed he had said it would be. Yet when the opportunity arose, some reflexive tourist instinct in me still wanted to follow in the footsteps of the old explorers, to see the deserts they had seen or visit the crusader castles that Lawrence knew, perhaps even to sleep where he had slept—for instance, in the Baron Hotel in Aleppo.

What you have to know about the Baron is that everyone tells you how wonderful it is. Intrepid travelers recount tales of its unique history, its Old World charm, the interesting Armenian characters who own it and the impressive signatures in the guest book dating back to 1909. Lawrence slept there. A glass case on the wall displays one of the bills he ran up. Amy Johnson, the aviator, stayed there when she flew to Aleppo. During the 1930s it was frequented by Agatha Christie and her husband, the archaeologist Max Mallowan. Even in the early 1980s there were celebrity guests, mainly diplomats like Phil Habib making the rounds in the region, trying to bring Syria into the peace process.

I went there with Carol on the tenth anniversary of the night we met, in one of those gestures of affection a marriage needs after a few years. I had been to Aleppo once before and thought it was spectacular. An enormous citadel built by the son of Saladin dominates the old city. The size and complexity of the fortifications—the moat, the gates, the trapdoors and secret passages—are like nothing else I'd ever come across. Most castles are a disappointment when you first see them: so understated compared with the fortifications Hollywood has taught us to expect. But the citadel at Aleppo was made to hold vast armies and repel still larger ones. The crusaders never took it.

Lawrence had loved it. The Arab quarters of the city, "like overgrown half-nomad villages scattered over with priceless medieval mosques, extended east and south of the mural crown of its great citadel," he wrote in *Seven Pillars.* "Aleppo was a great city in Syria, but not of it, nor of Anatolia, nor of Mesopotamia. There the races, creeds and tongues of the Ottoman Empire met and knew one another in a spirit of compromise. The clash of characteristics, which made its streets a kaleidoscope, imbued the Aleppine with a lewd thoughtfulness," Lawrence found. "They surpassed the rest of Syria. They fought and traded more; were more fanatical and vicious; and made most beautiful things: but with all the dearth of conviction which rendered barren their multitudinous strength."

We had been in Damascus, where I often went for work. It is a city whose charms are exhausted after a couple of days. People are reluctant to talk politics, which is what I was there to write about. The political system answers to one man, President Hafez Assad, and there is no second guessing his purpose, even when that purpose is not altogether clear. After twenty years of his rule every ministry is the Ministry of Fear. People watch each other closely and confide little in strangers. Those Damascenes who are rich enough for leisure spend their time at each other's parties or at a handful of restaurants, like the Sahara, which has imported food and drink in ample supply, unlike most of the country. It is owned by the president's nephew, and because of the many mirrors on its walls there are few hidden corners. It is just across the street from the Ministry of Information.

The night before we set out for Aleppo, we had dinner with Lena and Hanaan, two Syrian beauties married to men who made their fortune in Saudi Arabia. Living in Riyadh, they came home to Syria to blow out, relax a bit, get away from the veils and the tiny society of Saudi life, where their husbands lived in constant fear they would offend a prince. Lena wore a five-carat diamond and talked, in French and English and Arabic, of the American "peasants" who worked in Saudi Arabia, the holdovers from the Aramco cartel, which built the oil fortune of the House of Saud. She meant peasants, but she also meant good ol' boys. For the Levantine Arabs who went to the Gulf, sure of their sophistication and worldliness, the easy confidence shared by the Saudis with most of the Aramco Texans was hard to fathom. They tended to dismiss it as a meeting of arid minds. When Lena saw Americans arriving at Riyadh airport, she said she had the sense they had never before been anywhere outside the United States. "I mean, *yaanni,*" she said, "they are from, *je ne sais pas,* Alabama."

The drive to Aleppo takes a little more than three hours. The roads are long and flat and the countryside barren. Big tractor-trailer trucks driving from Turkey to points south barrel along two and three abreast on the two-lane highway. Mounted with as many as eight headlights, they look like enormous insects with faceted eyes. When they passed us, they sucked the air out of our taxi, leaving our ears popping. The driver spent most of the trip cruising on the gravel shoulder of the road.

There is a new Pullman Hotel in Aleppo, where I had stayed

before. It was booked solid and there seemed no way to get a room when we called ahead, but Syrian friends told us we could bribe our way in. In fact they told us we should pay almost anything to avoid the alternatives. But I wanted to stay in the Baron. How bad could it be? I thought. And Lawrence had slept there.

"Pullman?" asked the driver as we arrived in Aleppo. No, the Baron, I said. "The Baron? You are sure?"

Hotel brochures claim that when it was built, eighty years ago, ducks could be shot only a few hundred yards from the Baron's entrance. It was on the edge of an ancient city. Now it is just in the middle of urban sprawl. "I understand a lot of famous people have stayed here," I said tentatively to the clerk behind the desk. "Yes," he said. He told us he was giving us the Phil Habib suite.

One's appreciation of dirt is partly subjective. Dust, for instance, because it is inevitable, eventually becomes acceptable in Cairo. I'll always remember the feel of fine grit under my bare feet in the morning before the floors in our apartment were swabbed. But that was not particularly bothersome. The smell of garbage in the street eventually faded into the olfactory background. So did the particular odor of the fat women in black who sold vegetables on the corner. Even the sewage that erupted into the alleys, sometimes ankle-deep in the old sections of the city, could be tolerated in short spells as part of the ambience of ancient decay, a small price to pay for the beauty of the minarets and *mashrabiya* that rose above. When we first moved to Cairo, it took us a few weeks to realize the rashes we were developing came from bedbugs, but once discovered the insects were easily eliminated, and the faint scent of DDT in the sheets became tolerable when one considered the alternative. I confess the sound of snot being sucked, masticated and spit always grated on me, but I could live with it. The Phil Habib suite had dried snot on the walls. That seemed a bit much.

Carol tiptoed into the room, apparently trying to reduce her contact with the floor. "Where can I hang my clothes?" There was a closet, of course, but she eyed it suspiciously. "We can't stay here," she said. I was firm. "Think of it as an adventure," I told her. "Think of all the people who've stayed here." Tears came to her eyes. The suite was spacious, at least. There were, for some reason, two large sinks in the bedroom. The sitting room had an easy chair and table and a little balcony that looked out through some meager trees to the "casino," a restaurant with music, next door. The bathroom was large as well. In front of the toilet was a piece of carpet rigid with dirt.

We escaped to the bar. No one else was there, not even the bartender. On the wall were advertisements from an earlier day: a dapper man in a cricket sweater announcing that "Canada Dry makes the drinks." The light was dim inside, though the sun had not set. The tobacco-browned lamp shades were askew. I suggested we sit outside on the terrace. Exhaust fumes from low-grade gasoline wafted our way as, finally, we persuaded a sullen waiter to bring coffee. A golden retriever, tarnished with grime, eyed us warily.

I thought George Antaki would be our savior. Scion of an old Aleppo family, Italy's honorary consul and an indefatigable host to anyone remotely rich or famous who visits the city, he had offered to have us over to his house, briefly, for a cocktail. Having been there on my previous visit, I wanted Carol to see it. Antaki's home, in the center of the old city, is a monument to his good taste and good connections. The collection of ancient art and artifacts behind his high walls is more impressive than the one in Aleppo's museum. Built into one side of the courtyard is a large Byzantine mosaic taken from the floor of a local church the Antaki family razed and rebuilt. Second-century busts from Palmyra line the little colonnade. On that earlier visit he had given me a tour of the house. There's a trivial Roman mosaic in the kitchen. Down in the sub-basement, chiseled out of rock and dirt a century ago, are some broken Hittite relics. They were discovered during the excavation but were not up to the standards of the rest of his collection, Antaki said, so they were left there in a corner.

This evening, however, there was no tour, only a scotch on the rocks beneath the fig tree in the courtyard. Antaki preferred speaking in French. He had just been to Istanbul, he said. A Turkish billionaire friend had been feting Europe's titled gentry. There was a birthday party for Princess Margaret: a cruise on a boat with fifteen cabins. Prince Michael of Kent and his wife and their kids took three. "Fifteen cabins don't go so far, you know," Antaki lamented.

At his suggestion, Carol and I ate dinner at the Aleppo Club, which offers a certain faded elegance in the winter but moves outdoors in the summer to become a collection of battered tables and lawn furniture. Three cats positioned themselves around our kabob when it was delivered. The romance of Aleppo, and the romance of the evening, was fading. We went back to the Baron.

The driveway beneath our windows seemed to amplify noise from the street, but it was too hot to close the windows. Then, about midnight, the music began in the casino next door. The Middle East lives mainly at night, even in the provinces. The songs were loud and dissonant, and occasionally punctuated by shrill screams that seemed to come from a cat or a child. We lay there in the dark. "Maybe it's a circumcision party," said Carol. We laughed, but not for long. At 3:00 A.M. the mosquitoes began. The Baron, I thought, is where Lawrence didn't sleep.

THE GARDEN

....

IN THE WORST DAYS OF FAMINE IN WESTERN SUDAN I WENT TO THE VILLAGE called El Geneina, the Garden, as often as I could. It was situated on the border with Chad, in the middle of land parched white as bone. In those times it was impossible to see where El Geneina might have gotten its name. The streets were dust; the fields all around were dust; for years the riverbeds had been dust.

El Geneina lay about as close to the exact geographical center of the African continent as it was possible to get. Actually, it was closer to Doala, Cameroon, on the west coast, than to Port Sudan on the east. Remote as it was, it had a few amenities. Small, simple buildings were in the town, and on a rise nearby was a palace, of sorts, for the local sheikh. There was a rude airstrip, and even a little "guest house" provided by the government for visitors. But its basic civilization was nothing newly acquired; daily life had remained essentially unchanged for centuries.

El Geneina was a stop for camel caravans. Even now young boys rode into town on their ungainly beasts with the dignity of conquerors, and quivers full of spears beside their legs. Men walked the streets with their swords on straps over their shoulders, or simply held in their hands, while daggers were worn under the long, loose sleeves of their robes. Most of the market was a collection of rude lean-tos cobbled together from twigs and sticks where a handful of men half-reclined in the meager shade waiting to sell the articles of leather and iron they produced: slippers, scabbards, camel whips, knives, swords and the heads of spears.

Here on the fringes of Arabia, at its most remote corner, was the essence of savagery and nobility that the old explorers sought. Thesiger sharpened his passion for the primitive life serving with the Sudan Political Service in Northern Darfur from 1935 to 1939. It was here that he first learned to ride camels and ventured into the vast Libyan desert. "This was a new world," he wrote. "Hour after hour, day after day we moved forward and nothing changed. Always the same distance ahead desert met empty sky. Round us was silence where only the winds played, and cleanness infinitely remote from the world of men."

By the mid-1980s, however, a succession of disasters afflicting Sudan was attracting international attention. The nation was crumbling. The swamps of the south were the scene of civil war; efforts by Arab regimes to impose Islamic law on African tribal societies created merely chaos. The mountains and deserts of the east were filling with walking skeletons who fled neighboring Ethiopia. To the west, Libya and Chad were at war, trying covertly to outflank each other through Sudanese territory. Successive governments in Khartoum oversaw a process of relentless decay. Old postcards of the Acropole Hotel in the center of the capital showed it fronting on paved streets. Now the streets were rutted dirt tracks. Outside the capital, the railway system had collapsed. To drive as far as El Geneina was a cross-country expedition that took weeks, if indeed it was possible at all.

Aid workers, with their unique ability to impose bureaucracy on tragedy, arrived in Sudan by the hundreds. They colonized the

Acropole Hotel and the few livable villas left in Khartoum. They imported mountains of grain. They organized an "air bridge" to the western provinces of Kordofan and Darfur, using military transport planes loaned by the Europeans and Americans. They worked with the urgency of medics on a battlefield. But by 1985 the years of drought had all but destroyed El Geneina. The war across the border in Chad forced thousands of refugees onto territory already stripped bare. Then the rains came, and everything suddenly was much, much worse.

One summer morning before dawn I picked my way through the would-be travelers sleeping on the sparse grass in front of Khartoum airport to catch a flight to El Geneina on a C-130 transport supplied by St. Lucia Airways. (Later, St. Lucia Airways would show up as a footnote in the Iran-Contra affair, reportedly a CIA proprietary used to carry clandestine arms bound for Teheran. That's the way it is at the ends of the earth.)

The name of the plane was *Juicy Lucy,* and for most of the flight I slept in the cargo hold, stretched out on sacks of sorghum. It smelled as sweet and dusty as Iowa feedstores, I thought, half-dreaming of milk-fed, rosy-cheeked children and buck-toothed women. Then we banked sharply, dived low, and the runway rumbled rough beneath the wheels, its asphalt surface cracked like dried mud. The cargo door dropped down and men, singing and chanting, began to unload the ten tons of grain from *Juicy Lucy*'s belly. It emptied quickly, and as the floor cleared, another man, using his hands, swept the spilled kernels into a plastic bag.

I stood to one side, scanning the far horizon in all directions, listening to the song and to the sound of flies near my face. They covered my back and rose in swarms when I brushed them away.

A Land Rover sped down the dirt track. Relief workers from the Save the Children Fund and the European Community and the United Nations High Commissioner for Refugees (UNHCR) were upon us. Each time an airplane was heard overhead, they scrambled to meet it. "As far as anybody knows, we are completely cut off by land," said Chris Brown, a woman working for the European Community. "The truck convoy is two weeks overdue." I hitched a ride back to the UNHCR house: half office, half makeshift dormitory for aid workers and visitors. A UN staffer from Turkey was shouting into a large radio, trying to conjure some single-engine planes to deliver food from El Geneina to villages that were still more remote. There was talk that the Americans would send helicopters. Word had been sent out from the police chief of Beida, a village to the south, that shrouds should be sent along with whatever food could get there: fifteen people were dying every day. Predictions for the whole of Darfur suggested hundreds of thousands, maybe more than half a million people, were on the verge of dying. "If the food doesn't come in now, this one month will kill them all," said one of the aid workers. If that were true, then every minute became urgent.

In the heat of the day I walked out into the town. Little children huddled in what little shade they could find. Those who had lived all their lives in El Geneina were not suffering as much as the refugees. They laughed when they saw me coming and seemed unused to the sight of a white man on foot in the street. I thought they were shouting "How are you?" at me, although the accent with which the little children pronounced this first basic phrase of English struck me as odd—as if their instructor had been a Peace Corps worker from Brooklyn. "Howayya?" "And how are you?" I would reply. And they would laugh hysterically. "Howayya. Howayya," they would shout back, giggling.

What they were saying was *khawadja,* "foreigner." Ekber Menemencioglu—the Turk on the radio—told me that. He was grimly amused by my ignorance.

Ekber became my host and guide in El Geneina and the camps around it. Slight but handsome, very cosmopolitan, he managed to bring a little of Istanbul's worldly style to this remote corner where there was no love for Turks—the first *khawadjas* to arrive here in the

nineteenth century. Even his efforts to go native suggested sophistication. He was proud of his shoes made by local cobblers: soft, simple
slippers fabricated entirely from local hides. They were cut, coinciden-
tally it seems, more or less along the classic lines of Belgian slippers.
He bought several pair. Ekber was a graduate of the American University in Washington, D.C., and he had been, at one time, a broadcast director for Turkish television and radio. Having joined the UN
High Commissioner in a public relations capacity, he soon saw that
the action, and gratification from the job, were in the field. Like any
young officer looking for adventure and promotion, he wanted to be
at the front. His wife, a dancer, he left behind in Turkey.

In Darfur in those days there were an estimated 120,000
Chadian refugees, and 750,000 internally displaced Sudanese. All
were hungry. Only about 75,000 were being fed by the relief effort.
The battle against famine, Ekber would say, "is the same problem as
a war: logistics. It's to get the food here." To do that required assem-
bling infrastructure where none existed. Initial plans for the relief
effort had been based on rail transport. But the rails were gone, not
only washed out but washed up after years of strikes by one of Africa's
oldest Communist unions. Trucks were desperately needed—big ones
with low gears and big tires made for moving in rough country. "We
need six-wheelers, and only the military have these things now." Even
trucks, though, couldn't seem to get there. Dry wadis had turned to
torrents. "We need three or four pontoon bridges between Zilengai
and Genemar." Again, this was the kind of thing only an army or an
army's effort could deliver. "Only now it's a war to save lives."

A big refugee camp had grown over the previous year at
Aserni, just a couple of miles from El Geneina. Government officials
had been inflating the number of people there, sometimes by as much
as 50 percent. But there was no overstating the desperation of the
twenty-five thousand who were, all too verifiably, languishing in their
crude shelters of brittle twigs and scraps of plasticized grain sacking.
Since the rains Aserni had become a little peninsula on the far side
of a large lake. The only access was by a black rubber raft, paddled
by whomever was at hand. For the whole month of June there had

been no food. When I went to Aserni for the first time, workers were making the first distribution of grain in twenty-five days.

The European aid workers were dispensing arithmetic lessons along with the food, trying to teach the refugees who had volunteered in the feeding centers the basic notions of accounting along with the principles of nutrition. One OXFAM worker fretted that "each center is supposed to get a calculator," but like the helicopters and trucks and most of the food, the calculators had not arrived. "Five percent corruption you wink at," said Ekber. "But when you get 50 to 60 percent, you have to bring it under control." Some was sheer venality, some merely the product of desperation. When there had been no food to distribute, many of the refugees had wandered away from the camp. Now some returned, and new ones as well. Keeping an accurate census came to seem an almost insurmountable task. People registered two times, sometimes more. So the workers organized the hovels by grids, block by block, square by square, and were constantly counting. When "houses" were empty, neighbors were questioned about the occupants. Old men were enlisted as "observers" in each block. "They tell us, if not the truth, then near the truth," said a field director for one of the Arab relief agencies.

The sense of catastrophe, meanwhile, was multiplying geometrically. The floods had washed into the wells at the camp, destroying what measures had been taken to ensure safe drinking water. Habib, a health worker, pointed to a roped-off section of Aserni: "the cholera isolation unit." The disease had been moving steadily west, first hitting camps along the Ethiopian border, then the homeless of Khartoum, even the dock workers of Port Sudan. It had arrived in Nyala on a train bearing the corpses of people who died on the way. Fifteen thousand cases had been reported so far. "Of course," said Habib, "the government doesn't call it cholera." The genteel British-educated bureaucrats and politicians of Khartoum constantly solved problems by renaming them. Cholera carried the stigma of plague. No, this was merely a question of gastroenteritis.

At 4:00 P.M. the little skeletons in rags began to arrive at Aserni's German-run children's feeding center. One of them, alone, wandered absently, befuddled by hunger. Others came with still smaller children boosted up on their back. Mothers came with new-born babies in their arms, the children listless, their eyes clouded and distant. Five-year-olds wandered into line, their arms as thin and brittle as kindling.

The rains continued sporadically until early September, then stopped. Day by day the wadi around the Aserni camp shrank away, to become once again thin trickles of water and mudholes. Boys went fishing there. Somehow, deep in the mud or sand, in some subterranean way no one there could quite explain, catfish had survived, and they would bite, sometimes, at insects on makeshift hooks fashioned by the boys. Some of them were more than a foot long—hideous, almost finless, reptilian creatures of the mud. But there they were, in the isolated waters of the desert, alive.

And the people, too, had survived.

Finally the choppers had come. Big red and white Chinook-type machines with twin rotors that could haul sixty one-hundred-pound bags of grain on long flights, up to eighty on shorter ones. One morning I caught a ride with Dave and Roger, two American pilots working regular shifts flying out of Nyala up along the Chadian border. "Our principal function is to haul grain," said Roger as he waltzed the enormous machine into the air. When they had first arrived at some of the camps, starving men, women and children rushed through the hurricane blast of the rotors to tear the food from the lowering cargo nets. But now, a few weeks into the operation, routine had settled in. The cockpit bore hints of the pilot's homemaking. A sticker at the back of the control panel warned NO BOZOS showing a clown's face in a circle with a slash through it. In one recess of the cabin a fishing rod and spinning reel were stored. Roger and Dave wore red T-shirts, each with his own name stenciled on it.

These were veteran pilots, doing their jobs here as they had in Guatemala after the 1976 earthquake, or in Southeast Asia before that. "Most of us were in Vietnam," said Dave, shouting into the intercom. "Outside of med-evacs in Vietnam or the States or whatever, this is the most useful job that a helicopter can do."

We banked and headed west northwest, across a landscape just greening after more than five parched years. For mile after mile the terrain was almost featureless, flat with only the occasional low hill that seemed to pop up as if from nowhere, a solid rock dropped, somehow, out of place. Wadis where desiccation had given way to torrents were dry once again, but swirls and runnels of silt marbled the riverbeds. Here and there were aureoles of vegetation where water had overflowed and stood still, but these gave way to a pale reddish-brown terrain and rough scrub trees called *mokheit*. Low ridges were covered with dead trees. Rarely we saw small straggling herds of cattle.

The last detailed topographical survey of western Sudan was made by the British in 1929. "We've seen whole villages that aren't there," said Dave, pulling out a map. Roger ran his finger over some of the symbols on the chart. Key landmarks were mosques. "I found one," he said, "and it was just rubble." Now they used satellite photos of the region, each new settlement clearly visible, each hill, each tree in its place. Dave pointed out our itinerary: Zilengai, to refuel at a temporary depot; then to Beida, the village that had begged for shrouds a few weeks before; then Kongo Haraza, a major camp. "Lucy," said Roger. Then the smaller camp at Habila. "The girls," said Roger. Dave smiled. "Yeah."

At Beida the graves without markers stretched out beyond the edge of the camp like a low range of mountains. When the town had begun to starve, the local officials, fearful that the few remaining crops would be stolen, forced out the Chadian refugees who had been arriving by the hundreds each week looking for help and trying to find shelter. Mainly they were women and children. There were very few men. Now whenever aid was given to the camp that had been established, the people of the town objected. "The big problem here," said Robert Vermeulen of the Belgian Red Cross, "is that you cannot do something for the camp alone. You must also do for the village." In this famine any succor is a magnet that reaches out for hundreds of miles. "These people have nothing. So whatever you do is a pull factor. If you drill a well, it's a pull factor. If you start distributing plastic sheeting, it's a pull factor." Though the town suffered from malnutrition, few people migrated. Then the Chadians arrived after long treks through the desert from the nothingness of their homes to the bare subsistence of the camp. Everywhere the Chadian children had the puffy faces and the sickly orange hair of kwashiorkor, a severe form of malnutrition. They waited patiently, standing if they could, holding before them their empty bowls made of hollowed gourds—haunting, these little Giacometti sculptures all too real, alive, their stomachs bloated by disease.

Inger Nissen, a Danish worker for the International Commission for the Red Cross, had worked in the Ethiopian camps of eastern Sudan, where television footage and photographs had stirred the conscience of the world a year before. "It was heaven compared with this," she said.

And yet the death rate had not reached what was feared. Five hundred of the seventeen thousand people in the immediate area had died during the course of the summer. "There is always somebody who manages to survive," said Inger. "In one family they might have four or five children. And you can see that they have decided that one is not going to make it. You give the mother milk for the weak one, and she will give it to the healthy one because it's not worthwhile."

Doctors call this kind of unnatural selection triage, and the famine doctors practiced it on a massive scale. They were feeding the hungry, but they would not give medicine to the sick. "The big problem for this camp is the future," explained Robert. "We're only here for six weeks. I'm not going to start anything with medicine until I'm sure there's somebody to replace me."

Dave and Roger were back, having picked up some straw matting from another staging area. It served for walls in the hospital tents of the camp. "What would Beida have been like if it weren't for the helicopters?" Inger wondered. The matting came rolling out the back of the chopper as I scrambled to get aboard.

Dave looked at his watch. "You'll love Lucy," he said. By air we were only a few minutes from Kongo Haraza.

She spoke English with a French Canadian accent, and she looked, just a bit, like a gypsy. Her hair was short and businesslike, but she wore a long, flowing skirt, a red blouse, big, red, flat earrings and dark glasses. A black lace shawl was draped over her shoulders. "I don't know why I shouldn't dress well because I am in Africa," she said. "When people look at me, they smile. I like that." A few days before, Dave and Roger had taken her up in the helicopter, and she had waved the shawl from the window to the cheers of the refugees below. As we arrived, she was organizing a dance in the yard of the camp, with drummers taken from their cooking fires, singers from the ranks of the starving. "Because," she said, "I want the people to be laughing and happy."

A trained nurse, at thirty-five she had worked in Cameroon and in Quebec at a community health center, in Angola and now here. "It's a way to give what I can give." Lucy ran the supplementary feeding center that made the difference, for most of the children in the camp, between smiles and kwashiorkor. But she brought more than food. She had made discipline a game, but kept it discipline. "You have to have a fence," she would say. "Inside, you are the boss."

Registration and records had been turned into a competition. Children were given plastic hospital bracelets to identify them. And those with bracelets were given blue Save the Children Fund T-shirts as an added bonus. The center had been in existence two weeks, and had registered 205 children. "In the morning you can see the blue shirts coming from everywhere." There had been eight deaths. "Most kids here are around 60 to 65 percent of the weight they should be. When we began, we had twenty-seven who were below 60 percent." Already they knew to sit in neat rows, waiting patiently in the shade for food to be delivered, learning to accept the charity without shame, as part of a game, almost as a duty. "I have to push them to be proud of the feeding." The children sat cross-legged on straw mats eating porridge from plastic cups with plastic spoons. The compound was spotless.

"She appreciates to be the princess of these people," said one of Lucy's French co-workers, who did not appreciate her so much.

In one hand Lucy carried, almost always, a Swiss army knife and a piece of cardboard with an essential Arabic vocabulary spelled out phonetically: death—*mat*; wait—*istenna*; beautiful—*eloua*; clean—*nazafa*. On her red blouse she wore a little plastic pin of Antoine de Saint-Exupéry's Petit Prince. "You know it?" she asked. "Read especially the chapter about the fox, that we know well only what we take time to know." She knew her work and these people she believed; and she was constantly learning more. "I like to be a princess," said Lucy. Even the princess of Kongo Haraza.

"Watch that hooch for me," said Dave, as we took off again. "It's still there," said Roger. A bag of little goodies for the girls in Habila.

They came running toward the chopper looking like nothing so much as cheerleaders at a pep rally, wearing T-shirts and cotton slacks and leather tennis shoes without socks. They were in their twenties but looked younger, fair and fresh as a morning in Newport, even under the afternoon sun of central Africa. One, Rita Zemaitis, had the work in her blood. Half Italian, half Lithuanian, she had found her way here after visiting her father, who was working with the Food and Agriculture Organization in Juba, in the southern swamps of Sudan. But Phoebe and Daisy were from a different background altogether. They were Vreelands. Their father was an architect in Los Angeles. Their grandmother was Diana Vreeland, the doyenne of *Harper's Bazaar* and *Vogue*.

This was not something they advertised. Dave and Roger wouldn't have known and couldn't have cared. But once you guessed a connection from the name, it wasn't something they were going to deny. Phoebe, twenty-four, had bright blue eyes, light brown hair and freckles. Daisy was a year older, her features more angular; and her short blond hair was like a beacon in the desert. Phoebe had been going to UCLA, Daisy to Santa Monica College. But they decided it was time for some travel. Their grandmother encouraged them, apparently under the impression they were going to Europe. But they headed for the Middle East. In Egypt they heard about the famine in Sudan. Taking trains and boats along the Nile, they came down through Wadi Halfa, overland across the desert frontier. Such places are rugged even by the standards of *Vogue*'s fashion spreads; not a good place for Vreeland girls to be.

"When we went to Turkey, she was concerned, and when we went to Sudan she was frantic," said Phoebe. "She called the ambassador to the Sudan. He said, 'Don't worry, they're in the east. It's much safer than the west.' So I'm not sure what she thinks now." The refugees and the natives of Habila were not sure what to think either. Rarely had they seen white people, and never had they seen any like Phoebe and Daisy.

The girls spent their afternoon measuring children and preparing for the feeding. The babies were stretched out on a board to determine height, then placed in a kind of plastic swing hung from a scale to weigh them. Camp rules said that if the children weighed 75 percent of what they should, they were not eligible to enter the supplementary feeding program. Phoebe and Daisy bent the rules. "If they're above 75 percent but we still feel bad about them, we let them in." Triage gave way to noblesse oblige.

There were 123 children registered. The girls dutifully kept camp records, taking tidy little notes in a spiral notebook, as if working for extra credit. They had set up their proper feeding area; taking a cue from Lucy, they had an ample supply of Save the Children T-shirts. They dutifully prepared the mush of corn, soy, milk, oil and sugar.

"We're enjoying it," said Phoebe, "we really wanted to get out in the field and open up feeding centers of our own."

Phoebe had been majoring in English literature before she and her sister started traveling. Now she considered studying to be a nurse. And Daisy had doubts about returning to college at all. "It's very hard to go back to school when you're here doing things."

My friend Ekber had left El Geneina several days ago to try to drive to Beida. He was the first to make it through in a truck, but the going was still terribly rugged. Now he was on his way back, but the sun was setting and he hadn't arrived. Occasionally, faintly through radio static that crackled like a hailstorm, it was just possible to make out his voice. It seemed—although this was hard to tell—that he was making slow progress. Frances, a hearty Irish woman who had arrived in El Geneina a few weeks before, was handling the communications. "Ekber's stuck in a wadi, I think," she said. "Ekber's always stuck in a wadi." But we would wait a while before trying to find him. The desert tracks were hard to follow even in daylight, and little remained of that. Ekber was with his spanner boy, a local with some mechanical talents. It would be safer for everyone if the two of them could work their way out with winch and shovel, rather than us going in convoy to find them and getting more people lost or stuck along the way.

There was nothing to do but sit on the screened porch of the UNHCR house and wait. Frances was big-breasted, maternal, easy to be with. She told me to make myself at home. As the light faded, other aid workers came by to sit and talk and watch the dusk dissolve to the black of night. One was a young Canadian lawyer who had raised money in Halifax to feed starving children in Ethiopia. He had driven a truck for weeks through the desert from Khartoum and finally, to little end except to show it could be done, had arrived in El Geneina. He told stories of the times he was stuck in wadis and it took fifty Africans to pull him out. He was very interested in what he had to say.

Frances came to check on us.

"Now, would you be wanting a little of mother's milk?" she asked, looking at me. Perhaps in another place, at another time, I would have had a better idea what she was talking about. But, just then, I couldn't imagine what to say.

"I think you would," she said.

"Would I?"

"You wouldn't be wanting a little whiskey, then?"

Since the imposition of Islamic law, liquor had been banned throughout Sudan, and with special vehemence in the Muslim north and west. But many of the flight crews coming in on the relief effort were unaware of the prohibition, or didn't care, until they discovered that the law really was enforced. One Belgian transport plane had come brimming with cases of Stella Artois, then had no way of unloading them in the capital. So they got rid of it in small amounts as best they could. Once I flew back from El Geneina with the Belgians only to be offered a cold beer at 7:00 in the morning. One of these crews, it seemed, had donated a case of Johnnie Walker to boost the morale of the workers in El Geneina. Frances figured mine might need a lift as well.

Other aid workers drifted in, concerned about Ekber. Weapons from the Chadian war were spreading rapidly into the region, and travel had become a greater risk. Save the Children began mounting camel caravans to bring food supplies to remote villages. Eventually these ambitious anachronisms became a key part of the mad scramble to salvage lives after the rains finally came. A typical caravan had as many as 110 animals carrying four sacks of grain each. But the first one that went out was robbed. "It rather shattered people's confidence," said Chris Brown. "Since then all the camel trains going any distance have armed guards with them." Now Ekber was stuck out there somewhere in a Land Rover.

Arthur, a Dutch aid worker who specialized in water projects, suggested that we wait an hour or two more, then go after Ekber if he was still stranded. Most of us had another drink, starting to get better acquainted now, talking in the dark. Only Arthur declined the whiskey. His system was still recovering, he said, from the poison.

Arthur had been looking for some flowers, there in the desert town where there was so little food and so much dust. He had wanted to do something that would make his small house a little prettier, a little more like home. There was a girl, people said, who had flowers. She had been to Khartoum to be educated, and she had come back and, on her own, begun to grow flowers in a dry little garden. She was the only person in the town who did this or, it seemed, had ever done it.

Now I don't know at all what this woman, this girl, looked like. But that night, in the dark, drinking mother's milk, listening to Arthur, I had in my mind's eye a clear picture of her: tall and slender, with the Sudanese shawl like a sari draped around her shoulders and, loosely, over her hair. Her fingers were long and graceful but strong. It was easy to imagine them working the earth around flowers, or caressing, lightly, Arthur's tanned face while she smiled.

The women of western Sudan were, it seemed, full of surprises. They were stunning for their dignity and their strength. They were survivors like none I had ever seen before, and they amazed—again and again—the aid workers among them. In many of the camps there were virtually no men at all. As the famine had grown desperate, the men walked away, toward Nyala or Khartoum, concerning themselves only with their own survival and in the process relieving the women and children of the burden of their presence. The women, mother, daughter and granddaughter, knew a few things well, and one of those was what it took to survive a famine. They knew how to gather grass and cook it and eat it; and when the grass was gone, they knew how to gather the *mokheit* berries and cook them for hours and days until the bitter poisons in them were gone. Many of the women knew, also, how to hide, even bury, the food they had if there was any way some could be set aside for the future.

I imagined Arthur's woman as not too different, really, from the young mothers in the camps, their faces open and friendly and proud, despite all the hardships. I may have been completely wrong. Maybe she wore blue jeans and a T-shirt and looked and acted and carried herself in every way like the Western women who had come to El Geneina, or the ones she had known in Khartoum. Maybe she had a tawdry air of sophistication about her. But I suspect it was the flowers, and not her looks or clothes, that set her apart from everyone else in the town. And that she knew Arthur.

Of course, her brothers had found out. They had invited Arthur to a meal, and when he had left it, he was dying, or felt as though he were. He said that night that he did not die, finally, because he had been suspicious and hadn't eaten much. Or, though he would not admit this, perhaps the poison in the food had been of the accidental variety that the heat and the primitive conditions would create easily enough. If the brothers really believed Arthur had been having sex with their sister, surely they would have dealt him a more direct and effective blow than a dose of poison. But Arthur was, in his turgid Dutch way, not very enlightening on these points. He found it easier to discuss the nature of her circumcision, which, he said, had been only a token job, not the complete excision, so common and so horrible. The others who were there, who knew him and knew the girl, did not contradict his judgment, or even question it. The affair, and its dangers, were just part of the background of life in El Geneina.

By the time we went out to find Ekber, we were all quite drunk, and only a few blurred moments remain of the long drive, images flashing in our headlights like a slide show: the low, skeletal *mokheit* bushes slapping against the sides of the jeeps as we revved and raced and slithered along the desert tracks. I have no idea how anyone could know, exactly, in that wide, desolate territory and at night, where to find the Turk. But the lead driver in our little caravan found the place as unerringly as a delivery boy making his way to Fifty-ninth and Madison. There was Ekber sitting in the cab of the Land Rover with the door open, looking frazzled, nearly indifferent to our arrival, embarrassed that he had not been able to extricate himself from the wadi, but glad he wouldn't be sleeping in the bush. I have an image in my flickering eidetic retrospect, of a man with a rifle standing nearby. I do not know if he was a soldier. Perhaps he was the spanner boy doubling as a bodyguard.

Another random image from that night is a trip to the latrine.

Ekber's staff was proud of it. Aid workers, with good reason, make much of the salutary benefits of good latrines. It was, indeed, about as tidy as concrete gets. But nothing could be done about the cockroaches, which seemed as big as field mice. They crawled in large numbers over your feet if you remained still for even a moment. Of course, there are times when you must.

The next morning I woke at dawn, my mouth dry as sand. As soon as the first plane could be heard making its approach, I leapt into a car with the aid workers scrambling to meet it. I haven't been back to El Geneina since, nor to Sudan. The drift of the news was in other directions. There have been two changes of government in the Sudan since then, one peaceful, one not. The war goes on. Famines pass over the land with biblical fury; aid workers come and go. The men wander away, and the women survive.

I did see Ekber once again after that, but it was thousands of miles away, in another war, in another emergency. I asked him about Arthur and his Sudanese lover, whatever happened to them. But the question—the story—meant nothing to him. I asked him about Frances. He knew about her, certainly. She was working just then in Afghanistan. There, no doubt, one would be wanting a lot of mother's milk.

THE SHORE

SILKWORMS

....

Gerry blackburn, the workboat captain i'd known in dubai, had moved to safer waters. By the spring of 1987 the war in the Gulf was too much for a family man to handle. He had a wife, a thirteen-year-old son. But for a former fisherman from Yorkshire the money of Arabia was too good to leave behind.

The raid on Sirri Island that Blackburn witnessed in 1986, when he and his mate pulled the living from the water and left the dead behind, was the first stretch of the war's long arm to embrace the southern Gulf. Now mines riddled the waters and rumor had it that more were to come. The Iranians were setting up launch facilities for big Chinese-made Silkworm missiles. With aerodynamics out of Buck Rogers—so slow you could see them wending their way across the sea to a target—the Silkworms aimed into the Gulf were ship killers nonetheless. They carried one thousand pounds of explosives, potentially enough to sink the biggest tanker and all but the most

153

heavily armored warship. Silkworms were, true to the spirit of the Iranian arsenal, low-tech and high impact, the missile equivalent of a contact mine. And they were being used by the Iranians in a constant game of catch-me-if-you-can with the Reagan administration. Bluff or blast? None had been launched yet, but no one could foresee the consequences if they were deployed effectively.

So far, the main casualties in the fighting had been civilian sailors. So Blackburn had taken the workboat *Anita* around the tip of the Musandam and down the coast to Fujairah, well clear of the war zone, to an anchorage where supertankers waited for dark so they could pass through the strait or simply off-loaded their cargo and left. Either way, good, safe work abounded for a supply boat like the *Anita* and for a captain like Blackburn.

Fujairah wasn't much to write home about. It boasted the smallest Hilton Hotel in the world (ninety-nine rooms) and an international airport nobody, internationally or nationally, found much use for. The central monument in town was a giant Arabian coffeepot. Such were the icons of local civilization. The fishing boats pulled up on a beach that reeked of rotting sharks. The makos were caught by the hundreds, gutted for their oil and stripped of their dorsal fins, which were left to dry on putrid racks near the road. Countless soup pots in the Far East were the ultimate destination of these tidbits.

There were only a couple of decent bars along the entire coast of the Gulf of Oman, and nothing to compare with the subcontinental country-and-western, Tex-Mex, Filipino-Pak allure of Pancho Villa's. But there were a fair number of decent people. Captain Cecil Smiley, a jovial Scotsman, ran the Gulf Agencies Company operation there. Occasionally he and his wife, Elspeth, hosted black-tie dinners for the Fujairah–Khor Fakkan crowd. The beaches were long and empty. The people were peaceable.

On August 15, 1987, the *Anita* hit a mine. The proximity of danger should have been apparent. A few days earlier the supertanker *Texaco Caribbean* had been holed by another floating bomb. No one had been hurt on the *Texaco Caribbean,* with its compartmentalized hull and enormous mass. Perhaps it was just a stray mine, broken from its mooring, floating down from the upper reaches of the Gulf. The United Arab Emirates coast guard and Fujairah port officials had declared the Fujairah anchorage safe.

The *Anita* was a little boat. When the mine blew, her hull shattered, and she sank in seconds. Blackburn was trapped in the wheelhouse. Four other men went down with him. The six survivors were photographed lying wounded and in shock on the deck of the workboat that came to their rescue, and the wire services sent the image around the world. The workboat had picked up the living; the dead were beyond reach. Blackburn's body was not found until a week later, by divers searching among the schools of sharks, eighty-five meters beneath the surface of the Fujairah anchorage.

The danger was building everywhere in the waters near Iran, everywhere on both sides of the Gulf. But nobody wanted to stop doing business. Nobody believed the worst could happen to him. All imagined that the others, hit before them, had made mistakes they would not make themselves. The confrontation building out on the water turned ineluctably to chaos. Shrimp boats were blown to bits by Exocets; dhows erupted splintering from the water; newsmen in helicopters were lined up in the sights of Iranian gunboats; the radio traffic became a cacophony of distress calls and challenges, all interspersed with the obscenities of the Filipino Monkeeeeee. The hospitals of Bahrain, Dubai, Kuwait and Iran were taking in sailors, machinists, cooks and fishermen who had come from everywhere on the face of the earth. Some, who didn't know the Gulf, were lured by danger pay that would double their salary for the few days they were in the war zone. Others were just doing their job, thinking that somehow the odds would be with them to survive.

I found Luciano Zani, of Parma, Italy, in the Dubai hospital, his scalp torn, his arm wrapped in bandages and suspended above his head. He was forty-seven. He had first gone to sea when he was eighteen, and his life was now spread across the globe—a wife and apartment in Kobe, Japan, and employers in Denmark. He had sailed often through the Moluccan straits off Indonesia, where pirates still prey on merchant vessels. And he signed onto the *Estelle Maersk* with few qualms about a voyage to the Gulf. So many ships in its waters, he thought, the odds should be with him. "You come to the Gulf, you can't see it's dangerous. You have no worry," Zani said, shifting slightly in the hospital bed. "If you think about it—it's never going to happen to me—that's what you think."

In the dark before dawn, about thirteen miles off the Dubai coast, it happened. The *Estelle Maersk* had loaded up with 42,500 tons of volatile naphtha gas oil in Saudi Arabia and was hugging the coastline off the United Arab Emirates, trying to slip quietly out of the Gulf. As the ship's alarm sounded, shrill and deafening, Zani raced through the shadows to his station in the deck office. Artillery shells were whistling over the ship, some exploding above it. At any moment one might blast into the cabin where he stood. He didn't know whether to stay in the office or leave, to run or hide.

"There is so many warship around here, and the Gulf is not so big. Where is all those ship? There is bloody seven Italian, seven or eight British, there is I-don't-know-how-many American. Where they are?" But no one came. The captain never called. "He never try. There is no time. It is just like you meet a person in the street, he take the gun and he shoot at you."

Zani stepped outside. He could just distinguish the outlines of a small ship in the moonlight and the flash of artillery. A Danish crewman, Eric Johnson, followed Zani out and climbed up to a lifeboat to see what exactly was happening. The shelling did not relent. Zani started to duck back inside. He didn't hear the explosion above him, but suddenly he was reeling, his head bleeding, slivers of shrapnel cut into his scalp, his back, his foot, his arm. He managed to stagger to an alleyway and lie down.

Johnson was hit, too, and hit badly. He was crawling, shouting, trying to get inside, caught in the legs and the gut by the main force of the blast. "He start calling me, but I cannot do nothing." Other crewmen rushed to Johnson with first aid. They gave him three jolts of morphine to try to kill the pain. "They were talking about the legs. I really don't see the legs—because I really don't want to see the legs."

Finally the attacker, an Iranian frigate, it was thought, slipped off into the dark. Zani and Johnson were carried to the ship's helipad to wait for a chopper called from the coast. "My God, oh my God," Johnson was crying. "I want to die." Zani looked at him. "Just take it easy. We're gonna make it." The chopper descended toward the deck.

But somewhere, somehow, someone miscalculated in the dark, and suddenly the rotor caught a piece of the ship. The chopper faltered and crashed, shattering against the deck. By the time a boat arrived to evacuate the wounded, Johnson was dead.

It was not for money that Zani set out for the Gulf. "We never think about those bloody extra money because the taxes, they take it all away. You get paid 200 percent, but the tax take about half of that. So you have not so much left."

So, Luciano, what the hell you gonna do?

"In my future I think I gonna still sail. Sail again. Yes. What are you gonna do, change your job? If you start sailing in the sea—you know, we have another mentality, you know. If I stay ashore—you have to make new friends, you know. You have to go around to the other things. It's very hard to explain." He took a sip of water through a straw from the glass beside his bed and looked at me, unsure if I could understand. He told me, "You have to try to be a seaman. And after that you come ashore and be ashore. So then you find out."

Angel Valida was almost ready to be released from the Sharjah hospital. He sat up in the bed and pulled the sheet back to show the enormous scars on his leg. He said he was thinking about leaving the Gulf for good.

The young Filipino had signed up as first mate on the *Big Orange XIV*, a sister ship of the *Big Orange VII* I'd sailed on a few months before. It was based in Sharjah, operated by an American company there, but it was regularly chartered out to Iran's National Oil Company. Valida weighed the risks of the job and figured the southern Gulf would still be at the outer limits of Iraqi fighter-bomber range. The Iraqis' main objectives in any case would be tankers, not tenders. Then, too, the one area where mines did not seem to be popping up was in Iranian waters.

But once the *Big Orange XIV* arrived off Iran's coast, it was ordered north, toward Kharg, the main Iranian oil terminal at the northern tip of the Gulf. For more than three years the Iraqis had been trying to bomb this key oil installation off the map. Failing that, they ravaged the shipping lanes up and down the Iranian coast, Exocet Alley. The *Big Orange* never made it to Kharg. On September 1, a little north of Lavan Island, it was weaving its way past fishing boats and some Iranian coast guard vessels. Valida was at the controls. There was no warning when the Iraqi missile hit.

The superstructure of a *Big Orange* workboat is a tower, with access from the interior of the vessel by a steep, narrow stairway. Valida was blown back from the wheel, halfway down the stairs. Blood washed into his eyes from dozens of cuts on his face and scalp. One of his legs was twisted in a direction it was never meant to bend. Above him he could see the lolling head of the captain and that of a Sri Lankan seaman who had been with him on the bridge. They were dead, or looked it, half-buried beneath the rubble. Another seaman stumbled toward Valida. He thinks I'm dead, too, thought Valida. He was all but paralyzed by the pain. Before Valida could make a sound, the other sailor was gone. The corridor was filling with smoke. Lord, please, thought Valida, if I'm going to die, not here in the ship. A life jacket had been blown off a closet door into the hallway, just within Valida's reach. Almost by reflex he put it on. The fire had begun to crackle around him. Excruciatingly, like a ghoul rising from a grave, he dragged himself on his belly and side to the rear of the crew quarters. Other sailors saw him there, finally, and helped him down toward the broad, flat aft deck, a platform just inches above the water.

"The captain was killed, and the Sir Lankan on the bridge was killed. We abandoned the ship. The fire was already higher than the radio mast." A couple of sailors tried to help Valida into the rubber Zodiac boat beside the ship. But his broken leg wouldn't support him, wouldn't work at all. He fell, and the water closed over his head. Only the life jacket held him up. Another crewman grabbed his hair and held onto him to keep him from drifting away. Finally he was dragged over the edge of the Zodiac and onto its floor, which touched the surface of the sea and heaved like a water bed possessed by demons. Minutes later an Iranian coast guard ship was on the scene.

Valida was taken for treatment to an orthopedic field hospital outside the city of Bushehr, which catered to an endless influx of near-martyred Revolutionary Guards from the battles near Basra, in southern Iraq. There were few nurses, fewer doctors, still fewer orderlies. The patients, for the most part, had to care for each other. Many of the Iranian nurses, covered in their black chadors, did not want to touch them and did little more than hand out pills.

Valida's shattered leg was pinned together with three rods as big as knitting needles. They were left protruding through his muscle and skin on each side of his calf.

Few people in the hospital spoke any English. But one young soldier spent long, arduous hours trying in broken phrases to convert Valida to the Ayatollah's Islam. He gave him tracts from the revolution. There was little else to read. A copy of the Australian *Vogue* was smuggled to Valida by one of the more Westernized nurses. Valida kept it hidden beneath his mattress, as the fundamentalists didn't approve of the pictures. There he lay for thirty-four days.

Crewmen who've spent more time on Exocet Alley know to keep their passports with them in a waterproof bag at all times. Valida's had been left on the ill-fated boat. He was, officially, without a state, without status. The Iranian bureaucracy moved at a crawl. Finally he was sent to Teheran but still he couldn't get out of the country. Still the spikes protruded through open holes in his slowly healing leg. One week more, another week more, another day and another. After nineteen days in Teheran his papers were cleared and he flew to the Emirates. In the Sharjah hospital the spikes were removed. They had held his leg together, horribly but effectively. For the first time since Valida abandoned the *Big Orange XIV,* he was able to take a bath.

A few weeks later, after a vacation in the Philippines, he was back in Sharjah, back on the Gulf in another *Big Orange.*

The Americans were getting nervous, getting trigger happy. The minds of the sailors were filled with the threat of explosives-laden dhows or Boston Whalers ramming their thin-skinned ships in sea-borne suicide attacks, like the truck-bombs that had taken so many lives in Beirut. You could never tell what was going to happen, and if it did happen, well, hell, it was too late to do anything about it. The officers were worried, too. They had seen the career of the *Stark*'s captain go down the tubes. Thirty-seven lives lost and a career shot to hell. The level of rhetoric was skyrocketing, and the level of violence was rising steadily right along with it. The United States had caught an Iranian landing craft laying mines one night in the middle of the Gulf. Moving in with helicopters that seemed to whisper over the water, the Americans blew several of the crew to bits. They shot up encroaching Boston Whaler–type boats and all but cut the Iranian Revolutionary Guards in half with rapid-fire guns.

Most of the time the American sailors held their fire, but their fingers were on the buttons; and the newer they were to the Gulf, the more inclined they were to shoot. They hadn't seen enough dhows actually pass peacefully by, hadn't seen enough garbage bags and sheep to know they weren't the mines that would kill them in their sleep. Many, in fact, hadn't lowered their guard enough to be able to sleep.

A Barracuda is a simple, open fiberglass boat about thirty feet long with no cabin, no superstructure at all except the box to which the wheel is fixed. At night it is lighted only by small running lights fore and aft. Powered by twin outboard motors, craft like these travel anywhere on the Gulf. Occasionally they were manned by Iran's Revolutionary Guards staging hit-and-run attacks, but more often they carried Indian fishermen, hired on contract by enterprising citizens of Sharjah and Dubai who wanted a little income from the sea without having to work it themselves.

Jayanti Lal Govan Bhai Koli and Rama Bahai Madho were up from Kerala, on the west coast of India, working the Gulf waters for a small-time Sharjah businessman. They fished a stretch between the coast and Abu Musa, one of the islands seized for Iran by the shah back in the early 1970s. Iran's Revolutionary Guards operated out of a base there but paid no attention to these black-skinned Indian indentured servants. As the sun set one evening in November, Koli and Madho were pulling up their wire fish traps when their engine died. Another fisherman named Baghwan Bhai Kanji pulled up to see if he could help restart their balky Yamaha outboard.

By the time the engine roared to life, the sun had set. In the dark a large ship suddenly loomed near the three men. It was an American frigate, the U.S.S. *Carr,* flashing a spotlight. Madho signaled back with a hand-held light. The thunder of an approaching helicopter sent concentric waves of foam and spray off the surface of the sea. Kanji stood in the bow, steadying himself with a rope, watching the action. That should have been the end of the encounter. The fishermen obviously were not a threat. But someone on the *Carr* imagined they were, here, so close to Abu Musa. Bullets ripped across the water. Aimed high, they missed the boat itself. One caught Kanji just beside the right eye. The back of his head disappeared.

The *Carr* quickly sailed on, and the Pentagon announced the next day it had no idea what happened to the presumed attack boats. Later the United States apologized for the incident. And in the hard mercantile fashion of the Gulf, the owner of Kanji's boat wanted to know, "Who's paying for the man? This is the problem."

Filippo Tucci must have been a very handsome man, the kind of Italian who looked great in his uniform as master of the enormous Kuwaiti ship reflagged by the United States in the summer of 1987 as the *Sea Isle City.* He had worked for Texaco for eighteen years and knew the way Americans liked to think and talk. Ask him his name. "Filippo," he would say. "Foxtrot India Lima India Papa Papa Oscar." He smiled as easily as Vittorio de Sica. But when I met him in a Kuwait hospital, half his face had been peeled off; his ear had been all but severed. Some of the nerves in his face were cut, and his grin showed on only part of his mouth. A large bandage covered his eye, and in a vial by his bed were thirteen pieces of glass picked out of its socket. One was the size of a marble.

Tucci joined the Kuwait Oil Tanker Company in 1983, when the Gulf War already was well under way. But he had made countless voyages in the company's big tankers without problems. "Only one time I was really a little bit afraid. I was on the *Kassima*, on the bridge, and the chief mate said 'Captain, there is a helicopter coming.' And we saw this crazy copter, you know, taking the firing position, coming toward us. And we thought, Now what we have to do? The *Kassima* is about three hundred thousand tons. There is no possibility to move, because we are like an island, you know.

"Well, fortunately it was an American helicopter, inspecting us."

When the Kuwaitis decided to fly American flags to garner U.S. Navy protection, the reflagged Kuwaiti ships had to take on American crews. Tucci became, effectively, comaster of the *Sea Isle City* with John Hunt from Tampa, Florida. "It was possible to do a really nice job, Captain Hunt and myself, because, you know, we had about the same age. I'm fifty-three and Captain Hunt is about fifty-eight. The mentality is about the same."

Hunt skippered the eighty-one-thousand-ton *Sea Isle City* up the Gulf in a convoy protected by four U.S. missile frigates. These convoys, begun with the *Bridgeton* fiasco in July, had become almost routine by October, useful diversions from the real oil business. The press focused its attention on them; the Iranians shadowed them from a distance. Meanwhile as much as 90 percent of Kuwait's oil production was going out of the Gulf in other carriers, without convoys, for the most part unscathed. Business was good. The sense of emergency that surrounded the convoys and the U.S.-Iranian face-off kept oil prices high even as the world market was glutted. The great reflagging gesture was drawing attention, and it might draw fire, but Kuwait was thriving.

The Gulf Arabs wanted American protection but didn't want the political embarrassment of quasi-occupation by U.S. forces. Their expensive little armies, well trained and well armed and often well staffed by foreigners, had pride out of all proportion to their effectiveness. When the American convoys reached Kuwaiti waters, Kuwaiti pride dictated that the American fleet should peel off and sail away.

Secretly, but with Kuwait's blessing, the Americans created a pair of floating commando bases on barges offshore, so no single Gulf state would have to take responsibility for hosting the American combat troops. Armored and weighted down with electronic gear, the barges were guarded from beneath by trained porpoises. Based on them were special night-flying choppers, like the ones that hit the mine-laying *Iran Ajr*. Usually the Iranians just watched the convoys pass. Whenever they did make a move, or even a feint, the Americans came in hard and fast. Almost soundlessly they moved in on the speedboats working near Farsi Island and cut them to pieces.

Meanwhile Iran's own oil operations were being clobbered by the Iraqi air force. Kharg was hit again and again. Exocet Alley was popping with the high-priced missiles. In one long-range raid Iraqi bombers hit the 565,000-ton *Seawise Giant*, the biggest vessel afloat, sitting full of Iranian oil at the entrance to the strait.

Finally the Silkworms started to take wing. In the land war the Iranians had managed to capture the Iraqi town of Faw and the little peninsula around it, just at the Kuwaiti border. They brought in batteries of artillery, rockets and missiles, among which were Silkworms. The big old missiles' effective range fell short of Kuwait City, but with luck they could just reach the Al-Ahmadi oil terminal, a spidery network of pipes, hoses and gantries where the big tankers came to load offshore. On September 4 a Silkworm hummed past the terminal like an expired buzz bomb, smashing into the sand of Mina Al-Ahmadi. Windows were blown out in several nearby buildings.

Few people paid attention. Mysterious explosions were almost commonplace in Kuwait; and when no one was killed, headlines were brief, God was thanked, business continued.

Another Silkworm was spotted droning over Kuwait's desolate Falaka Island a month later. Kuwaiti antiaircraft batteries took aim, fired—and missed. The Silkworm slammed into the bow of the Liberian-registered supertanker *Sungari,* setting it ablaze as it sat at anchor off the Al-Ahmadi loading facility. No one was injured. Four American-flag tankers nearby escaped untouched.

Filippo Tucci had been on vacation and boarded the *Sea Isle City* when it arrived in Kuwait's waters. By the morning of October 16 he and Hunt were together on the bridge. They were up before dawn, maneuvering their big ship toward the Al-Ahmadi facility. The sun came up just as they passed the blasted, blackened *Sungari,* hit the day before. Everybody on the bridge was curious to see what kind of damage had actually been done. People had been talking about these Silkworms for so long, you had to wonder how potent they really were. The masters of the *Sea Isle* ordered it around to port, over toward the crippled tanker to take a closer look.

Chief Officer Robert Stanley Cartwright stepped out onto the open wing projecting off the bridge to take a picture. He fumbled a little with the controls of his Canon T70, focusing in on the *Sungari*'s bow.

Both Tucci and Hunt saw the Silkworm at almost the same instant. They were looking out through the thick glass windows of the bridge, built to withstand the smashing waters of the strongest storm. It was suddenly like a movie screen spread out before them, with a projected image of the placid dawn-gray sea, the damaged *Sungari* just in front of them, and "this crazy missile's coming in from our starboard side."

"It was about at sea level. I said to myself, I believe the missile, she will hit the forward part. I was also telling myself, The damage, maybe it will be sensible. The vessel is gas-free, and so it will be not explosive, you know? And then instead—instead of hitting the forward part—this crazy missile increases altitude and comes on back."

It rose over the bow and across the long deck that stretched like a football field before the wheelhouse, its little electric brain homing in on the biggest mass above the waterline it could find in front of it: the superstructure of the bridge and crew quarters. All it calculated were shapes, silhouettes. It didn't see the vertical funnel it hit, standing just inches from the front of the main superstructure. It blasted apart, blew up with all the force of its long flight and one thousand pounds of TNT, throwing the initial, enormous explosion across the face of the bridge. The heavy, half-molten remains of the missile continued on through steel wall after steel wall, seven bulk-heads in all—through the cargo control room, the galley—before the last fragments buried themselves, spent, against a steel beam on the port side of the fan room.

In that instant, "I heard 'plonk,' and then I lost my knowl-edge. Everything was confused, and I was . . . not crying . . . but . . . requiring help. I didn't know where my body was, which position I was in."

On the flying bridge, Cartwright's camera seemed to melt in his hands. "There was one almighty bang, an orange flash." His face and arms were seared by the blast, but the rest of his body had been protected by the open wheelhouse door. He made his way back inside and saw the bodies of the two captains and a Filipino seaman. Glass was scattered everywhere. The floor and walls were running with gore.

But Tucci was coming around. "I find myself close to the gyrocompass. And I start to see with one eye, and then I had my full knowledge again. I saw that Captain Hunt was on the floor of the wheelhouse. And at the same time I saw the other officer was close to Captain Hunt, and Captain Hunt was asking help. And then I saw, after awhile, the radio officer—the radio officer, fortunately for him, was in his cabin with no injury, nothing—and he tried to help Cap-tain Hunt." The blast had caught the captain full in the face. " 'Filip, I cannot see,' he was saying over and over."

In the Al-Ahmadi hospital, Tucci was sitting up now, telling his story eight long days after the event. Captain Hunt lay in a room down the hall, bandages across his eyes, without much hope of ever regaining his sight. The Filipino seaman's eyes were lost.

On October 19, three days after Tucci's ship was hit, the U.S. Navy retaliated against Iran with an attack on its Rostam and Rakash oil platforms—a couple of Erector Set villages on stilts in the Persian Gulf. A rain of high-explosive shells reduced them to abstractions of melted beams. The fires ignited in the sea beneath them would burn for months afterward.

THE GALLERIA

···

FROM THE ROOFTOP POOL OF THE HYATT-GALLERIA APARTMENT COMPLEX, thirty stories above the Dubai corniche, one could see ships in flames on the horizon and the clear blue of the sky stained with a spreading thunderhead of oil smoke. But the British flight attendant, called Big Orange by the journalists, for the color of her favorite bikini, would pay little attention. The young and indolent Arabs courting her would pay no attention at all. She had what seemed a nervous habit, poolside in the hot breeze, of opening her legs and closing them, opening them and closing them. Her suitors were mesmerized. The children in their water wings would splash and laugh as if nothing were happening on the horizon. Arab-American twin sisters, aged ten, strolled around the edge of the pool pulling their matching Barbie sports cars, oblivious to the black cloud that had come to obscure half the sky. The CBS news producer did care. But, stretched out on a chaise longue, working on her tan and sipping an iced tea, she could follow all the action through headphones, connected by the wire strung down past the barbecue pit and along the pristine glass face of the building to the CBS offices several floors below, plugged into a monitor that picked up all the naval distress signals. Filipino Monkey came on. The producer turned over and sipped her tea.

Altitude and electronics, Oriental and Continental cuisine, air-conditioning and elevator music cushioned life in the Galleria from the world and from the war around it. Dubai was full of places like this: the Intercontinental and Sheraton complexes; the Al-Ghurair Center, the Trade Center and the adjacent Hilton. They rose above the steamy souks of carpets, caviar, silk and gold, not to mention the newer Sony and Panasonic and pirate-tape merchants. The old trading post at the southern edge of the Gulf, the city that Thesiger himself found so remarkably exotic, had worked hard to become a convention-center oasis, a jumbo-jet-serviced ultramodern bazaar and playground on the edge of the desert, halfway between Rome and Singapore as the 747 flies. With Beirut dead, it was the best stop. Westerners lived here as if in a dream.

Dozens of nationalities inhabited the Galleria apartments; dozens more passed through the Hyatt Hotel. The Sikh doorman swung wide the tall glass doors to usher in bedouins just arrived in their Mercedes 500 SELs and Swiss bankers from Zurich. Saudis would arrive with their several wives, and show girls came in from Frankfurt. An elevator ride—a vertical rush hour at lunch- or dinner-time—would bring encounters with flight attendants in bikinis or women in long black veils, mothers picking up their children from nursery school packed in with former Rhodesian mercenaries. In the shopping complex was always a smell of popcorn, of the heavy perfume worn by Arab men, all mingled above the cool vapor of the ice rink.

Dubai had two ice rinks, just as there were rinks in Saudi Arabia and Abu Dhabi and Kuwait. This refrigerated luxury had become de rigueur for the Gulf sheikhs in the 1970s. But in Dubai such things had ceased to be incongruous: this supreme admixture of East and West, new and old, had seen it all. They were just part of the scene. Periodically homegrown versions of the Ice Capades would be staged with a handful of imported skating stars and such local talent as had developed. Rehearsals would go on for weeks. And then the show. Stage mothers looked on proudly as a little chorus line of expatriate children formed on the ice. They came from France and the United States and England. The skating skirts were short, the legs were long. Hundreds of Indians, Iranians, Arabs from the Emirates and Saudi watched from the railing. Just at the end of the show non-ticket-holders would be allowed to flood in, hot and sweating from standing outside, their beards wilted, their polyester shirts damp, pressing now tight against the rail, mesmerized, transfixed.

In the upscale apartments of Dubai and in the villas along the road to Jebel Ali there were people in the oil business and the shipping business, importers and exporters. But they were mainly in the business of losing themselves. A *Daily Telegraph* correspondent once called them "the cretinous flotsam of British society." They had come to the Gulf to "get away," then recreated the means of escape they'd always used at home: a life of mindless sports, screwing (or screwing as sport), eating and, especially, drinking.

The drinking was not always easy. In some parts of the Gulf necessity was the mother of truly inventive beverages. The Aramco compounds in Saudi Arabia were famous for their distilled spirits. One veteran engineer had authored a much-thumbed treatise called "The Blue Flame" to instruct newcomers. Houses were designed with laundry rooms separate from the main building in case of explosions. Relatives would send in regular care packages of juniper berries with which to flavor the bathtub gin. At least one American became a cooper, fashioning his own burned-oak casks to age his homemade whiskey. The best stuff was fifteen years old—the stuff of legend. Kuwait, it was said, had the highest per capita consumption of grape juice in the world. Actually, it was the American ambassador who used to say that. He prided himself on the white vintage he produced from the juice.

In Dubai wine came by the glass, the case or the spigot from a pasteurized bag in a box for the refrigerator. The taps were open, the minibars unlocked and the whiskey easy to find in any hotel.

"It's very easy to become an alcoholic here," said the woman at the bar in The Pub at Dubai's Intercontinental. I turned to look at her. She was telling Hassan, the Indian bartender in a tartan vest, something about one of her boyfriends beating her. She looked up at me over her half pint and crinkled her eyes and smiled as she sipped. Her hair was ginger colored, the dye job a little faded. Her eyes were lined in black. She was about twenty pounds overweight, with a chinless British profile.

She came out here from Wales with "a friend" almost a year ago, she said, and she decided to stay. She went back to England over Ramadan and didn't like it. It's much safer here, and you've got all the comforts. She was knocking back several half pints.

She was converting to Islam, she said, her voice a little slurred. She was engaged to a Dubai citizen who worked in the bank downstairs whom she was supposed to meet at 1:00. It was 1:15. He was waiting, and she was having another beer. She used to be an alcoholic and had been hospitalized. "It's very easy to become an alcoholic here."

When she left, Hassan looked at another of the Indian barmen and laughed. "This is about the fifth time she's changed her religion," he said, then added conspiratorially, "I think she is hooking."

Yes, now I recall, she said she was learning to pray, but it was difficult. And she said that when she converted to Islam, something really did come over her. It was a real sensation. One might think that would slow her drinking. She said it has. But, you know, it's easy to become an alcoholic here.

The girls on the team still had whiskers painted on their face. It was Halloween night, and they hadn't bothered to remove the makeup from their *Cats* costumes before slipping into their skin-tight baseball uniforms. They liked the way the uniforms made them look. ("You may in fact need to have them tailored in at the waist as these are men's pants," said the team newsletter. "No. Sorry, no men in them, girls.") At one point they had all tried making 69 their uniform number. They were the Enterra Rebels, part of the Dubai Softball League. All of them were British, and the team captain, Michele, was quick to tell you the average age of the team was twenty-four.

Jeff Johnson was American, an oil engineer. He'd been coaching the team since 1980, when Leroy set it up. Leroy was a big black American who had been in Vietnam and didn't much want to talk about his past or present occupation. But Johnson, what the hell, he'd talk. "Each season starts with new girls. I suppose that's why you call it softball. Then at the end of the season a lot of them leave. It's just the nature of Dubai."

They played at the Metropolitan Hotel, a little complex built near the Safeway on the highway to Abu Dhabi in the mistaken belief that the airport would be constructed nearby. Eventually the airport was built on the other side of town. So the Metropolitan gave itself over, almost completely, to partying for expats. It made a healthy income with its pub, wine bar, Chinese and Italian restaurants, the baseball diamonds and the rock bands it brought into its disco, Lucifer's.

Johnson was standing in the dugout sipping a beer. I was finishing up my hot dog. In the background, at the fast-food stand, the cook was playing a tape of Hindi love songs.

"We only have two married women on the whole team," said Johnson. "They're a wild and crazy bunch," he explained, rather matter-of-factly. "They're all shopping around for husbands, really. Ones with money." The expat community had four women to every man; a bumper crop of British secretaries.

Why stay out here, I asked the captain, Michele Motley. "You got your partying every night," came the ready reply, "water-skiing, sports." She was warming up for the game: short, smart, full of energy, a little impatient with this distracting interview. "One week is so much like another. It's just a fantasy world. And you don't pay any taxes." She handed me a copy of the Enterra Rebels newsletter she put together. It included the phone numbers of all the team members, and little descriptions:

> Ann Lenihan: For 2½ years Ann has been slogging away as a telesales person for a courier company. On the side Ann flaunts her body (fully clothed) about in front of the camera for a well known boutique in Satwa. . . . She is single and is absolutely mad on softball and even madder on Bruce Springsteen. She also enjoys the wild parties that we all get invited to.
>
> Carol Morley: A true exhibitionist, Carol has for the last 2½ years been up to all sorts of work at exhibitions. She wouldn't reveal much to us, but we did find out that this single, also taken, lady from Stockport in the UK, enjoys gyrating on the dance floor, swimming, music and party time.
>
> Michele Motley: Alias Captain Smelley! What do you want to know that you don't know already. She's nutty, single and loving it. (She says she has enough on her plate handling her engineers), enjoys horse riding, scuba diving, water and snow skiing, netball and an endless avenue of unmentionable pastimes.

Debbie Richards was twenty-one and had been in Dubai since she was seven. Her father was a pilot for Royal Flight, the air fleet of the princes. She had tried returning to England for a year. "I found I couldn't adjust. So I saved my pennies and came back. The people are so narrow-minded out there." From the newsletter: "This veteran of Dubai, for the last 14 years has been sleeping, sleeping and sleeping (that's what she says). A conscientious secretary for the waterworks, Debbie quotes that she tries very hard at softball, but even harder in the Red Lion afterwards."

They were all trying hard. A cumulative sense of desperation pervaded the place; it became a trap for people who could never live so well anywhere else but wondered why they were living there. It was a polyester existence—artificial, suggestive of luxury, but it didn't breathe. The parties never seemed as wild as hoped, and the life rarely as adventurous as imagined.

The Mad Hatter's Ball at the Sheraton each October was an odd celebration of expatriate culture. Mainly it was about funny hats. John Wallis, the normally dapper general manager of the Hyatt-Galleria appeared with an enormous vise clamped on his head and wearing mechanic's overalls. Another businessman wore a five-foot Big Ben. A British woman was graced with an enormous Swatch watch mounted on a hard hat. Another wore a Mobil-sponsored racing car. And then, to the rock and roll and wailing sax of a Filipino band, they danced.

Ann Lenihan, with a Benson & Hedges briefcase on her head, was talking about her boyfriend, who had left her to her own resources in Dubai while he went off to the Philippines. She said that she hoped to go live in Houston someday. A voluptuous Gurkha girl—the PR woman for the Emirates Golf Club—danced the night away in a tight black skirt and fuck-me high heels that looked honed to lethal points. I don't recall seeing her hat. Toward the end of the evening several people wound up in the pool. One of them, a tough-looking British girl, having failed to resuscitate her comatose boyfriend and feeling the chill of her wet clothes, simply took off her pants.

The younger expats gravitated to Lucifer's at the Metropolitan every Friday. The bash started in the middle of the day and ground on into the night, with the audience singing, drinking, standing on tables, the air thick with smoke and stale breath. "Tie your mother down," they shouted, singing over the superamplified voice of Cherie Beck, who looked and sang much like a female Rod Stewart. "Young hearts be free tonight." No one in Arab dress was allowed.

A year after my first Dubai softball season I was back again. The Enterra Rebels were the best team in the league, with a 10-0 record. But trouble was looming. The pitcher and her husband were being sent back to Houston four days before the championship. And number 19 was leaving at 11:00 that night, just after the game, to catch a plane back to the States. She'd met a sailor from a U.S. frigate and was going back to marry him. Carol, on first base, had been living with Billy, a Canadian oil worker.

The night of the game against the Metros, Billy was coaching the Metros, and had a new girlfriend, who was playing for them. Billy was philosophical. He was also handsome, with silvery blow-dried hair and a sense of style that led him to change his gold jewelry between drinks at home and dinner out. His background had taken him from the Canadian tundra to Brazil to here. He knew these things happened. Women changed, games changed.

"We used to play hockey." Ice hockey? "Yeah, if you go to Toronto and see the Hockey Hall of Fame you'll see us in there. We played at the Al-Nasr Leisureland. We were called the DuGas Flames." But that had to end. Billy shook his head and looked down into the dark recesses of his can of Amstel Light. "It got out of hand. They used to have to escort me through the parking lot to get home. They [the locals] didn't understand that when you fought on the ice, it's different. And when we'd play the Arabs—gawd."

The Metropolitan Hotel had added a Cajun restaurant to its culinary repertoire. But the Indian manager hadn't quite got the hang of it yet. Business was slow. So the after-game party was scheduled there instead of at the Red Lion. The greeter was a two-hundred-pound black woman who went by the name of Charlie. A band played "Leaving on a Jet Plane," over and over for number 19. The choruses grew stronger as people remembered the words.

Ann Lenihan was singing along but having trouble, it seemed, getting into the spirit of the thing. The sometime model for a Satwa boutique sweated in her softball flannels, slowly sipping a beer. It was four years now that she'd been here. She and Carol, from first base, had come to Dubai together. "In Kuwait and Cairo I was the sales manager for an advertising company. In Dubai we took a big step down. We were barmaids," she said in a voice as plainly cockney as

Eliza Doolittle's. They had worked in the Dubai Marine Hotel, figuring "the beaches, the sun, the people, the social life were about ten million times better than England." And so they stayed. "Every year I say I'll give myself another year," said Ann. "But I'll never go back to England. I couldn't go back and live there. There's nothing there." She was sixteen when she started working. "I was in a rut. I hated it. It was always the same old thing. Go down to the pub."

I looked around us.

"I know," said Ann. "Dubai is so small. You see the same people over and over again. It can get exactly like it is at home—except instead of it getting rainy and freezing cold, you can get up and go to the beach."

Do you do that?

"Well, no. I get freckles, actually, so I don't go out in the sun much."

There was a pause in the conversation. From the band, another rousing chorus of "Leaving on a Jet Plane."

"A lot goes on around softball," said Ann. "And they don't have ladies' night in England. You can go out for free in Dubai five nights a week." Thatcher's, Pancho's, Annabelle's, the Red Lion, Lucifer's.

"Of course, you meet a lot of people here, and nine months later they're gone."

What are the men like?

"Most of 'em are married."

"NQOCD," some of the older denizens of Dubai would say of the cruising crowd on the ladies'-night circuit. "Not quite our class, darling."

Brian Hopkins, a fifty-five-year-old former RAF squadron leader, was flying helicopters out of Doha, Qatar, running high-priced errands for the oil companies and combat missions for the American television networks. He'd retired from the air force, gone into land development in Britain, and nearly lost his shirt before finding his way to the Gulf. "Of course we're class conscious," he said one evening when I invited him to Pancho's. He eyed the crowd uncomfortably. "There are people in the Gulf in jobs they could never get in the U.K.: what we in the services would call a jumped-up corporal. You see a great deal of the man who's being paid more than he's worth, thinks he's a chief and not treating his Indians very well." Socializing, one stays with people of one's class, said Brian. "I never socialize with people I work with. There's no point, really."

Dubai has a country club, next to a military camp, near the shallow pond where the Creek peters out into desert. But the cachet of membership faded somewhat when the Emirates Golf Club opened on the Abu Dhabi road. After all, the golf course at the old club was made entirely of sand; the fairways and greens were bleak beiges and browns, oiled down to let the balls roll over their surface. Players carried little patches of Astroturf around with them for their drives and wedge shots. But the Emirates Golf Club was strategically located near the enormous aluminum smelter that doubled as a desalinization plant, supplying the quantities of water that kept Dubai alive and thriving. Even in the withering summer the grass was green over a full eighteen holes. The course invariably was booked solid from 6:00 until 10:00 in the morning.

"The grass is a lot cooler," Rod Boggs would explain. "It doesn't absorb the heat. And then there's a bit of a breeze when you ride in the cart." The 10 percent of the club's members who were locals wouldn't think of going out when the sun was high on the meridian; and the Americans, Canadians, Brits and Japanese who made up most of the rest of its roster were anticipated when the course was designed. Staff was trained to deal with heat exhaustion; shelters were built at strategic locations along the course. The ninth hole had an outdoor bar.

Boggs had been brought in from Malawi's Blantyre Sports Club. He was a veteran expat, having served his time in postcolonial Africa helping to keep up the old standards. But he was surprised and delighted by the standard of Dubai. "This is a lot more cosmopolitan than Malawi," he was quick to say. This was like nothing else, quite, in the world. Freshly arrived, he spoke with enthusiasm of the deep-sea fishing, wind-surfing and beaches. "It's amazing how many people brush up here by accident. Nobody ever says, 'I'm gonna go live in Dubai.' " The club had thirty-seven nationalities, many of them people who had never been anywhere before they got to the United Arab Emirates. "Malawi was the last vestige of colonial Africa. There it's like going back fifty years to the old colonial days. Everyone there had been somewhere else before." This was something sparkling and new. "How did people live here fifty years ago, when there was nothing green and no air-conditioning?" Boggs wondered.

It was one of those hazy days when on the horizon the white desert and the white sky merge and buildings on the Dubai skyline in the distance look ghostly. "We wouldn't encourage people to walk out at the moment. It's pretty hot, you know. I believe it's about 106 today."

We were looking over the course from the frigid air of a clubhouse designed to resemble a campsite of royal tents. Above us hung tastefully framed portraits of Sheikh Rashid, the ailing ruler, and his son Sheikh Mohammed, whose vision of Dubai encompassed golf courses as green as the fields of Ascot or Longchamp, where he raced his horses.

"Including the clubhouse and everything else we're using about a million gallons of water a day. About nine hundred thousand of that goes for the course," Boggs said, reciting. Construction of the course itself cost a relatively paltry $1.5 million. The total cost of the clubhouse complex, the dorms for the Filipino servants and grounds keepers—everything was about $10 million. It would soon break even, at least the way Sheikh Mohammed looked at things. "Of course, it wouldn't be feasible to run it if you had to pay for water."

The ecology of the immediate area was changing. Beyond the fence built to keep camels and goats off the turf new life had sprung into the desert, picking up the moisture that trickled out of the fairways' fifty kilometers of irrigation pipes. In the artificial ponds fish were thriving. And slowly the locals were acquiring a taste and skill for the sport of Saint Andrews. Very slowly. Three months after the course opened, the Filipino staff went diving in the main pond. They recovered eight hundred balls.

Kim had two cherries tatooed on the ample curve of her thigh. She had cantilevered breasts, long blond hair and big blue eyes as trusting as a puppy's. She had been in the Emirates about a year, working for a cigarette company whose main demands on her were that she pose at exhibitions and drive a car with the brand emblazoned on the door. "People keep saying to me, 'Kim,' " she said as she worked on her tan at the Galleria pool, " 'You know what Dubai's like. Keep your feet on the ground.' "

One ladies' night at Pancho's she came with Polaroids of her birthday party. One of the cooks at the Hyatt had baked a cake for her in the shape of an enormous cock and balls, with white icing flowing from the tip. Kim showed the picture of the cake around. She just meant for a few people to see it: Rudy Rivas, the Texan whose talent with sizzling *fajitas* and margaritas by the pitcher had been the secret of Pancho's success; a couple of flight-attendant friends; and maybe some of the journalists from the Galleria who had showed up that night. Then she showed the next picture: one of the girls she roomed with oohing and ahhing at the sight of the thing. Shots of other people at the little birthday party. Here's the knife; getting ready to cut into the cake. But wait, look at this picture. Kim is straddling the cake now, spreading her legs to see if, just maybe . . .

The pictures had somehow gotten out of her control. People were passing them around—not just around the table, but all over the bar at Pancho's—looking at the pictures, looking at her. Those big blue eyes seemed lost. It was all a joke, right? The moment of desperation in them was distilled essence of her life, raw and unpleasant and terribly clear. Kim, I thought, you know what Dubai's like.

* * *

Late at night most of the women were gone from Pancho's, the doors were locked and only the bar in the back, near the dart board, kept serving a private party. Dave Blakely, the manager and part owner, was back there with the boys.

He was a rock and roller in his late forties who had once played bass with a Beatlemania spinoff called the Mersey Beats. Then there were years playing American bases in Germany or working as a master of ceremonies at a nightclub in Manchester before he washed up in Dubai in 1981, first playing in bars, then managing a restaurant in the Ramada Inn. It was the height of the oil boom, and Dubai was full of Americans. But no one was catering to them. The Ramada management thought the roughnecks would "have punch-ups every night." The Americans kept asking for nachos with their beer. The Ramada didn't know from nachos.

Blakely got an American and an Indian backer; he scouted for cooks and got Rudy to come from Houston. And in 1984 Pancho's was born. "It was the right place at the right time and the right idea, and it took off like a bloody Atlas missile. It was absolute pandemonium."

On ladies' nights and rock-and-roll nights Blakely was known to get on stage and boogie with whatever band he had hired, rocking hard with a little bit of Jerry Lee Lewis, a lot of Hank Williams Jr., and some old favorites from the British pub scene in his repertoire. "Piss me off, you fucking jerks," he shouted. Or, "all my rowdy friends are comin' over tonight."

He glad-handed from table to table, cultivating the American sailors who came in. On a ceiling hung with state flags and baseball caps, a special place was reserved for the caps from the U.S. warships that called at Dubai, and a wall was covered with autographed photos of frigates and destroyers. British sailors, by contrast, were not so welcome. They tended to drink too much and danced mainly with each other. They wanted Rod Stewart, "Sailing," not Hank or Jerry. Many were turned away at the door. They could go try to get in at Lucifer's.

Late at night, the music long gone, Dave just played darts with the boys: Americans and Brits and Egyptians and local Arabs, and one Iranian. Over beer, and when they thought they weren't heard, the Brits would talk about all the niggers you had to deal with in Dubai.

The best player at the game of chase, a simple progression through the wedges on the dart board, was clearly the Iranian. With seven players the game took a long time; but each time it neared its end, the Iranian was a finalist. With about fifty dollars riding on the last match, he was in a position to walk away with the pot. Instead, he placed a neat little group of darts in a wedge that would ensure his loss. The Egyptian who won counted his money, apparently none the wiser. The Brits, over their beers, were talking about other things. But the final play had been such an obvious sacrifice I asked the Iranian why he had thrown the game away. He was mildly surprised anyone had noticed. "My mother would have wanted me to," he said. He had business interests; and he had only recently been given Dubai citizenship. What did this game mean, really? "Sometimes it is better not to win too much."

Christmas season was beginning in Dubai. At Fujairah mourning for Gerry Blackburn had given way to anticipation of the annual Dubai Caledonian Society Saint Andrews ball. Captain Smiley invited me. "It is very old-fashioned," he said proudly. "There's a lovely life here. I'm sure it's the last of an old style of empire."

Elspeth was elegant in her evening dress, and Captain Smiley was grandly pompous in his kilt and formal Highland regalia. The Zabeel Ball Room at the Dubai Intercon on the Creek was full of men with dirks and tartans and the short sharp jackets that made even the most stout and sedentary look imposing and, at the very least, like very serious figures. A Society officer read letters and telegrams of holiday greetings from the Bombay Caledonian Society and the secretary of the Istanbul Caledonian Society. They were toasted with a little athelbrose concocted of honey, oats, cream and scotch whiskey.

Thanks were given for the sponsorship of British Caledonian. Polite applause. Now the British navy. A hearty cheer. Sheikh Zayed. A cheer. Sheikh Rashid. Another. "To the Queen." The athelbrose flowed.

Then the Filipino band struck up, before a tartan backdrop. "La Bamba," they played. And "Demi Quando."

December 1987 was the cruelest month to date in the Iran-Iraq "tanker war." Lloyds of London counted more than thirty-five commercial vessels attacked—despite thirty U.S. warships in the region and an almost equal number of European and Soviet vessels committed to "protect freedom of navigation." Day after day columns of smoke billowed up from the once placid waters. Flames spilled like lava from the sides of stricken ships.

Attacks from helicopters had given way to the rage of the speedboats and mines. But on October 1 the Iranian frigate *Sabalan* shelled an Indian tanker called the *Spic Emerald* off the coast of Dubai and opened up a new, simple and deadly facet of the naval conflict. Using a handful of small British-built warships, acquisitions of the shah, the Iranians blasted dozens of vessels flying the flags of Panama, Liberia, Cyprus—any ensign without a navy nearby. The frigate's 4.5-inch shells were horribly effective, blowing off arms, blowing out guts. I remembered Zani, thinking of Johnson screaming on the deck. "I really don't see the legs—because I really don't want to see the legs." The Greek captain of the tanker *Pivot*, hit December 12, was challenged by an "Iranian war boat" that bid him good day, then came back a few minutes later and, as the captain put it, "Bam, bam, bam." More spectacle for those at the pool above the Galleria.

A helicopter chartered by CBS homed in on the flaming tanker before the U.S. Navy arrived on the scene. The navy regulations forbid its choppers to land on the deck. But correspondent Allan Pizzey had his network pilot set down, unloaded himself and his crew and filmed as the CBS chopper hauled survivors off the ship.

On Christmas eve a U.S. Navy helicopter drew fire near Iran's

Abu Musa Island. But fear of escalating the conflict, especially as the Pentagon was under increasing political pressure to justify its role in the Gulf, stopped the foreign navies from doing more, and the Iranian frigate took full advantage. Kuwait, which had most of its own tanker fleet under protective foreign flags, tried to sneak one of its unprotected tankers into the Gulf disguised as a Romanian ship. When the Iranians discovered the ruse, their little frigate hunted its prey into a crowded anchorage at midday only six miles off the coast of the United Arab Emirates. An American warship radioed a warning to the Iranian not to point its guns in his direction. The frigate obliged. It changed position—then blasted the Kuwaiti. The frigate then sped out of sight, unhindered.

Not surprisingly, sailors in the Western armada were seething with frustration. "You ought to see these boys with their fingers on the buttons," said a British military officer after touring part of the fleet that December. "It's like the subway in New York. Bernhard Goetz. 'Make my day.' "

REDS

"WE ARE GOING TO CONQUER THIS MARKET IN ONE OR TWO YEARS, THAT'S
for sure," said Eldar Younousov, straight out of Moscow but slick as
Madison Avenue: firm handshake, direct gaze through his thin-
rimmed glasses, preppy in his knit tie and blue shirt. He was sitting
in his little office at the Expo Center in Sharjah. His backdrop was
a row of identical posters showing a beautiful, sultry woman with dark
hair, bare shoulders and a brilliant gold and diamond necklace. Elegant enough for *Vogue*, she might look a little too exposed for the
local Islamic sensibilities. A group of nubile gymnasts brought to the
Expo by the Soviets had to don sweatsuits after their first shows
aroused the audience, and then aroused its indignation. So Younousov didn't pin up his diamond girl in the exhibit proper. But the wall
of the office was only a latticework of thin slats. "You can see her
through the cracks," he smiled. Such were the subtleties of seduction
as the Soviets worked their way into the Arab Gulf, a gradual policy—

"Moving slowly, that's our habit"—warming up to the reticent monarchies of the region and displaying some tempting openness through the calculated cracks in the Soviet facade.

Conquering the market, Younousov said matter-of-factly, was just a minor part of the picture. "That's not the reason we are here. Our trade with the U.A.E. is insignificant—around one million annually in U.S. dollars. That's nothing." The objective was to get a foot in the door. "In other countries the politics may be number one. But here it is commerce. So to get a good relationship, you have to do the trade. Otherwise you will not be known or recognized. So this is why we are here."

The Soviets had been sidling up to the Gulf Arabs for years, trying to recoup from the old days when they plotted socialist uprisings against the region's conservative sheikhs and, for the most part, failed. Under Mikhail Gorbachev they traded the veil of conspiracy for the more amiable face of commerce, and the results paid off with a succession of diplomatic victories in the Gulf. Where once they maintained relations only with Kuwait, now there were embassies in Oman and the United Arab Emirates as well. The Saudis, moving slowly toward warmer relations on the diplomatic front, continued to talk in friendly terms about possible trade with Moscow. "We understand the Soviets have almost as much legitimate concern about the Middle East as the United States does," one influential Saudi prince liked to tell his American friends. "You've got two superpowers to deal with in the world. Why should you make one of them mad?"

In Abu Dhabi, Ambassador Felix Fedotov was working overtime to smoothe the rough edges that remained on Soviet policy. A career diplomat originally from western Siberia, Fedotov had spent twenty years serving in Sudan, Aden and Syria. Rotund and jocular, more accessible to the press than his American counterpart, Fedotov would declare with a straight face that "if the motive of foreign policy is ideology, it is wrong." Perhaps the Saudis and other Gulf Arabs were suspicious of Soviet communism. But the Soviets, Fedotov would assure them in his thick accent, are "very realpolitik people."

Of course, the Americans still had their old worries, inherited from the British, that the Russians had grand designs on the Gulf. In the White House strategic thinkers like Marine Lieutenant Colonel Oliver North believed—or told their conservative friends in the press they believed—that the Soviets were poised to move in on Iran the moment Khomeini died: with troops, fifth-column subversives, the works.

The West's strategists looked at their globes and saw Reds in South Yemen, Ethiopia, Afghanistan. They looked at their almanacs and saw that 43 percent of the world's known petroleum reserves were in the region. The Soviets, they figured, were out to surround these resources, so vital to the West and Japan, maybe to choke them off someday. They looked at their history books and saw the long chronicle of Russian plots to move in on the Gulf. Hadn't Moscow always wanted a warm-water port, a year-round outlet to the southern seas? A senior official in Jimmy Carter's State Department declared it had been clear at least since the Constantinople Convention a hundred years ago that the Russians saw the Red Sea and its southern entrance, just around the corner from the Gulf, as a "legitimate area of Russian military hegemony." Before World War I the czars had messed around in Iran and even tried to establish themselves directly on the Arabian Peninsula. To reduce British influence, the Russians sent their navy to the Gulf, subsidized a steamship line linking it to Odessa and planned to build a railway with a terminus in Kuwait. When the Nazis were cutting deals with Stalin in 1939, they recognized the area "in the general direction of the Persian Gulf . . . as the center of the aspirations of the Soviet Union."*

But what the Western strategic thinkers tended to forget in this recitation of Russian ambitions is that all of them failed. Ethiopia was falling apart at the seams, with a discredited dictator presiding over multiple civil wars. Yemen was a collection of feuding tribes masquerading as a People's Republic. Afghanistan had become an unmitigated disaster since the 1979 invasion.

*For this little chronology I am indebted to Mark N. Katz, *Russia and Arabia: Soviet Foreign Policy toward the Arabian Peninsula* (Baltimore: Johns Hopkins University Press, 1985), pp. 3–5, 199.

Fedotov scoffed at American paranoia, sitting back in the armchair in the embassy living room and putting on a charming smile that made him look a little like Sydney Greenstreet. These days the Soviets no longer have any designs on the region except to ensure its stability, he said. No sponsoring of subversion. No territorial ambitions. No drive to conquer an outlet to southern seas. "All these old clichés about warm waters, it is all nonsense which belongs to the past." Ideology may "give certain nuances to foreign policy," Fedotov conceded, but "diplomacy, it is art of possible." All in all, "ideology, it is dangerous stuff." So *glasnost* and *perestroika* came to the Gulf, and while Washington was showing off its gunboats, Moscow went for style.

Its choice of a site for its commercial coming out was typical. Other city-states in the Emirates had more impressive exhibit halls, but Sharjah's was more fun. It looked a little like a Luna Park somewhere in the middle of New Jersey, with rides and lights and big exhibit halls where you'd expect to find lop-eared rabbits or chickens with feathers draped like mops. But the men were in white robes and the women in full veils. Sharjah, never quite as rich as its neighbors and always a little eccentric, was still a family kind of place. Construction of the international airport had all but bankrupted the emirate, and there were no flights to speak of, but families turned out enthusiastically on Fridays to picnic on the green lawns in front of the empty terminal. It was Sharjah's family atmosphere the Soviets liked, they said. Other exhibition halls might attract more business, "but here, the public is coming," said Younousov.

Other international exhibitors were, in fact, relatively few at the Sharjah Expo. In that small pond the Soviet delegation outclassed everyone else. The booths from the Iranian Poor People's Foundation, next door to the Soviets, looked a little like Goodwill stores, with elementary handicrafts, knitcraft sweaters, plaques clumsily inlaid with sayings from the Koran. The Thai booth offered, almost exclusively, counterfeit copies of Louis Vuitton handbags. Only the Chinese presented any real competition for the public's favor. Their exhibit came from a place called Jilin, which doesn't produce very much, it seems. But the Oriental medicines they displayed were in-triguing to many of the visitors. One, proffered as a boost for virility, listed its ingredients as spotted deer antler, donkey penis, dog penis and deer penis. It was in great demand.

"I say only for display, only for display," said exhibitor Zhao Wei-Zhuo, "but the Arabian people they want to buy. Some men is rich in money; they put a lot of money in my pocket and say, 'I take it now,' but I say, 'No, my boss is punishment me.' " If it were for sale, the price would be fourteen dollars for twenty capsules. "The cost of the raw material is high," he said. "But maybe they have more than one wife, so they want that one."

"It is a prestige thing to have the Soviets here," said Zafar Inamdar, sales director for the Expo Center. Along with Younousov's exhibits from the U.S.S.R. Chamber of Commerce and the cham-pionship team of rhythm gymnasts doing their thing with balls, clubs, hoops, ribbons and ropes, there was a documentary film, *The Bells of Chernobyl,* about clean-up efforts after the world's worst atomic disas-ter. But not all the Soviets in Sharjah were as smooth as the twenty-seven-year-old multilingual, multifaceted Younousov. "In a few years to come," he confided amiably, "we will have a whole new body, maybe you can call it a class, of professional managers who know how things work outside the Soviet Union. Previously the industry was oriented toward the internal market only."

At a nearby booth the display cases held nothing but dreary arrays of Soviet light bulbs. Behind them stood the Sovelectro man, the lapels on his suit as wide as the Volga, his tie as tasteful as Moscow's G.U.M. department store. He was reluctant to talk, even about the price of air conditioners. After several minutes dodging the question, a hitherto silent man in gray standing behind him said resentfully that the European community had "alleged" that the Soviets were "dumping" their products on world markets.

Younousov, the young technocrat, glittered against the gray bureaucratic backdrop. But even at his part of the exhibit, clumsy Soviet thinking spread a dingy film over his sales pitch like a drop of grease in a glass of wine. He was selling the diamonds in the poster, the stud services of Soviet stallions with old Arabian bloodlines, caviar, furs and, curiously, perfumes. One scent was called, with Wagnerian overtones, Ring. The other, launched with little or no market research, was called Brig. Direct from Moscow, *eau de prison.*

FORGOTTEN FRUITS

WHEN THE GUERRILLA FIGHTERS OF ISLAM START THEIR HOLY WARS, THEY target the video clubs. As much as petrodollars (and certainly more than politics), pirated tapes—both audio and video—have transformed the culture of their old, righteous world. They know well the power of the capstan and magnetic head, and they have turned them to their own use: the Ayatollah mobilized Iran's faithful with his mass-produced messages on tape. The muezzin of almost every mosque in modern Islam plays a prerecorded call to the faithful. The culture of the cassette is all-pervasive. On remote desert trails one may come across discarded tapes, jammed, cracked, tangled like spaghetti, spread across the rocks. In the souks, the heavy turnover is no longer in frankincense and water bags, but in multisystem videos and light-weight boom boxes. The electronic tide seems irreversible, and so does the culture it brings. In the hotels of Egypt or on the streets of Paris you can spot the young Saudis and Kuwaitis by their clothes.

Having taken off their *thobes*, they're trying to look like Michael Jackson.

There was a time when paradise was what they wanted, and what they thought they had. Bedouin living the hellish, ascetic life of the desert could dream of the Koran's promised eternity and find it as wonderful and distant as the stars: gardens planted with shady trees watered by a flowing spring, each bearing every kind of fruit in pairs, a place where the righteous shall recline on couches lined with thick brocade, the rich fruits hanging easily within their reach. The Koran promises believers they will dwell with bashful virgins whom neither man nor djinn will have touched before, virgins as fair as corals and rubies. They will drink of a pure wine, securely sealed, whose very dregs are musk. And toil shall not weary them.

This heaven used to seem impossibly far from the Empty Quarter. Now it was as close as the salesmen squatting and sweating in the tent. Paradise was there for the asking. With money the trees grew and the fruits ripened and everything else came to hand. Paradise became the road from Abu Dhabi to Sheikh Zayed's traditional seat of power in Al-Ain, a highway lined with flowering trees, irrigated all year, bringing green among the barren dunes. Paradise became a seaside mansion or the pool club of a hotel, or—a golf course.

Sheikh Surur, chamberlain to Sheikh Zayed of Abu Dhabi, invites you to his home by the emirate's azure coast, bids you wash your hands in one of the many sinks with gold faucets, asks you to sit comfortably on the white carpet before a table set this day, as every day, with dozens of delicacies. And when you have eaten the fish and the meat and the raisins and rice, he calls for the fruits. More than two of every kind are within arm's reach, perfect and ripe and sweet apples and pears, bananas, oranges. And this one—unlike anything you have ever seen before, oddly nubby in its skin, looking slightly syrupy when peeled, like litchi but not litchi—this fruit he bids you to eat. Of course you can't refuse. Nor do you want to look too tentative. So you take the peeled fruit, bite into its sweet flesh. Yes. Good. "What is it?"

··

And Sheikh Surur looks at you curiously and smiles. "I do not know. We get so many fruits here. Who can know?"

With the coffee afterward there is CNN, plucked from the skies by Surur's satellite dish.

Many make efforts to keep in touch with the traditions of the past, but bedouin culture—desert culture—was almost a vacuum forty years ago. What it offered was emptiness—the "silence where only the winds played, and cleanness infinitely remote from the world of men" that Thesiger wrote about. Compared to an influx of untold wealth, the ascetic life that fascinated the old explorers provided a remarkable paucity of diversions for the newly rich and indolent. Daily life was, at first, overwhelmed by the assault of electronic experience. In this new world of images, the sparse imagery of Arabia asserted itself through repetition—printed, broadcast, neonized and reflectorized, sprayed on black velvet, hung on hotel walls—until it lost whatever resonance it once had. The falcon. The dhow. The camel. The horse. The saluki. The sword. The coffee pot. The veil. The mosque and minaret. The tent. These are the icons; these are, to the Western eye, the ubiquitous clichés in architecture and decoration, advertising and art. After a while even paradise palls. The real symbol of daily life in Arabia, since the days of pink Cadillacs, has been the car. The susurrous ambience of the desert tent has given way to an envelope of vinyl, steel and glass and the all-encompassing sound of a Pioneer system.

Riyadh, the wild old capital of the Wahhabi hinterland, now looks more or less like Reseda, California. To clear the mind, there's nothing to do but drive. We pass a little BMW with a bumper sticker: SIT ON A HAPPY FACE. Lines are forming at the Kentucky Fried Chicken. In the hotels Western videos play most of the day, more or less indiscriminately chosen and run in oddly Islamized versions. Outside the sandstorm hangs thick in the air like a brown fog, giving even the air-conditioned room the scent of ashes. On the television is Andy Warhol's *Lonesome Cowboys*, considerably shortened.

"We had this boom," said Prince Sultan bin Salman bin

Abdul Aziz, the astronaut. "Everybody wanted to build a house. But there only seemed to be about twenty or thirty designs, like somebody threw them out of a helicopter." Sultan, son of Riyadh's mayor, grandson of the nation's founder, is a handsome young major in the Saudi air force and his country's only certified space traveler, having been sent aloft in an American shuttle in the days before the *Challenger* crash, when the Reagan administration was handing out public relations rides to schoolteachers. Now, meeting often with the press, Sultan offers a picture of Saudi Arabia that is smart, sophisticated, understanding of its past and present, mindful of the future. He can laugh about the grotesque excess of Riyadh mansionry. "Somebody had a dream in Dallas, and they wouldn't let him build it in Dallas. So they came here. When people thought luxury they used to think marble. And Italy almost moved here."

But Sultan is on the trailing edge of a waning generation raised to look to the West, educated there, skilled in the delicate act of balancing Wahhabi culture and Western tastes. His father's generation was mostly "palace educated" by tutors whose only text was The Book. Sultan's contemporaries were sent abroad for higher learning, many of them becoming Ivy League or Oxonian paradigms of multilingual urbanity. ("We had $320 a month. So you can imagine the overdrafts.") But now Saudi has seven universities of its own: enormous complexes boasting the latest hardware and a heavy emphasis on technical education. They are, of course, the best physical plants that money can buy. Riyadh's King Saud University boasts the second largest university library in the world—but the measurement is in floor space. It has 1.25 million volumes, roughly the number at a good, small New England college, but "any books that contradict the policy of the kingdom, we can't accept that," says the assistant librarian guiding a tour. The card catalog shows dozens of books about Karl Marx, none by him. Literature is sanitized: Western thought—even Arab thought—attenuated like a pirated copy of *Lonesome Cowboys*. *The Thousand and One Nights* makes no appearance. "It's not a big issue in my opinion," says the librarian. The collection is tailored to the teaching. Through the pristine reading area clerks are wheeling carts of books back to the stacks. Among them are dozens of volumes of *Jewish Conspiracy and Muslim World* by one Misbahul Islam Faruquhu, "with the complete text of *The Protocols of the Learned Elders of Zion.*" The library itself publishes these necessary adjuncts to the university's curriculum.

To balance the intellectual aridity there are the tapes, available everywhere. A pirated video costs ten dollars, and new releases hit the stands as soon as they hit the theaters in the United States, sometimes before. The music tapes cost about two dollars apiece. Any title imaginable is available: rack after rack of Ronstadt or The Clash, Clapton or, of course, Madonna. "Like a Virgin" seeps from the smoked windows of a stretched Mercedes carrying one man's veiled wives on their daily expedition to the shopping malls.

The generation that was educated abroad developed the strongest and most immediate sense of the culture from which it had come, and the culture to which it had been sent. Their experience was firsthand, not cut, spliced and packaged.

"My father, who was dragged out of school when he was thirteen or fourteen, sent me to learn English and to school in England to learn engineering, which I hated to do," says Prince Abdullah bin Faisal bin Turki. He had arrived in Britain in 1968. "It was very political. You either became a hippie or a Weatherman. It was very moving. At least the music moved you, if not the people." Ten years later he went back to Saudi Arabia to take over the ambitious efforts to build industrial cities where before there had been only sand.

The sons of King Faisal were meant to be examples to their countrymen. They went to the Hun School in New Jersey, then on to British and American universities. Saud al-Faisal, now foreign minister, is a Princeton man. Another brother went to Sandhurst. Turki al-Faisal, chief of intelligence, was educated by the Jesuits at Georgetown University.

But they will never succeed to the Saudi throne. Old Abdul Aziz's fecund loins gave them forty-three uncles, the youngest born in 1947. The generation of Faisal's sons is relatively small, sandwiched between its palace-educated elders and the younger products of Saudi's own school system. They are no longer the hope of the future but vestiges of the past. By the time their uncles' claims have petered out, their children will be chafing for power. There are four thousand princes, a kind of inflation that has reduced the prestige of royalty—if not the demands of the princes—almost to a par with ambitious commoners. Already the younger generation is jostling for positions held by expats.

"Saudiization? It all started, of course, when the first Saudi learned to fix the first car that came," says Abdullah. But the demands now are for the top positions.

The same thing has been happening in Kuwait and Oman—all over the Gulf. Expats had come first as a class of explorers, entrepreneurs, exploiters, then as the training class. But they have stayed, in diminishing numbers, to be the service sector of Arabia. They are needed less and less to interpret the world, more to fill jobs that the Arabs themselves didn't want to bother doing. They are useful adjuncts to paradise; assurance that toil will not weary the faithful. But the world they helped create has its obsolescence built in as surely as the old cars that rolled out of Detroit. What is rising to replace the old world of the Arabs and expats is a curious hybrid of East and West, the desert and paradise, something streamlined but with a falcon on the hood, something powerful but a little ungainly—a new culture where there is no doubt that the Arabs themselves are in the driver's seat.

His swimming pool was in the shape of a crescent moon, and the old sheikh looked at it longingly in the warm Dubai night as his Pakistani butler served up skewered chicken from the grill in his garden. He could remember when there was nonstop fucking there, among the peacocks and the flowers, in the old days of the big money and the big times. He would invite twenty girls to parties with him and his friends. One, he remembered, was insatiable; she would take on two men at once—just there, in that far corner of the pool there. She couldn't sleep without being fucked.

Those had been great times. Those were the days when the old sheikh would go to London and pay whores two hundred pounds a night for two basic services: sex and information about the other sheikhs of the Gulf. The whores told him their preferences, performances, sins and secrets.

But then this thing with AIDS had started. He had been a poor man once and was a rich man now, the pride of his family, a power near the throne. "I couldn't imagine the shame for my family if I got AIDS," he said. So he gave up sex. The parties—or at least the orgies—ended.

He drew on a Romeo y Julieta Churchill, sending a little cloud of smoke up into the light of the moon. He wore a loose white *thobe* and sat with his bare feet pulled up, idly massaging his toes as he talked. The pleasure he took in wealth and luxury was simpler now. Inside his home the marble floors glistened. He had become fascinated with cleanliness, and had a commercial-style laundry installed in his house so he could always have clean, crisp sheets on his bed.

The sheikh would sit on his white sofa watching television, always watching television. The local news would come on. The Gulf Cooperation Council interior ministers were meeting in Abu Dhabi. He snorted. "They look like ice cream," he said, as if they were frozen and sugary and about to melt.

"You know," he said, "this is all going to end."

It was something he thought about often. Eventually the oil would run out; the money would run out. "It will be like a garden without water." It would dry up and blow away.

But no, you hasten to say, as any guest would, repeating the wisdom of the rulers that the infrastructure, the investment, the playground and trading-post aspects of Dubai would remain and prosper.

"Really?" he said. Look at the golf course. Dubai consumes fifty-three million gallons of water a day. The golf course used a full million of that. Or the dry dock—there's a major investment. It cost £250 million to build, approaching half a billion dollars. In 1985 it turned a profit of $700,000. Look at the armed forces. At one military exercise more than half the tanks couldn't be started.

There was a rueful shaking of heads. Among the sheikh's guests that evening were a Roman Catholic Iraqi businessman and a British lawyer, an old friend and an old acquaintance. The Iraqi was overtly obsequious. The Englishman attempted to leaven his own servility with condescension and cajoled the sheikh with off-color jokes. The sheikh wearied of him.

Had the lawyer heard about old Alex? Ah, yes, poor old Alex. Another of the sheikhs had been paying for Alex's string of polo ponies all these years. But it seemed there was a falling out. Now Alex didn't have any more ponies. There was a rueful shaking of heads. The old sheikh looked for something between his toes.

Falcons fly all over the Middle East during the fall, mainly in business class and first. Black-winged peregrines and the big brown-winged sakers sit, hooded and silent, at the feet of sheikhs from Bahrain and Qatar traveling to their hunting grounds aboard 737s and Tristars. Other passengers take note only in passing. The cabin attendants calmly spread paper or plastic beneath the portable perches.

"Please, do not take my picture with this bird," said Ahmed, a retainer of one of Bahrain's princes. "This is a cheap bird. My friends will see and say, 'Oh, look at Ahmed with that cheap bird.' "

Ahmed sat with his *thobe* pulled up toward his knees and his bare feet propped up, sipping a screwdriver. "Smirrrrnoff," he smiled. Two days before, he said, he had brought "a big, strrrong peregrine" from the Gulf to a friend hunting near Alexandria. But Egyptian customs officials told him he would have to take the bird out again or pay a twenty-five-hundred-dollar fine. So he bought this cheap one to show Egyptian customs when he left the country. He glanced down at it with an air of amused derision. "He is just for the airport."

On another flight a military officer from the United Arab Emirates is headed for Egypt to catch migratory peregrines in the Sinai, then give them as gifts to Abu Dhabi's leading sheikhs. He shows off snapshots of his falconers and their camp and of a wooden racing boat he has built with a lateen sail modeled on ancient dhows. He talks passionately about ancient traditions that endure among the Gulf Arabs; he is a young officer on the make who has joined the right club, preached the right values, owned the right things and given the right gifts. "They are part of us. The camels, the sea and falcons. We cannot leave them behind."

But many of the wooden-hulled dhows have massive inboard engines; jockeys on racing camels carry walkie-talkies in their silks; falcons are fitted with tiny radio transponders in their tail feathers and tracked with portable telemetry systems. Some have microchip implants in their skin that can be scanned for identification purposes like the bar codes on a cereal box.

Modern camel racing and falconry are marred by a kind of conspicuous or, rather, rapacious consumption that cares little for the needs of man or beast.

The gyrfalcon, a native of the Arctic, is twice the size of a peregrine and a truly regal bird. In medieval Europe it was reserved for kings and is much coveted by Arab princes. Kept in air-conditioned rooms, released only to hunt, it cannot survive more than twelve hours in the wild if it escapes into the debilitating heat of the desert.

The Arabs' favorite prey is a big, ungainly desert fowl called the houbara bustard, seen only rarely in Arabia these days, due to relentless hunting. Each fall Saudi princes rent whole rooms at the Damascus Sheraton for their falcons, hoping to find the birds in the plains and hills of Syria. Pakistan, Iran and India also are favorite houbara hunting grounds. Falconers who stay closer to home employ professional trackers to search day after day for signs of prey— houbara or smaller curlews. When word comes of a sighting they drop everything in the office or at home to race into the dunes.

Sheikh Faisal bin Khalid bin Sultan al-Qasimi, formerly of California State University in Turlock, California, and now head of Sharjah's royal guard, phoned ahead from his Mercedes 560 SEL to his falconer's jeep about fifteen miles north of town. Some curlews had been found, but the sun was setting. The speedometer moved easily past 135 miles per hour. Faisal fumbled with his tapes, looking for some new music. "Dire Straits?" Too cool for his taste. He wanted something with a little soul. The Pointer Sisters. He propped one foot up, almost on the seat, as he drove, distracted, hot for the hunt.

The falconers, with their birds in the back of four-wheel-drive Daihatsu Rockys, came into view on a freeway off ramp that led directly into the bare red dunes of the desert. Faisal traded the wheel of the Mercedes for a Toyota Land Cruiser, and the chase was on: a race through the long shadows of the wadis, up over ridges, the axels shimmying and wheels shaking, now half-sliding sideways, now surging over hilltops, crashing through bushes, slithering through sand. Where signs of curlews had been found, the cars suddenly came to a stop. One falconer, Gareeb, slipped the hood off his hawk's head. Another tracker scoured the land in his Rocky, circling inward like a motorized bird dog. The curlew sprinted forward on the ground, then froze. The car horn blasted angrily behind it, and the bird took off. Gareeb, his right hand on the wheel, launched the hawk from the gauntlet on his left. It coursed in a wide arc, up and down over the dunes after the curlew. On the first pass the falcon missed its prey. The bird was flushed again with the rush-hour blast from the car horn. Again the midair chase. This time the curlew came down in the peregrine's talons. The bird of prey looked around, idly curious, as if this dying thing had just appeared in its claws, studying it. Gareeb stalked the trained bird and in a deft move substituted a dead pigeon for its game. The falcons were loaded into the jeeps again. The curlew was tossed into the trunk of the Mercedes when we rolled back across the highway. The wheel-spinning hunt, the blasting horns, the flight and the kills went on until dark.

One of Faisal's favorite hangouts is the Canary Coffee Shop of the Continental Hotel in Sharjah, where his uncle is the ruler. He and his entourage sip fruit juices beneath a geodesic skylight that soars sixteen stories over the empty lobby. His falconers are with him here, too, with young hawks, which perch unhooded, surveying the vaulted expanses of glass and steel. But Faisal is mainly talking, this night, about his growing string of racing camels.

Sometimes he goes to the big new track south of Dubai, where the white-robed sheikhs are served coffee, tea and sweets by white-gloved waiters. The Arab owners finger their digital stopwatches like worry beads, glancing back and forth between the track in the distance and a battery of ten Sony Trinitron televisions nearer at hand. Camera cars are poised to cover the four-mile race. The Dubai track has few physical barriers, but the trainers and the sheikhs are as separate as those in morning coats and those without at Ascot. Trainers and grooms, their feet bare, heads haphazardly turbaned, wait expectantly for the start. Suddenly the starting wire springs up, and the camels are off and loping.

But Faisal prefers Sharjah-style racing, in Dhaid and other outlying towns. There the owners and trainers can drive alongside the galloping beasts, blasting ahead in their Range Rovers, shouting instructions over bullhorns and walkie-talkies. Every race quickly becomes two races, the camels and the cars. As a local newspaper put it, "For the bedu there is no conflict between his love for the camels and his love for fast driving." Faisal concedes the point easily. The cars are as much fun as the camels.

"We lead two different lives," says Sultan bin Salem, one of Faisal's guests, as he sips mango juice in the Canary.

In this schizoid world camel racing has become one of the few reassuring links to the past. Camels used to be at the center of bedouin life, acting as beasts of burden, giving wool and milk—racing was incidental; now racing is all that's left. Otherwise camels just get in the way of cars; they wander through the carefully nurtured grass of the median strips and trespass on putting greens. The sport of sheikhs has become an obsession in the post-petrodollar world, especially among the sheikhs themselves. Like real and would-be aristocrats anywhere, they are fascinated by bloodlines—the notion that breeding is the true test of substance, and sport is the test of breeding. The best camels sell for hundreds of thousands of dollars, in a few cases millions of dollars, and they are tremendously pampered.

Among the dunes around the tracks you can see them eating their alfalfa off of picnic blankets.

In the 1980s racetracks sprang up all over the Gulf, and a season was established that ends each spring with a series of spectacular events. On the outskirts of Riyadh more than six hundred camels run in a single race, charging around the track on a scale that might have stunned Lawrence of Arabia. But the jockeys are hardly desert warriors.

On the camels' backs are children. Little children. "Sure," says Faisal, there in the geodesic calm of the Canary Coffee Shop, it used to be pretty reckless having little kids on these crazy, enormous beasts. "There were many accidents. Many children died." But, well, measures were being taken. The boys were all supposed to be ten years old, at least, though some of them looked five or six. The parents, in India and Pakistan, were paid a good price for their childrens' services. "And the children will get paid—like any laborer in the market." They are used for as long as they are useful, then sent back, like other expats.

The Indian press deplores the practice, accusing jockey brokers of stealing children and accusing parents of selling them. But the practice goes on. The featherweight jockeys are easy on the spines of the young bloodstock. The poverty from which the children come is almost as fraught with risk as the races in which they ride; maybe more, the owners claim. And meanwhile, fans talk about the improvements made in safety precautions. An ambulance follows close behind each race. Trainers used to tie the riders to their saddles. But after some of the fatal accidents the practice was banned. Now after the camels thunder across the finish line with little boys clinging to their back or flailing their whips, seeming magically balanced, the trainers rush up to help the children off and the paddock is filled with the rasp of peeling Velcro sewn to the saddles and the seats of their pants.

THE NEW WORLD

FRIEND OR FOE

....

THE AIR TRAFFIC CONTROLLERS HAD BEEN WORRIED FOR A WHILE. IN THE bar of the Dubai International Hotel, across from the terminal, they talked uneasily about the dangers of so much civilian traffic flying, almost nonchalantly, through the war zone. Dubai was a hub—like Atlanta or Amsterdam—not only for flights within the region but for long hauls from Europe to Asia. The Maktum dynasty had set out to attract the air trade with every means at its disposal, from modern runways to duty-free liquor at the world's lowest prices. "FLY BUY DUBAI," beckoned the posters. But these were not friendly skies. In October 1987 the *Khaleej Times* in Dubai ran a concerned editorial: "One shudders to think of what would happen if an airliner was mistaken for a hostile warplane or a warplane tried to take advantage of the presence of an airliner to carry out a military operation." The controllers were not the only ones tracking the planes. The nervous fleets of the Americans, the British, the French, the Dutch, the

Belgians, the Italians, the Soviets, the Saudis and the Iranians were all out on the water, saturating the air with radar, vigilant for the moment when something would go wrong, someone would fire, someone would turn them into another *Stark*. Their minds danced with attack profiles.

The boys sitting before the blue screens and white blips, watching shapes and numbers, could only imagine the danger. It was like a video game, only the bells and lights of a miscalculation might turn suddenly to screams, explosions, the rush of steam, the stench of burning insulation, metal, flesh. This blip seemed to be a civilian airliner. So did that one. But—what's this?—one blip suddenly becomes two. Another plane is peeling off where before there was only a jumbo jet. It's making an attack run against something on the water. The controllers in the Dubai tower had seen it happen. So had the boys on the ships.

On June 8, 1988, at 20:47 local time, a British Airways flight from London to Dubai entered the control area of the Dubai tower. A Balkan Airlines flight was taking off from Sharjah's little-used airport at the same time. There was no problem, normal traffic. But then an American warship broke onto the airwaves. The British Air flight was about to pass over him, and the warship ordered it to change course. The warship ordered British Air right into the path of the Balkan flight. Now the Dubai controller came on the air, livid, his voice barely controlled, countermanding the warship, narrowly keeping the two planes out of each other's way.

There were no headlines about that incident. Just diplomatic notes. Just the kind of thing that controllers talked about when they were finishing a beer at the end of the day. "Why don't they just call us?" one of them said. "It's easy. We can tell them all about the bloody aircraft. I mean, have these guys seen a radar screen before? We really do wonder." These were cool men, but they were getting upset. "You can't mix a war zone with civilian aircraft. Something's got to give."

* * *

I was on vacation in Italy when the news broke. I was diving off a pedal boat about one hundred yards out in the Mediterranean when Carol's sister came running down to the beach. The cold water felt good. The sun was warm on my face. And the first thing I could make out over the waves, as my sister-in-law shouted, was that no one had died. She meant no one in the family. It was just David Mills, the *Newsweek* photographer, calling from Cyprus. He normally worked with me in the Gulf. We had been on the *Big Orange* together. He liked to chat about news and was always ready with a hot tip on one thing or another. But this seemed more urgent than usual. He had insisted I call back as soon as possible.

Someone *had* died, as it turned out. An American warship, the cruiser *Vincennes,* had been attacked—or maybe it hadn't—but in any case it had shot an Iranian Airbus out of the sky over the Strait of Hormuz.

Twenty-four hours later I was back in Dubai. "Thank God, it was those bloody Iranians and not a real airplane with real people," said one of my friends in the tower when I called him. "It could have been British Air, or Pan Am or Singapore Airlines."

Iran Air 655 was a commuter flight, a regular 140-mile, thirty-five-minute jumbo-jet milk run over the war zone. The pilot, Captain Mosen Rezaian, was trained in the United States. His five-year-old daughter was born there. His sister-in-law lived in Norman, Oklahoma. His job was simple: take off from the Bandar Abbas airport in Iran, climb to an altitude of about fourteen thousand feet, then start to descend. Stay within a twenty-mile-wide commercial airline corridor, and stay in touch with the towers, first at Bandar Abbas, then at Dubai. To identify itself to controllers his airplane carried a transponder that showed it on monitoring equipment as a civilian flight. The signal was called IFF: Identification Friend or Foe.

Later, months later, the U.S. Navy's internal investigation would determine that Captain Rezaian had done everything right.

The U.S.S. *Vincennes* was a billion-dollar warship, outfitted
with the highest-tech systems the navy could procure. In the sparest
Pentagonese prose it was a "563-foot Ticonderoga class AEGIS
cruiser with about 360 officers and crew. The ship displaces 9,600
tons and is armed with Standard missiles, five-inch guns, Harpoon
antiship missiles, a Phalanx close-in weapons system and two Sea-
hawk Lamps Mark 3 helicopters. It has the capability of engaging in
antiair, antisubmarine and antiship warfare simultaneously." Or it
was supposed to have.

Reporters would later discover that the AEGIS system, the
computer-driven soul and psyche of the ship, the collection of hard-
ware and software that had pushed the vessel's price tag to a thousand
million dollars, had never really been tested. It was bought on the
basis of trials in which the operating crews already knew what situations they were supposed to deal with, what they were supposed to
see, how they were supposed to react.

On July 3, 1988, the crew of the *Vincennes,* too, knew what
it was supposed to see. The cruiser had been positioned in the Strait
of Hormuz a couple of weeks before because of intelligence that the
Iranians were building underground launching sites for their Silkworms. Iran seemed increasingly determined to fight back directly, if
need be, against the American presence in the Gulf. In April they had
managed to cripple the frigate U.S.S. *Samuel B. Roberts* with a mine.
The Americans hit back by sinking or pulverizing six Iranian boats.
The new Silkworms looked like Iran's parry, and the *Vincennes* was
the riposte. Its Tomahawk missiles were reported to be equipped with
warheads that burrowed into the ground after their target.

The Iranians had also moved their dwindling squadron of old
American F-14 fighter planes, left over from the shah, from the
interior to the Bandar Abbas airport on the coast. Their obvious
purpose was to counter the long-range Iraqi raids into the southern
Gulf. Short of kamikaze missions, they could do little against ships.
But the *Vincennes* crew was looking for those F-14s. Kamikaze was
possible. Anything was possible with these Iranians. The *Vincennes*
was there to cool them out, intimidate them, show its stuff. Robo-

cruiser is what the crews of other American warships called the *Vincennes*, a billion-dollar high-tech enforcer, like *Robocop* the movie, Robocop the comic book, Robocop the video game. "My guess was that the crew of the *Vincennes* felt a need to prove the viability of AEGIS in the Persian Gulf," the commander of an American frigate sailing nearby wrote later, "and that they hankered for an opportunity to show their stuff." None of them had been in combat before.

And suddenly they were. And things started to go wrong. Things went so wrong that nobody could believe, in the first moments and then in the long weeks afterward, that such a tragedy of errors could take place. The *Vincennes* had skirmished with Iranian speedboats at about 10:00 in the morning, Dubai time. As that engagement was drawing to an end, at 10:47, the Airbus took off from Bandar Abbas, a few minutes behind its scheduled departure. The *Vincennes*, only sixty miles away, spotted it immediately and started pumping electronic data; AEGIS went into action. UNKNOWN—ASSUMED ENEMY came the message on the screen. Bingo. An F-14, everyone thought, and kept on thinking. A crew member checked a book of commercial flight schedules. Somehow he missed IR-655. The navy never did figure out why, but it might have been because the idiosyncratic Iranians set their clocks a half hour later than Dubai time. The plane was late, too. Nobody called the towers. The *Vincennes* started issuing warnings over the radio. Maybe Captain Rezaian had the right frequency on; maybe he didn't. But in any case, the warnings were explicit. "Iranian F-14 this is USN warship bearing 199, 20 miles. Request you change course 270 immediately." Rezaian was flying an Airbus, 177 feet long, with a wingspan of 147 feet and weighing 170,000 pounds. The *Vincennes* was warning off an F-14 a third that size (with 38-foot wings, 62 feet long, weighing 40,000 pounds).

In the darkened war room of the cruiser, the Combat Information Center, where the captain and his high-tech team were watching the computer screens, one man shouted out "Possible COMAIR." Possible commercial airliner. The captain raised his hand to acknowledge the information. But everyone else was still saying F-14. And the action against the gunboats on the water wasn't over yet. The *Vin-*

cennes suddenly heeled over thirty-two degrees, racking around to get the little Boghammer speedsters in its sights. In the Command Information Center coffee cups were falling, lights were flickering and, in the background, guns were booming.

The Iran Air milk run continued. Robocruiser went into action. Captain Rezaian's flight was at twelve thousand feet and climbing. The *Vincennes* concluded it was at nine thousand feet and diving. The Airbus was flying normally at 350 knots. The *Vincennes* concluded it was speeding along at 450. The commercial flight was barely off the center line of the twenty-mile corridor. The *Vincennes* concluded it was more than four miles outside the commercial flight path. The crucial electronic sign of attack—indicators that the plane was sweeping the ship with radar to aim its rockets, bombs and guns—never showed. But the *Vincennes* fired—or tried to. The first few efforts to launch two Standard sea-to-air missiles were fumbled. Eventually the rockets shot aloft. Nobody on the ship had seen anything yet with his own eyes. The Standards were supposed to be aimed at a fighter plane diving now at seventy-eight hundred feet. But since the fighter didn't exist, they homed in on the airliner. The two Standards hit one after the other, blowing the plane to bits. Even as it was spiraling in flames toward the water, sailors on the *Vincennes* would believe the wreckage they saw was of a swept-wing fighter plane.

In its final report the navy concluded the AEGIS system had performed just fine. The problem was the nervousness of the inexperienced crew. Captain Will Rogers III was exonerated. Investigators recommended that one officer, the "anti-air warfare coordinator," receive a "nonpunitive letter of censure," the mildest reprimand in the military. But the chairman of the Joint Chiefs and the secretary of Defense rejected the recommendation. Officially, though everything had gone wrong, nobody was to blame. On Iran Air 655, where nothing had been done wrong, everybody was dead.

* * *

At the entrance to the Mostaan cold storage warehouse in Bandar Abbas some of the Iranian officials thoughtfully unrolled handfuls of toilet paper for visitors to hold over their noses and mouths as they went inside. Three days after the jet went down, people were still arriving in Bandar Abbas to search through the corpses for relatives, friends. Where boxes of vegetables and sides of beef were normally stored were open coffins made of fiberboard. A few were draped with Iranian flags. The corpses were twisted, bloated; some had been chewed, some dismembered. Ice had crystallized across their features, man-made hoarfrost settling over hair and lashes. Many had been found nude, their clothing stripped from them by the blast and the rush of air as they fell twelve thousand feet into the strait. Most of the dead women in the cold store had been covered in woolen blankets. On the makeshift shrouds of those who had been identified were pinned names and addresses and the slogan DEATH TO AMERICA.

Of course many were mutilated beyond recognition. In some cases whole families were wiped out, and no one came looking for them. Of the 290 people on Iran Air 655, 170 corpses had been retrieved. Forty were unidentified.

A handful seemed at peace. Leila Behbahani, three years old, was still dressed in her tidy blue dress, black shoes, white socks, and little gold bangles on her wrist. Twenty-year-old Fatima Faidazaida had been found in the water three hours after the crash still clutching her baby, Zoleila-Asham. They were together now in the same coffin.

For almost three years I had been trying to get into Iran, but my visa request repeatedly was refused. When an editor in New York went to plead my case with an Iranian diplomat at the United Nations, the diplomat told her there were two problems. They didn't like some of the articles I had written (they wouldn't say which ones). And they didn't like American newsmagazines. "For us," he said with revolutionary conviction, "*Time* and *Newsweek*, they are the two eyes of The Beast."

After the Iran Air atrocity reporters from all over the world were given visas, even I. But now that I was there I wondered who, exactly, imagined I was an eye of the Great Satan, the beast of American intelligence. I wondered whether we could have a calm conversation about the subject.

That was a talk I never had to have, as it turned out. Through three days in Teheran the people on the street treated me and other American reporters with impeccable courtesy. Even as I worked my way through the crowd at a funeral for seventy-six of the flight's victims, no one displayed any hostility toward me. Ritualistically, en masse and on cue, they shouted, "Death to America." But I was right in the middle of them, and when they asked me where I came from I told them: the United States. Then they asked, "Why?—why had the United States done this thing?" They were sure the American people must regret such carnage. I heard again and again, "The American people are not our enemies." They couldn't quite figure it out. So many of them had known individual Americans, worked with them, eaten and played and studied with them in the days of the shah. The country had teemed with expats then, and if the shah had brought corruption and eventually paved the way to chaos—with the backing of the U.S. government—the American people the Iranians had known were mostly agreeable types. "I myself was a student of the RCA company, a computer technician," said one of the mourners. "Four of my family are dead. One of them has not been found yet; three were found. I cannot say anything about the American people. It is the government."

Think how an American crowd would have reacted if an Iranian reporter had been walking around in its midst after 290 American civilians, more than 60 of them children, had been blown out of the air by an Iranian warship. Would the American people differentiate between that Iranian and his government? After nine long years of agony with the Iranian revolution, Americans had come to see all Iranians as something not quite human—but as something quite capable of the most atrocious, inhuman acts. The Iranian mullahs call the United States the Great Satan, and their people remain skeptical. A big part of the American public, however, was perfectly willing to believe in the satanism of Iranians, all Iranians. Just before I went to Iran, I was called in Dubai by a radio talk show from the States that wanted to know if the Iranians might have set up this whole thing, then just dumped all those naked corpses of women and children in the water. . . .

I didn't know what to say.

America found it very hard to be sorry after the downing of Iran Air 655. Captain Rogers's statement that he would have to live with this for the rest of his life was one of the few made by an American official that seemed to be genuinely felt. Iran's Brigadier General Mansour Satary, trained in the United States, made it clear he did not think the Americans actually intended to shoot down an unarmed civilian aircraft. He just said they didn't care enough to be careful enough not to do it.

Iran Air 659 from Teheran to Dubai took off a little before 3:00 P.M. Saturday afternoon, not quite a week after the downing of Iran Air 655, and the passengers in the packed jumbo jet were much the same. Lots of women, lots of kids running up and down in the aisles, meeting each other in the corridor by the bathroom and giggling.

Why was the flight full? Because life in Teheran—in Iran generally—was so tough. The man who sat next to me was a former teacher at an American school in Isfahan. Before the revolution he taught foreign students, mainly American kids, about contemporary Iranian culture. "I used to tell them religion was really very central." Then the revolution came, and he found himself out of a job. "I don't really do anything. There are no jobs in Iran." So he carefully accumulated enough hard currency over a couple of years to fly to

Dubai—that wide-open port and trading center—to buy a television set, a vacuum cleaner, maybe a video, to take back to Iran to sell. At black-market rates you could make a living that way.

As we talked, three little girls were trying to play musical chairs in the seats beside us. I got up to walk around.

One of the stewards was smoking a cigarette during a break. Many of the crew members wore black ribbons on their white shirts. "Our best friends died, you know," he said. "Very nice friends. . . . It is very bad." He was looking out the window at the Gulf below us.

The schoolteacher sitting beside me loved the Americans. "When I heard the Americans shot down the Airbus, I couldn't believe it," he said. "I thought at first that something was wrong with the Iranians—the Americans would never do such a wrong thing."

All the anti-American slogans, the propaganda jingles that little kids sang to themselves almost unconsciously, had been around so long that they became mere background to the daily life of many Iranians. Earlier in the year the Iraqis had rained missiles on Teheran as indiscriminately as the Germans had dropped V-2s on London in World War II. The war had been brought home, terribly, indiscriminately. The resources, the will to fight were waning. And now this tragedy of the Airbus, horrible and senseless, evoked more sadness than anger. As for the hostage taking by Iran's friends in Beirut, the terrorism, the long chronicle of humiliations directed at Uncle Sam, those were done by "them." Iranians, at least of the English-speaking class, rarely seemed to talk about their clerical government as "the government" or even "the regime." It's "them." And "they" did these things. "We have no connection with those taking the hostages in Lebanon or wherever," said one bureaucrat at the funeral of his friend shot down on flight 655. Hostage taking is something "they" do. Even the head of the air force, Brigadier General Satary, when asked why the war went on and on, said reporters would have to talk to the politicians about that. Ask "them."

On Iran Air 659, my flight, a rough-hewn Iranian peasant who seemed new to air travel was seated near the window, looking down.

He didn't speak much English, but when he saw we were over land once again he smiled. He looked at me and after searching for the word said enthusiastically, "Finish." No warships below now. He made his hands like a gun shooting up at a bird, then shook his head, grinned and laid his head on his hand to show he could relax, sleep.

One of the stewards on flight 659 wanted to know how I felt about what had happened. Awful, obviously—I mean, isn't it obvious? Two hundred ninety people dead are two hundred ninety people dead, and these were pretty clearly innocents. But I asked him what he thought happened. "I don't know," he said. "It was a mistake. An American mistake and an Iranian mistake." He was the one whose friends were lost. He was willing to admit there could be gross errors on both sides. I wondered why it was so hard for Americans to do the same.

A few weeks later the Iran-Iraq war ended. Accepting a U.N.-sponsored truce, Khomeini said, was like drinking poison. But he drank it anyway. The years of suffering, the foundering economy, the succession of tragedies had finally taken too much of a toll. Zeal had given way to bitterness, and popular resentments began to present a greater challenge than war to the mullahs' regime.

Not quite six months after the downing of Iran Air 655 a Pan American airliner exploded over Lockerbie, Scotland, killing 270 people. Civilians. Children. Little girls playing musical chairs. Even with the war against Iraq over, some of the mullahs were still keeping score.

On June 3, 1989, exactly eleven months after Iran Air 655 and six months after Pan Am 103, Ayatollah Ruhollah Khomeini died. His nation mourned him passionately but briefly. His successor as de facto leader, Hashemi Rafsanjani, declared the country open for business. Expats were welcome once again, it seemed. But by then I had left the Middle East.

UNICORNS

....

I HAD HOPED TO FIND BIN KABINA AND BIN GHABAISHA, THE BOYS THESIGER loved, the men he no longer wanted to see, and I'd hoped that by finding them I might discover something unexpected—I wasn't sure what—about the transformation of Arabia. In my last months assigned to the Middle East I scrambled to pick up loose ends of experience I had thought, through almost four years, would eventually be tied up elegantly and serendipitously. I wandered the back alleys of the Khan Khalili looking for the world of Mahfouz, went up to Aleppo to find that decrepit hotel where Lawrence didn't sleep. I went to the mountain in Lebanon to drink the rich red wines of Serge Hochard and wandered the alleys of frozen time along the Green Line in Cyprus. Now I wanted, as a last discovery, to find those two sons of the desert. A reporter for the Omani oil company's public relations magazine had found them in 1987 in a remote corner of Dhofar, living with their children, camels and cars not far from the military air base at Thumrait. His article was painfully bland. Bin Kabina had become "a dignified man with a trim appearance. . . . He no longer has the long hair but possesses the same white teeth that sparkled as he talked and laughed about old times." However banal, at least the piece made the search seem possible. Before, I had really had no idea how to begin.

But visas for Oman—"no-objection certificates," as they are called—were rationed out by one Anthony C. Ashworth, a distinguished British gentleman who had worked for Her Majesty's various services before entering the employ of His Majesty the Sultan as consul in Hong Kong and, in Muscat, adviser to the information minister on, well, the advisability of letting certain foreign journalists into the country. After I had written about the listening posts at Musandam for *The Washington Post,* I was a long time reestablishing myself as unobjectionable. It was only in the last weeks of my time in the Gulf that Ashworth finally let me into Oman. To be fair, he also found my wife, Carol, unobjectionable, so we were able to go together.

I thought I'd made it clear my main goal was to seek out Bin Kabina and Bin Ghabaisha. But we arrived in Oman to find that this was not clear; in fact, for reasons of logistics, time and, I suppose for reasons they did not want to explain, having to do with the sultan's idea of Omani dignity or security questions about the Thumrait air base, it would not be possible. But, the ministry wanted to know, hadn't I said I was interested in the oryx?

Sure, I said, the oryx.

At least I would make it out into the desert for a few nights, perhaps get a sense of the primitive roots of the people far from the Bustan Palace and the Galleria or experience that cleanliness and peace the old explorers had found. The oryx, after all, are in the Jiddat al-Harasis, a vast plateau in the center of Oman with no wells and no oases. The only water comes from the morning fog blowing inland off the Indian Ocean. It is a land less spectacular, perhaps, than the Empty Quarter, but no less desolate and empty. Its people, the Harasis tribe, are not Arabs but a primitive bedouin clan with their own customs and language from an age before Islam, before history. Traditionally they lived and traveled light, without tents, sleeping beneath the rare acacia tree. In the evening they would spread blankets over the branches and in the morning wring the dew from them. The Harasis numbered perhaps twenty-five hundred, spread over more than twenty-five thousand square kilometers. That was about all the desert could support.

Sure, the oryx, I said. Which is how I came to meet, instead of Bin Kabina and Bin Ghabaisha, Debbie Forester and Tim Tear, from Acton, Massachusetts. They lived with the oryx, and with the Harasis.

On the long, lonely road from the ancient city of Nizwa in the north across the center of Oman to Salalah in the south we passed only one truck stop, at a place called Adam. To that point there had been little to see but occasional sparse acacias and, in the distance, punctuating the flat horizon, arid mountains. We stopped briefly for gas and something to drink. Along the shelves of the little store were Pampers and Palmolive Citrus Shampoo, Stripe toothpaste, Vaseline hair tonic. The selection of Styrofoam coolers and soft drinks and crackers was not much different from what you'd find at a 7-Eleven in Arlington.

Then the real desert began. It passed by for hours, almost as flat as a calm sea. The only plants readily visible were forlorn spots of weeds six inches high. Occasionally a microwave tower loomed beside the road. But for most of the drive, for 360 degrees around us, the land stretched flat to the horizon. Finally, our eyes sharpening to the subtle contours of desolation, we saw two black spots floating on the brink of the world. Two camels.

Haima is the settlement at the center of the plateau, our last stop before the driver from Muscat would leave us and a new driver, from the White Oryx Project at Yalooni, would take us across the open desert. The new driver was late, and we were left drinking coffee with local officials who offered us hospitality but spoke no mutually intelligible language. Opposite the filling station was a school, from which echoed the sound of children playing. Finally the new driver arrived, bearing a note on Sultanate of Oman stationery.

"Dear Mr. Decay," it began, with my name as it had come across the radio. "Welcome to the Jiddat al-Harasis. Your driver's name is Hamad bin Aziz and he will guide you to Yalooni.

"It is 1½ hours from Haima to Yalooni, so you may prefer to grab some lunch from the restaurant there. We will have some lunch ready for you here if you prefer, but there is no rush in case you are hungry and want a break. Your driver may prefer it as well." Considerate with the help, I thought.

"We look forward to seeing you when you arrive.

"Sincerely,

"Tim Tear."

The desert was no longer trackless, though it had no discernible road through the barren waste. Tire tracks were everywhere, running in all directions. Trees were still rare. Abandoned trucks were almost as common—irreparable hulks, rusting skeletons.

We arrived in Yalooni to a meal of homemade bread, quiche Lorraine and carrot cake. The camp, it turned out, was a well-ordered collection of trailer homes, like the offices used on construction sites. A large water tower graced the premises. And the house where the camp directors lived was a small prefabricated home suitable for a pleasant Florida vacation: living-dining area, two bedrooms, big kitchen, a Japanese stereo system, a Guatemalan hammock on the porch. We became acquainted over cold drinks. The amenities left us relieved yet disappointed. I asked about the tire tracks and the abandoned trucks.

Tim Tear, twenty-nine, tall and trim and clean-cut, looking like a young lacrosse coach and history teacher at a New England prep school, nodded his head in the direction of the fenced-in yard consisting of sand and rock and a few large potted desert plants around the front of his house. "This is about the only place in the Jiddat with no tire tracks," he said. The others had accumulated over decades, like footprints on the moon. No rain came to wash them away. The trucks were old Bedfords, bought from Pakistani merchants. They were big enough to carry an entire Harasis household across the desert from tree to tree, camp to camp. But they broke down quickly and were left behind where they died.

The last twenty years had changed the life the Harasis led for millennia. Roads brought them into contact with people who would never have braved the desert before. By petty commerce and the sultan's decree they had been set on the path to civilization. They still wandered, still slept beneath the trees, but now they rode in their trucks. They carried folding wire enclosures to keep their goats and camels at a little distance when they slept and ate: the animals roamed free; the people were in the enclosures. And they had begun to send their boys to get a rudimentary education at the boarding school in Haima. When the children arrived, their ages were determined by looking at their teeth. When they left, they knew more of the world beyond the horizon than their fathers ever imagined.

"I'm afraid that one day they'll wake up and see themselves as poor," said Debbie as she stood in the kitchen washing dishes. She, too, was twenty-nine, with long blond hair as straight as if it were ironed, her clothes simple enough for a farmer's wife, her demeanor more than a little reminiscent of a commune in 1972. "The worst part about going back to the States: putting on shoes," she said.

Except for a brief crisis when a loose camel broke through the fence to eat one of the potted plants in the yard, the scene was as perfectly domesticated, as perfectly American as a New England afternoon: sketching out details of work and outlines of personal biography while drying pans, putting away the knives and forks.

Debbie and Tim had met in their eighth-grade English class in Acton, Mass. His father "makes missiles" at the Raytheon plant, he liked to say. Hers owned a lumber business. They were high-school sweethearts. But when they graduated he went off to the University of New Hampshire to study in the environmental program and she went to the State University of New York to study forestry, and their lives began to spread steadily farther apart across the globe. His advisers told him to forget wildlife studies; maybe 1 percent of the students ever went anywhere with that; think hazardous wastes—that's where the future is. Or think public relations. But he kept thinking wildlife.

She "fell for the Peace Corps advertising" and wound up in Guatemala, living with the Indians. He went to Kenya and fell in with another American, "an aging hippie with a pony tail and earring, working for the Kenya police. He'd come through Kenya on his way from California to Papua New Guinea, climbed the mountain and stayed." Debbie went to Tanzania, spent a few months with Tim in Kenya, then returned to the United States. He went to Sudan, to the south, watching the migrations of the antelope called white-eared cob. "My houseboy, Charles, wrote out a list of the Arabic phrases people were using to abuse me. There was one translation: 'having intercourse with one's mother.' That was the beginning of my Arabic." Debbie went to the Comoro Islands, north of Madagascar, with CARE. She was near Tim, or nearer than before. Somewhere between Zaire and Kenya, while standing in a potato field, they decided to marry. "We'd just gone to see some gorillas."

The dishes were done. The sun was getting low on the horizon.

Mohammed Aziz and Mohammed Saif of the Harasis tribe prepared themselves for prayer. Even rocks and small pebbles sent long shadows across the sand. The sun was behind us, and in the middle distance white shapes—brilliant white with the golden tinge of evening—seemed to float above the surface of the desert, suspended and still. Tim handed me binoculars, and the white shapes took on new form through the lenses. Their heads were visible now, with long, gently curving horns so elegant and symmetrical that, from the side, they seemed to be one. Centuries ago, when oryx thrived across the desert, the crusaders had seen them in the distance and thought they were unicorns. Their legs were black, blending with the evening shadow, giving the magical impression that they hovered lightly there near a patch of scrub. Seven were in this herd. As the Harasis prayed beside their Land Cruiser, we moved closer to the big antelope. Now through the binoculars colored tags became visible on the ears of two of the oryx. These had been born not here, in the desolate interior of Oman, but in the San Diego Zoo.

"I have a hard time thinking of them as wild oryx because I know so much about them," said Tim. "But they are very wild."

A Saudi hunting party in cars bagged the last truly wild white oryx in Arabia in 1972 with automatic rifles. Conservationists had foreseen the end of the species and had begun trying to build up the captive stock from zoos and the private menageries of Arab princes. In 1982 the first handful bred in captivity was introduced to the open desert. Now there were regular releases of zoo-bred antelope every few months, dashing excitedly from the holding pen.

"That feeling of expanse is just what every released animal feels: 'Wow! It's *big* out there!' And then you look around, and you're glad to be with someone else."

By 1988 the majority of the fifty-nine oryx ranging across the Jiddat were born in the wild. Each was watched over by the tribesmen, who followed the movements of the herd, tracking, observing, living near the animals all the time. "We're still at the stage where we want to know where they all are," said Tear. For years the fear lingered that a disease might wipe out the whole oryx population. Now that threshold seemed to have been crossed. They ranged far and wide, in small, separate herds. In the trailer headquarters their movements were radioed in, plotted on maps, fed into computers. And yet, "without the Harasis, I could never find an oryx," said Tear.

He and Debbie and their predecessors who developed the project over the course of more than twenty-five years were not so much preserving the wilderness. They were trying to re-create, to resurrect the wild—for the people as much as for the antelope. The project cost the sultanate a million dollars a year: it was kept on the sultanate's books as the Jiddat al-Harasis Development Project B. Stalking the antelope through the still desert air, protecting them, following their every move, the Harasis were given back a little something of what civilization had taken from them, not only a reason to be, but a reason to be where they had always been. "This project is totally within a tribal boundary. There's not a single example of a poached animal, a harrassed animal. The Harasis protect their wildlife."

Their prayers over, Mohammed Aziz and Mohammed Saif offered us coffee. Mohammed Saif is a young man, his face bright with quiet intelligence. His eyes are the color of tea, the same color as his skin. Mohammed Aziz is in his forties, a man who knew the old ways. He quietly filled his tiny pipe with tobacco taken from a little bottle. In earlier days he had lived with no desert transportation but his camels, no wealth but his goats. He would ride for days to a salt dome in the middle of the desert, then trek for weeks up to Nizwa, the forbidden city ruled by the imam, to sell his salt for a few Maria Theresa silver dollars. With some of these he could buy cloth. Down on the coast below the escarpment where the rains fell when the monsoon was caught and turned back by the cliffs, he would buy himself some dried seafood—abalone strung on a rope or the tough, dry skin of a shark—before making his way back to the plateau, to the tree that the family would call its house.

Now Mohammed Aziz talks Toyota four-wheel-drive prices with Tim when they're not talking oryx. But mostly they talk oryx. The big, slightly sheepish antelope with the elegant horns has become a kind of lingua franca between and among the several cultures converging here in the wide-open desert. It is the medium through which the Harasis have learned to deal with the world that rushed in upon them.

Their skills and their bravery are understood; and they show them off. An older Harasis named Loti made his house and his work near the edge of the plateau, along the escarpment. He had grown up around the cliffs, and unlike the other Harasis he was not afraid of the djinns who lived there on the precipice where the clouds met the edge of the plateau. Loti captured ibex, the rugged mountain goats that roamed the rocks, with his bare hands. Stalking them, seizing

their horns, he could wrestle them into his truck. He caught snakes
as well. One day he called Tim on the radio. He had found a large
viper, and he tied it to a tree. Would Tim be interested? Tim wasn't,
but his praise was fulsome. Loti's renown grew among the men.
Bragging and bravery still had a place on the Jiddat, just as a place
remained for the djinns on the escarpment, and for the oryx.

"For the Harasis, this is a halfway measure," said Tim. You
could wish their lives would never change. "But who are we to deny
anyone the benefits of the modern world? They should stay the way
they are because we think they're neat?" These are people, not speci-
mens in a human zoo, he said.

Thesiger would have hated this. He would detest the conscious artifice, these zoo-spawned antelopes, this tire-tracked desert,
the very accessibility of the place and the time. But in that long
twilight on the flat sand and rocks I had to think, This is the moment
Thesiger must have been waiting for each day in those long walks
through the Empty Quarter, this moment of serenity on the edge of
night, with the oryx grazing in the distance, shimmering figures of
light, the last things to fade in the dusk. This is what is left of Arabia,
I thought, after all that oil and blood spilled, all those riches squan-
dered, those paradises built to be lost. It was not what the explorers
had found; it was what they dreaded. They had come to Arabia
looking to find a life they had never led—the solitude or the license
the Orientalists imagined—or to retrieve their youth, to prove their
manhood. Or they came looking for fabulous riches or, most often,
just looking for work. Today foreigners still drift up onto Arabia's
shores, wander its deserts, but they find what they never quite expected: bits and pieces of their own civilization mixed and modified
and distorted and absorbed, something new that is different, still,
from anything else in the world. And after all that had happened, I
thought as the twilight faded, it is not bad. Against the warnings of
T. E. Lawrence, I was in love with the glamour of strangeness. The
new world created by juxtapositions of Arabia and America, Islam
and suburbia, had won me over. I could leave Oman, leave the desert
now, with less regret for the experiences missed and the past that was

lost, if only I could make one more trip. But, well, there are some things that are not meant to be.

In the desert you hear stories and tales, and those about the escarpment fascinated me. Tim and Debbie, when they could arrange the time, would go there on camels to the brink of the Harasis's world. I wanted to go, too, but there was no time left. My life still ran by a New York clock, and all I took away with me was an imagined picture of something Debbie told me in passing. It was just an image conjured from small talk as we drank wine on the front porch and watched desert foxes scampering along the edge of the light around the house. But after I left Yalooni, it stayed with me, as convincing and real as a mirage in the middle distance. Once, said Debbie, Tim's brother visited, and they took along a Frisbee on a trek to the escarpment, flipping the saucer back and forth as they might have done on the Boston Common, throwing it to the Harasis who were with them, watching them catch the Day-Glo dish in hands that wrestled ibex. You can see it there—can't you?—this Wham-O toy. On the edge of the land of the unicorns, there it is spinning, sailing, swept up on the breezes rushing up the cliffs, hovering lightly over the world of the djinns.

POSTSCRIPT

....

WILFRED THESIGER RETURNED TO THE UNITED ARAB EMIRATES FOR TWELVE days in February 1990. He was almost eighty years old. The Shell Oil Company flew Bin Ghabaisha up from Muqshin to meet him. Bin Kabina also appeared, as if from nowhere, and was given a free room at the Abu Dhabi Holiday Inn. After a few minutes, Bin Kabina decided to stay elsewhere with friends.

Thesiger returned to the Emirates to launch an exhibition of his photos that eventually toured Abu Dhabi, Dubai, Al-Ain, Fujairah and Sharjah. "Thesiger Praises Bedu Nobility," read one typical headline in the local press. He was celebrated as a hero.

The old explorer's evaluation of what he found was courteous and tactful after so many years away and such public bitterness about his last experience with the new Arabia. "When I returned in 1977 I was looking for the past and found it gone. I was disappointed and resented the apparent destruction of all that I had valued. But on this visit, I have been most impressed by the dignity of the city of Abu Dhabi," he said in his parting statement.

But why had he decided to go back at all? In one interview he gave to *The Gulf News* Thesiger suggested a reason. A condition he put on his visit was that his book *Arabian Sands* be made generally available in the Emirates. "I want it to be put into Arabic as a monument to a proud people," said the old man. "And I want it to be read by every young Arab who has never been a Bedu."

A BRIEF BIBLIOGRAPHY

....

This is a short list of books I consulted often while writing *Expats* and occasionally cited in the text.

Ajami, Fouad. *The Vanished Imam: Musa al Sadr and the Shia of Lebanon.* Ithaca, N.Y.: Cornell University Press, 1986.

Dawood, N. J., translator. *The Koran.* New York: Penguin, 1974.

Dickson, H. R. P. *The Arab of the Desert.* Edited and abridged by Robert Wilson and Zahra Freeth. London: George Allen & Unwin, 1983.

Dickson, Violet. *Forty Years in Kuwait.* London: Allen & Unwin, 1971.

Graz, Lisl. *The Omanis: Sentinels of the Gulf.* London: Longman, 1982.

Holden, David, and Johns, Richard. *The House of Saud.* London: Pan, 1982.

Katz, Mark N. *Russia and Arabia: Soviet Foreign Policy toward the Arabian Peninsula.* Baltimore, Md.: Johns Hopkins, 1985.

Lawrence, T. E. *Seven Pillars of Wisdom: A Triumph.* New York: Garden City Publishing Co., 1938.

Mahfouz, Naguib. *Miramar.* Translated by Fatma Moussa Mahmoud. Edited and revised by Maged el Kommos and John Rodenbeck. Notes by

Omar el Qudsy. Introduction by John Fowles. Cairo: The American University in Cairo Press, 1978.

———. *The Beginning and the End.* Translated by Ramses Hanna Awad. Edited by Mason Rossiter Smith. Cairo: The American University in Cairo Press, 1985.

———. *Midaq Alley.* Translated by Trevor Le Gassick. Cairo: The American University in Cairo Press, 1975.

———. *The Thief and the Dogs.* Translated by Trever Le Gassick and M. M. Badawi. Revised by John Rodenbeck. Cairo: The American University in Cairo Press, 1984.

———. *Palace Walk.* Translated by William M. Hutchins and Olive E. Kenny. New York: Doubleday, 1990.

———. *Autumn Quail.* Translated by Roger Allen. Revised by John Rodenbeck. Cairo: The American University in Cairo Press, 1985.

Mansfield, Peter. *The British in Egypt.* New York: Holt, Rinehart and Winston, 1972.

Page, Bruce; Leitch, David; and Knightley, Philip. *Philby: The Spy Who Betrayed a Generation.* Introduction by John le Carré. London: Andre Deutsch, 1968.

Peyton, W. D. *Old Oman.* London: Stacey International, 1983.

Randal, Jonathan C. *Going All the Way: Christian Warlords, Israeli Adventurers, and the War in Lebanon.* New York: Vintage, 1984.

Said, Edward W. *Orientalism.* New York: Vintage, 1979.

Thesiger, Wilfred. *Arabian Sands.* London: Penguin Books, 1984.

———. *Desert, Marsh and Mountain: The World of a Nomad.* London: Collins, 1979.

———. *The Life of My Choice.* New York: W. W. Norton, 1988.

I am indebted to the reporting of George Wilson and Molly Moore at *The Washington Post* for comprehensive background material on the *Vincennes* investigation used in the chapter "Friend or Foe."